SERVICE IN CHRIST

SERVICE IN CHRIST

Essays Presented to
KARL BARTH
on his 80th Birthday

Edited by
JAMES I. McCORD
and
T. H. L. PARKER

WIPF & STOCK · Eugene, Oregon

Wipf and Stock Publishers
199 W 8th Ave, Suite 3
Eugene, OR 97401

Service in Christ
Essays presented to Karl Barth on his 80th birthday
By McCord, James I. and Parker, T. H. L.
Copyright©1966 Epworth Press
ISBN 13: 978-1-60608-417-5
Publication date 12/29/2008
Previously published by Epworth Press, 1966

Copyright © Eptworth Press 1966
First English edition 1966 by Epworth Press
This edition published by arrangement with Epworth Press

Contents

Service in Jesus Christ: Professor T. F. Torrance, D.D., Edinburgh	1
The Classical World: Professor J. B. Skemp, M.A., Ph.D., Durham	17
Old Testament: Principal N. W. Porteous, D.D., Edinburgh	27
New Testament: Reverend C. E. B. Cranfield, M.A., Durham	37
Early Church: Professor G. W. H. Lampe, D.D., Cambridge	49
Middle Ages: Professor G. Barrois, Princeton	65
Reformation:	
Luther: Reverend J. Atkinson, D.Theol., Hull	80
Butzer: Reverend B. Hall, M.A., Cambridge	89
Calvin: Professor J. K. S. Reid, D.D., Aberdeen	101
England: Professor G. W. Bromiley, D.Litt., Pasadena	110
Puritans: Reverend G. Yule, M.A., Melbourne	122
Eighteenth and Nineteenth Centuries: Professor F. Herzog, D.Theol., Durham, N. Carolina	135
Christological Understanding: Reverend W. A. Whitehouse, D.D., University of Kent, Canterbury	151
Diakonia in some of the Churches Today:	
Anglican Communion: The Most Reverend A. M. Ramsey, D.D., Archbishop of Canterbury	162
Roman Catholic: Monsignor H. F. Davis, Birmingham	166
Reformed: Professor J. L. M. Haire, D.D., Belfast	174
Methodist: Reverend G. S. Wakefield, M.A., B.Litt., London	182
Diakonia in Modern Conditions: Professor D. M. Mackinnon, D.D., Cambridge	190
The Church's Diakonia in the Modern World: Reverend Alan A. Brash	199
Ecumenical Diakonia: Reverend John Coventry Smith	212

Foreword

It has long been the privilege of Christians in the British Isles to greet Karl Barth on successive decades of his life's journey. Sir Edwyn Hoskyns began this custom in 1936 with his open letter on Barth's fiftieth birthday. Dr F. W. Camfield continued it with the essays entitled *Reformation Old and New* when the next ten-mile stone arrived. The *Festschrift, Essays in Christology for Karl Barth*, was our Siegfried Idyll (but Dr Barth would not doubt prefer us to say 'Haffner Serenade') for 1956.

Now we come to 1966 and Karl Barth's eightieth birthday. Once again we are sending our greetings to him in the form of a volume of essays. The theme of this book, suggested and largely worked out by the Reverend Charles Cranfield of Durham, is the Church's service of Christ. When Christology was chosen a decade ago it was regarded not as one possibility among equal doctrines but as the central doctrine of theology. We did not wish, therefore, to choose another doctrine as the theme of the present book. But as soon as *diakonia* was suggested it was clear that this was the step in the right direction—from active faith in Christ to faithful activity in Christ. We do not now leave Christology to write about *diakonia*, but we are trying to understand what it means that, because Christ the Head is the servant, the Church which is His body is both His servant and the servant of mankind.

Since 1956 Karl Barth has conquered new worlds, or rather, the New World. His visit to the United States in 1962 is already becoming something of a legend, with a host of stories, not to mention photographs, surrounding it. What more proper, then, that the Declaration of Independence should on this occasion be quietly set aside and that Americans should join with those who speak the same language as themselves (if with a less pure accent) to express their gratitude and respect to him on his eightieth birthday? We send him our congratulations and good wishes, which perhaps we may frame in the words of Psalm 121: 'The Lord shall preserve thee from all evil; he shall keep thy soul. The Lord shall preserve thy going out and thy coming in from this time forth for evermore.'

JAS. I. MCCORD
T. H. L. PARKER

Service in Jesus Christ

T. F. TORRANCE

I

The Scottish divines of the sixteenth century used to distinguish between what all Christians should do 'of their charity' and what some have to do 'of authority'. That was a distinction regarding not so much the *kind* of service as the *mode* of service rendered. All members of the Body of Christ are constrained through love to bear witness to Him and to pray for others, but some have this ministry laid upon them as a special task, so that they fulfil it not only out of love but in obedience to a specific commission from the Lord and with the definite authority of that commission behind them. It was this authoritative 'sending', they held, which distinguished the 'solemn' preaching of God's Word, accompanied by the divine 'seals', from the service of all the faithful in their proclaiming of Christ and His Gospel. While that is no doubt a valuable distinction, it would be wrong if it were interpreted to mean that, in contrast to the special ministry within the Church, the service of all members of the Body of Christ is to be referred back only to the free movement of their love and to be understood as its spontaneous expression. The great characteristic of all Christian service or διακονία is that while it is certainly fulfilled under the constraint of the love of Christ it is a service *commanded* by Him and laid by Him as a *task* upon every baptized member of His Body.

We must not forget that even love is commanded by God. As Jesus Himself taught us, the love of God and the love of our neighbour are the supreme commandments upon which all the others depend, and in our love to Him we are bound in a relation of unconditional obedience to His commandments, among which is the specific commandment to love one another. This is the context in which διακονία is to be understood. Christian service is commanded of us. It is to be referred back to the Lordship of Christ and is to be understood as the pure service rendered to the Lord by those who are His servants.

In the New Testament two principal terms are used to speak of the servants of Christ, δοῦλοι and διάκονοι, slaves and waiters. The former refers to status rather than function and describes the relationship that determines the very structures of existence in Christ. The δοῦλος lives under the total claim of God and is completely subordinate to Jesus Christ, to whom he belongs body and soul. The latter refers to function rather than status and describes the service of those who exist in an absolute relationship to Christ as Lord. The διάκονος is one who has been given a task by his Master, and who does only what is commanded by Him, not what he thinks out for himself. The servants of Christ (whether we think of them as δοῦλοι or διάκονοι) are not their own masters, for they belong to Another. They do not carry out their own wishes or minister to their own glory, but they do only what they are told and serve only the glory of their Lord. The way in which the New Testament uses δοῦλος and διάκονος lets us see that Christian service or διακονία is not something that is accidental to the Christian, but essential to him, for it is rooted in his basic structure of existence as a slave of Jesus Christ. It is a form of service in which he is not partially but completely committed in the whole of his being before God, and which he discharges not occasionally but continuously in the whole of his existence as a follower of Jesus Christ.

We would misunderstand this servant-existence of Christ's followers if we did not see that their servitude in the Lord is the mode of their freedom, and their service of the Lord is the movement of their love, the true freedom and true love into which they have been redeemed. It is Christ's to command and theirs to obey, but both commandment and obedience are modes of the divine love in Jesus Christ in which service and freedom are the obverse of each other. But we would also misunderstand Christian service if we construed it simply as the expression of Christian love, intrinsically intelligible in its own requirement and inherently compelling as an end in itself, for then we would detach Christian service from its heteronomous ground in the Lord Himself and give it a basis in the autonomous existence of the Christian; we would think of it as arising out of himself and explain it as the Christian's self-imposed way of life in which his existence comes to its truest self-expression. Christian service is not the service of love for love's sake, but, service of love though it is, the duty rendered by *servants* to their *Lord* in obedience to His commandment. Hence while it is fulfilled in the form of service to others in the world, it is not fulfilled as something they have freely chosen for themselves but as a task which Christ has laid upon them in the entirely new situation that has overtaken them in Him. Faithful servants do not arrogate to themselves the authority for their actions, nor do they assume responsibility for the results of their service. They act simply as servants who live in subjection to their Lord, but who are free from the necessity, and the anxiety, of having to justify their service. They act responsibly by doing obediently what He commands, and act freely in leaving to their Lord alone the responsibility for the consequences of the service He has laid upon them. Obedience is demanded without any secondary motive, and likewise service is rendered without secondary motive, without any thought of claim upon the Lord and without any thought even of thanks from those to whom service is rendered.

Διακονία is pure service fulfilled in accordance with the requirements of an external Authority, that of the Lord, yet διακονία is intrinsically related to that Authority through its content of love. The content of the commandment and the content of the service in obedience to it derive from the self-giving of God Himself in Jesus Christ the Lord. He gives what He commands and commands what He gives. He commands a service of love, and He gives the love that empowers that service. It is this inner relation between commandment and love, or between 'authority' and 'charity', that is so distinctive of service in Jesus Christ.

Διακονία of this unique kind is possible only because the Lord Himself has come in the form of a servant, incorporating our servant-existence in Himself and incarnating among us the self-giving of God in sheer love and compassion for mankind. He came not to be served but to serve, to live out on earth the life of unconditional obedience to the Father in heaven and the life of pure love poured out to all men in unrestrained mercy. He was Himself the complete embodiment of the commandment of love and of the love commanded within our human existence, and as such He constitutes in Himself the ultimate source for the inner relation between commandment and love and the creative ground of all true Christian service. This is particularly apparent in the Sermon on the Mount, which is at once the self-portrait of our Lord in His life on earth as Son of Man and the promulgation of the will of the Father as unconditionally binding on all men. This is the life of the Servant: 'Be ye therefore perfect as your Father in heaven is perfect.' This is the service of the Lord: 'Be ye therefore merciful as your Father also is merciful.' It is only in this Jesus that we learn what διακονία really is, the loving service in mercy that looks for no reward beyond the knowledge that we do what is commanded of us and looks for no thanks from those to whom mercy is extended, but it is only because this Jesus has made our cause His very own, sharing our existence in servitude and sharing with us His own life of love, that we may and can engage in this kind of διακονία in Him.

Our particular concern here, however, is not with the structure of the Christian's existence as δοῦλος of Jesus Christ and therefore with the general ethos of life in Him, but with the form of the Christian's service as διάκονος of Jesus Christ and therefore with the specific function of life in Him. That is to say, we are concerned with διακονία in its concrete sense as *deaconing*, both as the charge which Christ lays upon the Christian community and as the office to which some are called within the community. Διακονία describes not only the relationship of service to which the whole membership of the Church and specific individuals within it bear to Jesus Christ, but the form which that relationship takes in the mutual service of members to one another and in their service to their fellow men in the world. It is natural that at this point the spotlight, so to speak, should fall upon the *deacon* himself, for it is his specific office, as a humble representative of the people of God, to prompt them in their response to Christ and His Gospel and to seek the fruit of that response in their life of deaconing toward their fellow men, and thus in his special vocation as a deacon to fulfil in an exemplary way the kind of διακονία we are all called to exercise in Jesus Christ. It was for this reason that the Early Church saw delineated in the deacon's office more than anywhere else the likeness of Jesus Christ the Servant of the Lord.

II

Before we consider this diaconal ministry we must examine its source and ground in Jesus Christ, for it was the kind of person He was and the kind of ministry He undertook that determined the form and mode of all Christian service. He was sent by the Father to carry out the redemption of human existence, not by dealing with it from the outside but by operating from within it, not by the sheer fiat of divine power but by humble acts of service in all the weakness and frailty of human creaturehood, i.e. as a Man among men, holding messianic office and exercising ministerial function. And so He came qualified by His incarnation to act for the human race within its structures and limitations, and consecrated in His capacity as a humble representative of the people for messianic office within their conditions of alienation and subjection. Hence His mission took both a human and a menial form, the ministry of the Son of Man and of the Servant of the Lord, the *Christos*. Now, we have been accustomed to expound this ministry of Christ in terms of His threefold office as the anointed Prophet, Priest and King, but this has tended to obscure or to discount two essential aspects of His ministry: (*a*) that He fulfilled His ministry as a human office within the conditions of the community which He served and sustained by direct personal and individual acts on His part; and (*b*) that He gave this ministry content and pattern by deeds of love and compassion in the healing and succouring of sick and suffering and outcast human beings. That is to say, the *diaconal* nature and significance of our Lord's ministry of mercy have tended to fall out of the picture, so that the Church throughout history has had great difficulty in relating to their proper source and ground not only the diaconal office within the Church but the deaconing of the whole community.

It is to this neglected aspect of Christ's ministry that we turn our attention in order to lay bare its permanent significance for Christian διακονία. Christ was Himself the διάκονος *par excellence* whose office it was not only to prompt the people of God in their response to the divine mercy and to be merciful themselves, not only to stand out as the perfect model or example of compassionate service to the needy and distressed, but to provide in Himself and in His own deeds of mercy the creative ground and source of all such διακονία. He was able to do that because in Him God Himself condescended to share with men their misery and distress, absorbed the sharpness of their hurt and suffering into Himself, and poured Himself out in infinite love to relieve their need, and He remains able to do that because He is Himself the outgoing of the innermost Being of God toward men in active sympathy and compassion, the boundless mercy of God at work in human existence, unlimited in His capacity to deliver them out of all their troubles. Thus through the Incarnation it is revealed to us that God in His own Being is not closed to us, for He has come to share with us the deepest movement of His divine heart, and so to participate in our human nature that the heart of God beats within it. We know that in the springs of His own eternal Life God is ever open and ready and eager to share the weakness and sorrow and affliction of others and to spend Himself in going to their relief and in saving them. It is the very property of God's nature to be merciful, and in mercy it is that nature that He has come to share with men in Jesus, that they, too, may be merciful as He is merciful.

This is mercy that is quite limitless in its extent, mercy that will not stop short at any point in being merciful. It is not just mercy to man in his creaturely weakness and abject need, but mercy freely and unstintingly extended to him at his wickedest and worst, in his revolt from the divine love and his opposition to the divine grace; mercy that regards man's resistance to God's mercy and man's inability to be merciful as his most desperate affliction and his greatest need. It is in man's proud contradiction of God's love and in his contempt of mercy, in man's sin and guilt, that the real sting of his misery lies, but it is precisely at that point of ultimate extremity, in the terrible sharpness of his distress, that God's mercy is extended and refuses to be limited even by man's arrogant scorn and refusal of it. But this is mercy that operates by stooping to suffer all the worst that man can do and be, by entering into his revolted and alienated existence and by dealing with sin from within the depths of human life, by attacking and vanquishing guilt from the inside of its own movement, imparting itself where there is no mercy, until it begets mercy even where it has been scorned.

Now, what distresses God so deeply as He looks upon man in his fearful condition is not simply his sickness and pain, nor even the torment of anxiety that gnaws at his inner being, but the fact that in his hostility to God man has become possessed of sin in his very mind and is caught in the toils of a vast evil will that extends far beyond him, and what vexes God also is that man's existence breaks up under the pressure of his guilt in it all and under the threat of the divine judgement upon him. In view of this tragic state the mercy of God takes on a dynamic and creative form in miraculous acts of grace and power in which He allies Himself with man against the evil that has entrenched itself within him and against the threat of demolition that has come upon him. That is what we see actually going on in the miracles of Jesus in which He was at work reclaiming lost humanity, not by accusing men in their sickness and sin but by shouldering all their ἀσθένεια upon Himself, i.e. not by throwing the responsibility back upon them but by taking their responsibility on Himself. That is surely the most miraculous thing about the healing acts of Jesus, the fact that in Him God has come into our enslaved existence in such a way as to make Himself responsible for men and even to assume their sin and culpability upon Himself. That is why there took place in Jesus such a struggle with evil, a struggle that was waged between God and evil power not only in the heart and mind of man but in his bodily and historical existence, and a struggle to reclaim the existence of man as human being from its subjection to futility and negation.

That is the pitiful condition of man that lies at the root of his anxiety, for his deepest being is menaced by chaos and slips away from him into corruption and destruction, since his existence is subjected to vanity in its contradiction of God and in its judgement by God. Here God's mercy takes a real form, for it is of the sheer mercy of God that He enters into this very being and existence of man under the dominion of evil power and under the doom of unavoidable destruction, and takes this human being and existence upon Himself. That is to say, God penetrates into the very negation of evil as it is entrenched in man, suffers it in Himself, and so, as it were (how can we find words to express what is so unutterable here?), 'hazards' His own existence and being as God for the sake of man. Moreover, He enters into this banned and sentenced state of man to live in it precisely *as man* under all the assaults of evil, within the entire limitation of the creature exposed to evil power and to the judgement of divine Holiness, in order to struggle with evil and vanquish it just where it has dug itself in so deeply, in the self-will and resistance of the creature toward God, and in the obdurate and brazen character of its hostility gained under God's rejection.

That is the meaning of the incarnate life and ministry of the Son of God and the whole passion of His existence as Man among men, made under the Law, and obedient unto death, where evil pays its fullest wages and delivers its ultimate assault upon God's creatures and where that assault gains its fateful force from the very judgements directed against it. No wonder St Paul insisted that our sin gains its strength from the very Law of God! That is why the 'hazard' to which God submits as He stakes His own being on our behalf and for our salvation comes not from the attack of evil itself by itself but from the judgement and negation of evil—it is that fact that makes the Cross and its *Eli, Eli, lema sabachthani* so indescribably terrible, the sheer anguish of God bowed under His own judgement on sin, a judgement not mitigated in the slightest but utterly fulfilled. Thus the existence of man into which God enters, and within which He lives as Son of Man, is a lost existence that is already breaking up and crumbling away not only under the negation of evil but under the negation of the divine judgement, where the rejection of evil serves to harden and make final the threat to demolish human being. It is into that dark and doomed existence under the divine judgement and into its corruption and destruction under negation that God enters in unutterable mercy in order to save mankind.

Now we can grasp something of the extreme gravity of man's plight, and the nature and extent of his need in the inseparability of his spiritual and physical existence and in the disintegration of his whole creaturely being as man before God. Now we can understand also something of what lay behind the Cross and the descent of the Saviour into our bottomless pit of evil and guilt and death, and so of what was involved in every act of healing and mercy in which Jesus through sharing our human existence sought to release distressed humanity from its subjection to evil and vanity, from its imprisonment in chaos and disorder and disintegration, and sought to restore it to the truth of God's creation, in which God affirms as good that which He has made, and so makes good His own Word in the creation of man.

The miracles of Jesus were concerned, then, with the saving of creation. In them God asserted His claim over the human beings He had made and proclaimed His will to maintain them in integrity of being in face of everything that threatened their existence and to restore them to natural life in the freedom and joy of His creation. The miracles reveal not only that the salvation of man involves a total negation of all that is opposed to God's creative purpose but that it can take place only within the healing and remaking of a human being in his actual physical and spiritual existence. Only through the Creator's full participation with us in our human life on earth can atonement for sin and redemption from evil power issue in the actual restoration of what God has made. The miraculous acts of Jesus are thus the luminous points in His ministry, proleptic to His resurrection from the dead, where it is disclosed that the whole life and sojourn of Jesus Christ among us is the absolute miracle within which and through which the New Creation takes place.

Without the Incarnation of the Creator Word the fallen world would crumble away finally and irretrievably into nothingness, for then God would simply let go of what He has made and it would suffer from sheer privation of being. But the Incarnation has taken place—once and for all the Creator Word has entered into the existence of what He has made and bound it up for ever with His own eternal being and life, yet the Incarnation had to mean, in this union of the Creator and the creature, the final negation by God of all that resists His creative will. That is the stupendous and bewildering miracle of Jesus that just because in Him divine nature and human nature are united in the unity of His one Person, the judgement and expiation of sin had to take place as an inner determination of the life He lived among us from birth to death (and how He was straitened until that inexpressible agony was accomplished!); and the new creation took place in the healing and sanctifying and regenerating of the human nature He assumed from our fallen and corrupt existence (and how joyful and radiant was the fulfilment in His resurrection from the grave!). It was through the sovereign παρουσία of the Creator Word within our flesh at the points of enslavement and disintegration that the integrity and wholeness of man in his spiritual and physical being was restored and that human nature was reclaimed for the heavenly Father. That is what Jesus was in His healing and helping acts. He was the Redeemer at work serving the creature from below and from within his broken and divided existence delivering him from inner bondage, redeeming him from deeply-rooted tension and anxiety; the Creator Himself at work re-creating what He had made by sharing in its humble creaturely existence in all its distress and trouble and futility, and sharing with it the healed and sanctified humanity in the perfect life of the Son of Man.

III

This work Jesus Christ fulfilled from two sides: from the side of God toward man, and from the side of man toward God. He came as God Himself, drawing near to man in all His sovereign freedom and grace, bringing His Kingdom to bear directly upon human life and history. He came as the mighty Son breaking into the realm of darkness to deliver men from their thraldom and shame, and to redeem them from the whole power of evil in triumph over sin and guilt and death and hell itself. Yet, Son of God though He was, He came among us as an infant of days in great humility within the darkness and helplessness and poverty of man, in order to work out through His own human life and deeds among us the faithful answer of man to the saving grace and power of God. Hence He came issuing out of human history as a son of Adam, of the seed of David, in order to wrestle with our perverse human nature from within our disobedient life until He had converted it back in obedience to the Father and offered it to Him in the perfection of filial trust and love.

Within this twofold work Christ came identifying Himself with man in his hopeless misery and abject need and making man's cause His very own. By incarnation and atonement He who had been the ground of man's existence from beyond his existence now forged such a bond of union between man and Himself that He became the ground of man's existence in his existence, undergirding and sustaining it from within and from below, overcoming its vanity and privation of being and giving it meaning and reality in Himself. Hence Christ is to be found wherever there is sickness or hunger or thirst or nakedness or imprisonment, for He has stationed Himself in the concrete actualities of human life where the bounds and structures of existence break down under the onslaught of disease and want, sin and guilt, death and judgement, in order that He may serve God in ministering His mercy and realizing His relation toward man, and serve man in re-creating his relation to God and realizing his response to the divine mercy. It is thus that Jesus Christ mediates in Himself the healing reconciliation of God with man and man with God in the form, as it were, of a meeting of Himself with Himself in the depths of human need. And it is thus that the Father looks upon every man in his need only by looking at him in and through the atoning presence and suppliance of His incarnate Son that meets Him there, for the incarnate Son is the outgoing of His own divine being toward every man and the pouring out of His own eternal love upon him in unrestrained mercy and grace.

As we have already seen, Jesus ministered this divine mercy as a humble representative of the people into which He had incorporated Himself and within which He had been consecrated to the vocation of the Messiah, the Elect One, the Servant. This office of *Christos* He fulfilled as *Man*, not therefore by a compelling display of mighty power, but by meek and personal service as He went about doing good, helping and healing others, and so through fellowship with men in a shared existence. That was His diaconal ministry to men in their enslavement and disintegration which gave meaning again to human life and sustained it in such a relation to the Father that within it atonement could issue in communion and redemption in new creation. It was indeed only in continuous fulfilment of this diaconal ministry that He went forth at last to offer Himself in sacrificial expiation for the sin of mankind, so that when His atoning work was accomplished in death and resurrection and ascension and the message of reconciliation with God through Christ was freely proclaimed, it could be heard and received by men whose very existence was sustained in its relation to God by the hidden presence of the incarnate and crucified and risen Christ within it. That is the permanent and immense significance of His humble διακονία in the flesh, which has been given continuing effect through the pouring out of Christ's Spirit at Pentecost, for it is that διακονία in the flesh that gives material content to His presence through the Spirit.

Now, in the fulfilment of His earthly ministry Jesus drew to Himself a company of disciples whom He formed and instituted into one Body with Himself as the inner nucleus of the Church, incorporating them into His messianic mission and sending them out to exercise His own διακονία in helping and healing, in preaching and forgiving. He set Himself in their midst as their Lord and their Example in the service of mercy. Through their union and communion with Him in His mission He gave structure to the Church He founded upon them and shaped its ministry of the divine mercy in His Name. That is to say, in constituting them as His Body, baptized with His baptism and partaking of His cup, He so assimilated them into His own diaconal life and service on earth that He made διακονία an essential mark of the Church redeemed by Him and built up round His own Person as the Christ. They were in Him a messianic community anointed for service, through sharing in His own anointing and His own self-consecration for mankind. It cannot be doubted that this diaconal character of life and service in Christ is a basic and permanent sign of the Church sanctified in Him, for it is here that Christ's own image and likeness most clearly appear: in the διακονία of the divine mercy within the spiritual and and physical existence of man. The Church cannot be in Christ without being in Him as He is proclaimed to men in their need and without being in Him as He encounters us in and behind the existence of every man in his need. Nor can the Church be recognized as His except in that meeting of Christ with Himself in the depth of human misery, where Christ clothed with His Gospel meets with Christ clothed with the desperate need and plight of men. It is never the διακονία of the Church to be itself the *Christ*, but through its humble service to Christ clothed with His Gospel and its service to Christ clothed with the misery of men to seek and to pray for their meeting and so to be in history the bodily instrument which Christ uses in the proclamation of the divine mercy to mankind and in prompting their responses to that mercy.

Διακονία in this sense is not only the charge which Christ has laid upon the whole membership of His Body but an office to which some within it are specially called and for which He bestows through His Spirit the appropriate χάρισμα. Here Jesus stands among us both as the Κύριος who gives the charge and as the supreme Διάκονος whose example is to be followed in all διακονία of the divine mercy. He would have us minister to one another and to others as He ministered to His fellows in the form of a servant.

SC-B

What were the distinctive features He exhibited in this ministry?

(i) He served God in His mercy and man in his need with the secret of the Cross in His heart. As He went about doing good, He healed not as a doctor but as a Saviour, and He helped not as a wonder-worker but as the Holy One who absorbed into Himself the affliction of men. Though it was by the Finger or Spirit of God that He brought divine power to bear upon the realm of evil and broke through the thraldom of sin and sickness in miraculous deeds of mercy, He fulfilled His ministry in meekness and lowliness in order to bear the onslaught of evil upon Himself and so to get at the heart of it. It was by living a life of holiness among us in perfect obedience to the Father that He engaged with the inhuman forces of darkness that had encroached upon the bodies and souls of men. Therefore when Jesus healed a man even of a physical affliction He did so only through a struggle with evil will. Nowhere did He heal simply as a kindly physician, but as one who wrestled personally with evil and overcame it through the conflict of His own holy will with the powers of evil spirit. That is why again and again Jesus groaned in agony and grief of spirit as He cured men's bodies and minds and had to renew His strength constantly through prayer, while prayer itself was a battle with the rebellious will of an alienated creation. This was not simply the service of kindness for kindness' sake, but a far profounder service of mercy that dealt with the real sting of evil by penetrating into its sinful motion and undoing its guilt in atonement. It was the kind of service which could not be rendered apart from vicarious divine sorrow for the sin of the world.

(ii) He ministered the mercy of God to man at the sharpest point of his need and misery, where he is not only unmerciful but resents mercy, and is therefore bitterly hostile to this ministry. Although it was the mercy of God freely minitered by Jesus that provoked the resistance of man to its sharpest point of hostility toward God, yet in this ministry of mercy Jesus met the hostility of man by making it the supreme object of His compassion, by accepting it and bearing it in Himself and then by making an end of it in His own death. It is easy enough, as Jesus pointed out, to be merciful to others when it meets with some return, but to be merciful without any hope of return and without ever looking for any return, to go on being merciful in the face of unremitting unthankfulness, and always to make every act of ingratitude, no matter how bitter and obdurate, the very occasion for mercy, is to minister a mercy that is quite limitless. That is real mercy, and that is what it means to be merciful as God is merciful. Such was the mercy ministered by Jesus, triumphant mercy which drew out human unthankfulness and resentment to their ultimate point where He limited it by absorbing it in Himself and put a final end to it in the very death which it inflicted on Him—mercy that cannot be defeated.

(iii) Jesus carried out His ministry as a humble servant on earth in utter reliance upon His Father in heaven, refusing to do anything except what He had been sent to do and refusing to discharge His mission except in the weakness and selflessness of pure service. At no point did He seek to change the nature of

His ministry as service, and therefore He rendered it only through constant recourse to prayer in order to let it take effect solely through the good pleasure of the Father. The true and faithful servant does not arrogate authority to himself or build up round him instruments of power or even an aura of prestige through which he may exert pressure to attain his ends; otherwise he would betray the essential nature of his service as *service*. Hence Jesus warned His disciples, as He washed their feet in menial service at the Last Supper, to beware of allowing their service in His name to gather a worldly prestige in which its nature as service would be lost or to take the form of a munificent patronage that could lord it over mankind. Διακονία in the Name of Christ has only one source of power: in prayer and intercession, for Jesus Christ Himself, the supreme *Diakonos*, will rule over the ages and the nations only through the weakness of the Man on the Cross.

Such, then, is the pattern of service which Christ has instituted in Himself for the Church and for all who within it are called to be deacons. It is a charge to be merciful as the Father is merciful and a call to follow Christ in the form of a servant, that all members of the Body of Christ may be fellow labourers in His work and that deacons, reflecting in themselves the pattern of Christ's service, may prompt the whole people of God in the ministry of divine mercy.

IV

Without doubt this is a very difficult charge which Christ has laid upon His Church, and one that is desperately hard for the Church to fulfil in its corporate capacity as Church and therefore in the form of a service rendered by the Community as such. How can it render this service as *service* and render it *effectively* within the power-structures of humanity?

Here the Church is up against a twofold temptation. On the one hand, it is tempted to use worldly power in order to secure the success of its service. As an organized community within the national, social, and economic structures of human life the Church cannot isolate its ministry of the divine mercy from the organized services of the State for the welfare of its people. The Church knows only too well that the need of men is bound up with the injustices inherent in the national, social, and economic structures within which people live, and is often directly traceable to them, and therefore in order to meet human need adequately and rationally attention must be given to the factors that create it and aggravate it. Certainly as far as hunger and poverty and want are concerned what is required is the application of scientific methods in the production and distribution of goods from the vast wealth with which God has endowed the earth. But how can this be done without economic and political power? And so the Church is constantly tempted not only to institutionalize its service of the divine mercy but to build up power-structures of its own, both through ecclesiastical success and prestige among the people and through social and political instruments, by means of which it can exert pressure to attain its ends and impart power to its service in order to ensure its effectiveness. What church is there that feels deeply the burden of human need, and takes seriously its service of mercy, that does not fall into this temptation?

On the other hand, the Church is tempted to leave the corporate responsibility for the need of men wholly to the State and to restrict itself to the ministry of forgiveness. How can the Church participate in the planned and controlled welfare of mankind without actually compromising its freedom and secularizing its life in the worldly forms of society? And so the Church is tempted to retreat into an area where it could not come into conflict with the power-structures of organized social welfare and where it thinks to avoid the subtle snare of using its success in the relief of human suffering as a means of enhancing its own image or of pressing its own claim upon the people. This could take a quietist and other-worldly form through the restriction of Christian service to inward 'religious' concerns, but it could also take the form of a flight into the anonymity of 'religionless' behaviour or the so-called 'meta-christianity' of the 'new man'. But in either case the Church would decline the burden of human need at its sharpest point and deflect the real force of Christian witness, and so run away from the agony of being merciful as God is merciful.

Whichever alternative the Church chooses, on the one hand or the other, it contracts out of the actual charge Christ has laid upon it and betrays the essential nature of Christian service as *service*. Can the Church engage in the pressure groups of organized society in order to ensure the success of its own enterprise, and so suffer assimilation to the forms of this world, without compromising its real nature as the Body of Jesus Christ? Can it hide its light under the natural forms of man's cultural and scientific development without losing its soul? Can it follow Christ, the Servant of the Lord who steadfastly resisted every temptation to use compelling demonstrations of glory and power to fulfil His ministry, without like Him suffering the hostility and ridicule and ignominy that are heaped by the world on powerless and selfless service of God's mercy? Can the Church really fulfil the charge Christ has laid upon it and therefore take up His Cross without renouncing itself for Him, without, as it were, hazarding its life or losing its identity in recognized historical existence for Christ's sake and the Gospel's? Can the Church go forth from Christ clad with His image in the form of a servant without laying aside the pride and glory and power of the nations, and without taking into its own mouth in triumphant agony His cry before the judgement seat of Pilate: 'My kingdom is not of this world'? And how can the Church go forth from Christ to engage in authentic service in His Name without immersing itself in the need and misery and desperate plight of men in complete solidarity with the world under the judgement and grace of God, without participating deeply in the divine mercy that has put an end in the crucified Body of Christ to our restless striving for power and vain snatching at glory, and to our resentment of meek and humble reliance upon the heavenly Father?

Difficult though it is for the Church as such to carry this burden and fulfil the role of a servant, God in His mercy has instituted within it special ministries to dispense to it the Word of Life and to seek the fruit of it in the lives of its members, to guide the Church and to prompt it in its service. This is the two-fold ministry which we may speak of as 'the service of the Word', and 'the service of response to the Word'. *The service of the Word* is the ministry of Word and Sacrament through which Christ is pleased to be present, offering Himself as Saviour and implementing His salvation by the power of His Spirit. But it is a *service*, a διακονία, in which ministers only *serve* the proclamation of Christ and cannot make that proclamation effective by imparting to it their own strength, and in which they only dispense the Sacraments as *stewards* of the mysteries in utter reliance upon Christ to fulfil His own ministry of Himself in Word and Spirit, in Grace and Power. *The service of response to the Word* is the ministry of the divine mercy to the people in which Christ Himself is pleased to be present, acting as their Representative in lifting them up to the Face of the Father in thanksgiving and worship and in making them His fellow labourers in the pouring out of the divine mercy to all mankind. But it is a *service*, a διακονία, in which deacons only *prompt* the people in their responses of prayer and praise and do not act on their behalf, and in which they guide them in their service to mankind and do not undertake it for them, but in which they remind the people of Christ's own promise to meet them in all their deeds of mercy to the hungry and thirsty and naked and sick and imprisoned, and so to give effect to their service in the depths of human need.

These two ministries are essentially complementary and are mutually dependent, since each requires the other for its proper fulfilment and one is obstructed by the lack of the other. It is through that double ministry that Christ communicates Himself to man by bringing God's presence to bear upon man and by bringing him in his need to receive that presence, by ministering the mercy of God toward man in his guilty estrangement and by freeing him in his desperate need for the response of faith and trust in God, and He does that by incarnating God's love in Himself for man and by sustaining through His own presence the existence of man for fellowship with God. It is thus that Jesus Christ mediates in Himself the healing reconciliation of God with man and man with God in the form of a union of His own presence in the Gospel with His own presence in the depths of human need. The service of the Word serves Christ clothed with His Gospel, so that through it He draws near to man with forgiveness in unconditional grace; and the service of response to the Word serves Christ clothed with the misery of man, so that through it He sustains and upholds man in unutterable compassion until He finds the sheep that is lost and counts that He has found it when it hears His voice and follows Him.

Now, while the New Testament uses the term διακονία both for the service of the Word and for the service of response to the Word, it is especially used and indeed technically used for the service of response to the Word, that is, for the ministry of the *deacon*. We may thus distinguish between the two forms of ministry as the *presbyteral* ministry through which the Word and Sacraments are dispensed and the *diaconal* ministry through which the responses of God's people in worship and witness or intercession and mercy are guided and prompted. The term διακονία is peculiarly appropriate to the latter ministry, for while the presbyteral ministry is one in which the ministers act not as representatives of the people but only as those sent by Christ and commissioned by Him with authority to dispense His Word of forgiveness, in the proclamation of the Gospel and the administration of the Sacraments, the diaconal ministry is one in which the deacons act as representatives of the people and as examples of the way in which Christ identified Himself with their need, and therefore as sent by Him to engage in a ministry of pure, unassuming service without any commission to exercise authority or pastoral control. They are as necessary and as indispensable to one another as husband and wife, and father and mother, in the same family.

It is an immense tragedy that throughout its history the Church has so often lacked a proper *diaconate* to guide it and prompt it in the ministry of the divine mercy, and to seek the full fruit of that mercy in the activities of the community and in the lives of its members. This has had disastrous consequences for the ministry of Word and Sacrament, for left on its own, without its other half, it has succumbed to the temptation to arrogate to itself a false glory and to fulfil its authoritative commission not by obedient *service* but by usurping control and mastery over the Lord's inheritance. But it has had disastrous consequences also for the service of the Church in its corporate capacity, for without the example of pure service, which it is the office of the deacon to set forth, the Church has fallen into the temptation to give itself out as the patron of goodness and welfare and to assume worldly powers in order to achieve success in its works of relief, and thus has betrayed the very nature of its ministry as service of divine mercy to mankind. This has also meant that the ministry of Christ clothed with His Gospel has been kept apart from the ministry of Christ clothed with the need and plight of men, with the result that the ministry of the Gospel has so often lost its relevance to men in the concrete actualities of their existence, and the ministry of the divine mercy has lacked its penetrating power to strike into the deepest root of human need in man's guilty estrangement from God—thus grave disorder has appeared in the life of the Church and its mission is often fraught with a deep sense of futility.

The Church needs today a massive recovery of authentic *diakonia* if it is to hold forth the image of Christ before mankind and is to minister the mercy of God to the needs of men in the deep root of their evil and in the real sting of their misery. Such a recovery would go far to heal the breaches in the life of the Church and to supply what is lacking in its mission. Three areas in particular call for drastic amendment and far-reaching reform.

(i) *Intercession*. There is no more basic form of the Church's ministry than prayer, for it is in prayer that it renders its supreme service of worship and thanksgiving to God, and it is only through prayer that the Church can engage in the pure service of divine mercy in utter reliance upon God and in the renunciation of every attempt to put the Word of God into effect through its own cunning or strength. The Church does not minister through the power of its own action but only through the power of its Lord, and therefore it cannot fulfil its *diakonia* on earth without continuous engagement in intercession through its great High Priest at the right hand of God Almighty. The frantic attempts of the Church in modern times to find ways and means of making its message relevant to men, of clothing its ministries with worldly power, or of evolving methods and instruments which will ensure the popularity and success of its enterprise, are open admission that the Church has ceased to believe that the Gospel is really able to effect what it proclaims and of tragic disbelief in the power of intercession, i.e. in the active intervention of the Church's heavenly Mediator which is echoed through the Spirit in the Church's stammering prayers on earth. The intercessory prayer of the Church is direct engagement in the mighty apocalyptic battle between the Kingdom of Christ and the kingdoms of this world and in the triumphant reign of the Enthroned Lamb over all the forces of evil and darkness in history. The Church's greatest need is to *believe again* in the intercession of Christ and to find through prayer the sole source of power in its mission. Nothing can ever take the place of this basic service, the *diakonia* of intercession.

(ii) *Witness*. Witness is the form which service takes as it moves from worship and intercession in Christ toward men in their estrangement and separation from God. It is open and transparent witness to Jesus Christ as the incarnate love of God, the Lord and Saviour of men, and witness directed above all to the deepest point of man's misery in his guilty alienation from God and to the sharpest point of his need in his hostility to God's grace. It is thus witness in the face of resistance and even persecution. The Christian Church is under constant pressure by the world to conform to its ways and thoughts, to adapt its message to its desires and ambitions, and thus the Church can only bear witness by entering into affliction. It is because the Church is a servant of Christ and is assimilated to His mission in its essential life that it suffers the same hostility as He suffered and shares with Him the weakness and helplessness of His passion. It is because Christ crucified and risen again dwells in the Church and makes it the earthly and historical form of His Body that He leads it into the unavoidable conflict between the mercy of God and the inhumanity of man and between the holiness of God and the sin of mankind. The Church cannot withdraw from the affliction and suffering which this conflict brings without contracting out of its witness and betraying its Lord. Yet this is the very point where the Church today in its faint-heartedness and scepticism seems to have lost its nerve, and where under pressure from the world it makes its message easy and acceptable to human hearing, adapting the Gospel to modern man instead of bringing modern man face to face with the Gospel. But the actual point of relevance and communication lies at the point of offence where the real hurt of man is exposed and divine healing takes place. It is a betrayal of *diakonia* to heal the hurt of God's people lightly, saying peace, peace, where there is no peace. The Church cannot discharge the task which Christ has laid upon it without offering unadulterated witness and engaging in pure evangelism, cost what it may in scorn and ridicule or oppression. If at this point the Church seeks to save its life it will lose it, but here if it is ready to lose it for Christ's sake and the Gospel's it will find it. It still remains true that the blood of the martyrs is the seed of the Church, and that it is through bold and suffering witness that men and women serve Christ most faithfully.

(iii) *Reconciliation*. The Church that is committed to the *diakonia* of the divine mercy must live the reconciled life. It cannot proclaim reconciliation to the world without standing in solidarity with the world under the total grace and judgement of God and without carrying within itself a solidarity of communion in the redemption through the blood of Christ. It cannot offer healing to mankind without being healed in its own body. It cannot minister reconciliation to humanity in its bitter divisions and hostilities without being reconciled in its own membership and purged of its internal bitterness and strife. What can obstruct or damn the service of the Church more than to act a lie against what it proclaims and by perpetuating division within itself to blaspheme the blood of Christ shed to make men at one with God and at one with each other? What is demanded of the Church by Christ is that it should serve the divine mercy in the actualities of physical and spiritual existence where the bounds of human life break up under the divisive forces of evil, and that instead of allowing the divisions of the world to penetrate back into the life of the Church, to make it equivocal and futile, it should live out in the midst of a broken and divided humanity the reconciled life of the one unbroken Body of Jesus Christ—that is διακονία.

Until the Christian Church heals within itself the division between the service of Christ clothed with His Gospel and the service of Christ clothed with the need and affliction of men, and until it translates its communion in the body and blood of Christ into the unity of its own historical existence in the flesh, it can hardly expect the world to believe, for its *diakonia* would lack elemental integrity. But *diakonia* in which believing active intercession, bold unashamed witness, and the reconciled life are all restored in the mission of the Church will surely be the service with which Jesus Christ is well pleased, for that is the *diakonia* which He has commanded of us and which He has appointed as the mirror through which He reflects before the world His own image in the form of a Servant.

Readers of Karl Barth will be aware of how much this essay owes to him and not least to the last volume of his *Church Dogmatics*, 4.3. It is highly appropriate that *Diakonia* should be the theme of this tribute to him, for rarely has any theologian so consistently directed his theological work to stimulate and prompt the *diakonia* of the divine mercy as the charge which Christ has laid upon the Church as a whole.

Service to the Needy in the Graeco-Roman World

J. B. SKEMP

Though the word διακονεῖν is Greek, there is little help to be gained from a study of its usage and that of its cognates in the classical period when our task is to elucidate its meaning in the Christian Church. A study of the use of *minister* would not help very much more. The Greek word undoubtedly achieves its Christian signification (though not, of course, its significance) through its special use to name 'attendants' who were officials of religious guilds or societies in Hellenistic times. One may, however, note an interesting passage in Plato's *Laws* (vi, 763a, 5, 6) where the companies of twelve young men between 25 and 30 years of age chosen from each of the twelve tribes to be 'rural warders'—a kind of police and 'home guard' under para-military discipline—are to live frugally together and 'do and receive menial services mutually'—διακονοῦντες καὶ διακονούμενοι. These same young men are to lead the waters of springs into conduits and in sacred groves or precincts near them to provide exercise-grounds for themselves and their elders, with warm baths for the latter. They are to give a friendly reception to the sick and those worn out with labour on the land and plan for their benefit. Such a reception will be worth far more to them than treatment by a second-rate doctor. Plato, however, does not call this notable piece of διακονία by that name: it is a desirable 'incidental' service of the young men doing this form of 'national service' (*Laws*, 761b, 6 seqq.).

The evidence for the treatment of the poor and outcast among the Greeks and the Romans need careful assessment. The great work of Bolkestein, which has rightly come to be regarded as 'standard' on the subject,[1] has the demerits which go with its excellencies. By making Egypt and Israel the model cases and asking what in Greece and Rome coincides with Egyptian and Israelite customs and attitudes, it necessarily fails to show the bases upon which the Greek and Roman practices themselves were built—though, in fact, it offers excellent material for a unified study of these practices. In a brief sketch like the present one only a few instructive passages from literature can be adduced, for most of the evidence is necessarily literary: there is almost nothing inscriptional until

[1] Hendrik Bolkestein, *Wohltätigkeit und Armenpflege im vorchristlichen Altertum* (Utrecht, 1939).

Hellenistic times, and then very little on this particular matter.[1] But the literary evidence, if used cautiously with a sense of context, is valuable, since we are concerned with attitudes and assumptions rather than with detailed historical events. Where epic or tragedy is drawn upon, the needs of the dramatic situation have to be allowed for: thus it would be easy to say that Euripides, *Medea*, 82–87, reflects a Greek cynicism rebelliously refusing the command to love one's neighbour as oneself. Two household slaves, the nurse and the *paedagogus*, are discussing the reported intention of Jason to exile his foreign wife Medea with her children—these are on the stage with the nurse—because he is to ally himself to the princess at Corinth. The nurse says, 'Children, do you hear how hard your father is toward you. I do not wish his end—he is my master—but he is being shown up as a wicked one to his own.' The other replies, 'What man isn't hard to his own? You're learning this late in the day: everyone loves himself more than he loves his neighbour.' But this amateur cynicism is less important than the nurse's concern for Medea and the children; and Jason's act in exposing a foreign-born wife to exile along with his children is a form of self-love which goes far to excuse Medea's fatal jealousy and murderous deed. There is no evidence that either Euripides or his audience would applaud the Paedagogus here.[2] In the case of epic, the obviously interesting passages are those concerning Odysseus's return to his own land disguised as a beggar. Here, too, allowance must be made for the fact that this particular beggar must succeed in defeating those who had pillaged his home in his absence. But this leaves much that indicates accepted Greek attitudes embodied in the story. We need not inquire for our purposes what historic society the *Odyssey* portrays: it certainly involves memories of 'Mycenean' feudalism, as well as material relevant to and understood by the audiences of bards in the so-called 'Dark Ages' between 1000 B.C. and Homer's own time.[3] The later audiences hearing the poem recited in the Greek city-states would regard its environment as an earlier one than their own, but not as discontinuous with them in basic attitudes to life and duty. It is not in any significant sense true to say that 'Homer is the Bible of the Greeks'; but Plato (and many others from Xenophanes in the sixth century onwards) would not have censured him so severely had his epics not been so much part of the common life of the Greek cities that they influenced social and individual values, or perhaps *reflected* those values.[4] If Homer and Hesiod are taken

[1] For relevant inscriptions see B. Laum, *Stiftungen in der griechischen und römischen Antike* (Teubner, Berlin, 1914). No. 28 Delphi (school founding). Nos. 29 (Delphi), 86 (Philadelphia), 129b (Didyma, Miletus) refer to corn for distribution: so later Patara (Lycia) No. 139. Other cases are discussed by Bolkestein, op. cit., pp. 232–5.

[2] It must, however, be said in fairness that Greek New Comedy is reflected in Terence, *Andria*, 426 seqq.: *verum illud verbumst quod volgo dici solet, omnes sibi malle melius esse quam alteri.*

[3] For purposes of definition in time, I would place the author of the *Odyssey* round about 700 B.C. I doubt whether he was very much earlier than Hesiod. But opinions on these matters are never stable.

[4] A very interesting study of Greek ethical values has been made recently by Dr A. W. H. Adkins in *Merit and Responsibility* (Oxford, 1960). This studies Greek conceptions of ἀρετή, of

together—and this means the Hesiod of *Works and Days* in this connexion—we have a remarkably reliable index of the minds of ordinary unheroic Greeks.

Bolkestein is inclined to argue that because Odysseus is a stranger he receives protection and consideration he would not receive if he were only a beggar.[1] This is no doubt true in some measure, but Bolkestein overstates his case very seriously. When Odysseus is smitten by Antinous's footstool as he begs of the suitors, he cries, 'If there are gods and avengers for beggar-men, may the doom of death grip Antinous before he weds.' He has to say '*if*', Bolkestein argues, because there are no avengers of beggars as such. But this is legalism gone mad in argument. We know Antinous will be killed in fact. The violation of a guest-stranger is clearly, in this episode, worse in the eyes of the rest of the company because the guest-stranger is helpless (or seems so at the moment) and a beggar.

There is really no parallel with entertaining angels unawares (cited by Bolkestein, p. 179). There is a risk in *not* entertaining gods unawares (xvii, 485–6), as the other suitors warn Antinous; but this really covers and 'rationalizes' their normal habit of giving to beggars. Odysseus, making up one of his stories about his past, tells Antinous himself a little earlier that he was once a rich man and 'regularly gave gifts to vagrants of all sorts in whatever need they might be (xvii, 419–20); and these lines are probably true of Odysseus's practice twenty years earlier—certainly they are truer than the rest of his tale. Similarly Nausicaa's remark that 'from Zeus come all strangers and beggars and even a small gift is acceptable' must not cause us to suppose that Homer means us to think that prudent religiosity accounted for her reactions. This is as blind an interpretation as to say that she only stood her ground when the other girls ran away because Athene put courage in her limbs. The protection of the obviously helpless is part of the picture even if—as it is now fashionable to suppose—romantic potentialities are there from the beginning of the encounter.

There is the other side of the picture, of course. If Odysseus had been led to the home of Melanthius the goatherd instead of to Eumaeus the swineherd, his reception would have been very different. Professional rivalry gives point to Melanthius's abuse (xvii, 217 seqq., 'Here is a villain with a villain in tow', etc.), but his estimate of a work-shy beggar and his kicking of Odysseus on the hip are

---

courage and excellence in a man, from Homer's time to Alexander's. Dr Adkins would see essential 'Homeric' valuations persisting into the fifth century B.C., but 'quiet' conceptions of 'responsibility' and 'equity' beginning to predominate by the time of Plato and Aristotle in the common man's view of what is 'good' and 'excellent'.

Like all classifications, this forces the evidence somewhat, both early and late. Moreover, one may note that the Homeric superman can be kind to suppliants in need, even though the 'responsible citizen' is more likely to feel a public duty to the underprivileged. To take Dr Adkins's thesis further than he takes it, one may say that Alexander himself was something of the Homeric hero once more, but the magistrates and officers who lived in the many Greek cities in Asia Minor in the centuries before Christ were more liable to show what Dr Adkins terms the 'quiet' virtues of the responsible citizen—that is, if they had any virtue at all!

[1] op. cit., pp. 177–81.

not examples of *diakonia*. Similarly Irus, the licensed beggar among the suitors, is prepared to defend his 'pitch' against all other beggars, and old bent men would not usually have the punch in them which Odysseus proved to have. Hesiod said that 'beggar is jealous of beggar' just as bard is of bard or as potter has feud with potter. Yet the vivid sketch of Irus at the beginning of the eighteenth book clearly depicts a not uncommon type. The suitors, when Odysseus has laid him low, turn against him—it is ingrained in mortal men, according to Clytemnestra in the *Agamemnon* (885), to give another kick to the man who has been thrown down—and they threaten to send him off in a black ship to the mainland to the maimer of men, King Echetus, who will slash off nose and ears and drag his inwards out for the dogs to rend raw. It is very doubtful whether there were many exports of this kind in fact. At any rate Odysseus props him in his groggy condition against the house wall and puts his staff in his hand and 'his miserable wallet full of holes' about his neck. Honour is satisfied: Irus henceforth must know he cannot lord it over strangers and beggars (xviii, 106).

In sum, then, feudal Greece has a *de facto* tolerance of the outcast and gives some protection; so that no one was likely to end his days as Odysseus's faithful hound Argos did 'in the deep dung of mules and cattle'. How well he fared would depend on his wits and his strength not a little; but acceptance into some place in the feudal structure would not readily be denied to a man who was not an open robber.

The rest of our evidence covers Graeco-Roman humanity living in city-states. This condition Aristotle considered to be specifically human: man is ζῷον πολιτικόν. It is important to remember that Rome, too, was a city-state: the present papal proclamations *urbi et orbi* reflect this early consciousness, and ordinary Romans in Roman streets share it still. But city-state humanity is almost certain to seem inhumane to those outside itself as compared with feudal or theocratic humanity. The consideration for the weak is for weaker brethren—weaker fellow citizens that is. One should realize who the 'outsiders' were in most cases. First there were slaves, and discussion of slavery in Greece and Rome must be a separate issue. There was certainly more than a prudential and utilitarian humanity (like old Cato's, who would work neither slave nor beast to death unprofitably) towards many slaves, household and other. Onesimus had many predecessors. Slaves at Athens, at any rate, were very free spoken and indeed cheeky at times. Plato complains of an extreme of freedom where the bought are as free as their buyers and where animals have the right of way in the streets (*Republic*, VIII, 563b c). But one of the Homeric quotations that was universally believed comes from the books of the *Odyssey* we have considered. Eumaeus says that Zeus whose voice is heard afar takes away half a man's 'worthiness' or 'status' (ἀρετή) when the day of slavery comes upon him (xvii, 322). The lines immediately before it are not so often quoted: Eumaeus is saying that slaves when their masters lose grip no longer do an honest day's work. This failure goes with their diminished humanity. More can properly be expected of a free man. This assumption lies behind much seeming harshness to beggars in the city-state. Plato's ideal state in the *Laws* will be such that no human being *need* beg: therefore that kind of creature will be strictly rejected at the frontiers or expelled across them (*Laws*, xi, 936b c).

The whole of Hesiod's treatment of these things in *Works and Days* is relevant here, for Ascra is a very primitive πόλις and yet more than a κώμη. His brother Perses has received the greater portion of the patrimony and wasted it: he is now warned to wrest a living from a poor soil. To 'sponge' on the neighbours is dishonest (397–402):

Foolish Perses, get on with work and do such tasks as the gods have indicated for man, lest bitter in heart with wife and children you look for livelihood among your neighbours and they will have none of you. Twice or thrice maybe you will get what you want; but if you still pester, you will fail in your attempt and use many words to no purpose.

Perses must pass by the smithy full of gossipers and go home and put his house in order (493), but the city must give straight judgements to strangers as well as to natives (225) and his brother is told (and might he not rejoin *tu quoque?*):

Never dare to taunt a man with deadly poverty that devours the spirit of a man: it is sent by the deathless gods (717).

We may avoid inconsistency by the device well known to theologians of saying that this is a loose adage attached to the 'pericope'. Maybe, but it serves us well as stating the morality and the social conscience of the *Kleinbürger* of Ascra.

The other 'outsiders' in city-state society were the 'metics'—settlers for trade reasons with recognized rights and duties to their place of settlement. These were often wealthy and could find employment if necessary. Traders were normally citizens of some city and formed a peripatetic confraternity in all the harbours, large and small, they visited; but they were home based. Other 'strangers' normally had guest-friends on all lawful occasions of travel. We come upon more interesting characters, it is true, in the ἀγύρται or 'collectors'. They were not attached to state shrines, it would seem, but were free-lance collectors, normally for themselves. It is a vile taunt of Teiresias by Oedipus (Sophocles, *O.R.*, 388) when he calls him 'a crafty collector with an eye on the bag and on nothing else'; but it is even more interesting to find Aeschylus as early as 458 B.C. making Cassandra upbraid Apollo as he deprives her of her prophetic symbols before she is killed and telling how she 'put up with being called "poor miserable starveling"' like some itinerant beggar-woman (φοιτὰς ὡς ἀγύρτρια, *Agamemnon*, 1273).[1] Earlier she has challenged her hearers as to her effectiveness as a prophet: is she true or a false seer—a babbler who knocks on doors

---

[1] I read καλουμένη with the MSS., not κακουμένη with Murray (following Musgrave), which would mean 'put up with being ill-treated'. It may also be questioned whether φοιτάς means 'itinerant' or 'maddened' like Io or the Bacchanals or the Cybele priestesses. Aeschylus's other usage (*Prometheus Vinctus*, 598) of the word seems to me only to have the colour of 'mad' or 'wild' wandering because of Io's special fate. Fraenkel's discussion (Commentary, vol. iii, pp. 590–1) should be consulted for another view of the passage.

(1195)? We need not worry with Fraenkel whether Priam really made his daughter an allowance or turned her out of doors: the interest lies in the clear implication of the passage that ἀγύρται of this type existed. Adeimantus complains of Orphic tractsellers who are vendors of 'indulgences' (Plato, *Republic*, ii, 364b–365a), though this is eighty years after Aeschylus wrote the *Oresteia*. Let us at least conclude that there were Athenians ready to give money to such ἀγύρται, whether out of pity or out of a prudential gamble on future bliss. Let us also note that really poor citizens might make a little honest money 'on the side' by offering initiations as Aeschines's mother did, in the name of Sabazius. The Greeks were not all abstract philosophers or beautiful aristocrats.

The final 'non-political' group that we must consider is that of the voluntary poor: the wallet and staff and single cloak taken over from Irus in the *Odyssey* and Socrates in the streets of Athens. Antisthenes was commonly held to have 'founded' cynicism: he is, however, chiefly important as having moralized Odysseus as a man of many sufferings and wanderings and—above all—as having taken further an understanding of the Heracles story which he inherited. Heracles is the toiling servant of men himself suffering injustice. This figure is of no small significance.[1] But the actual Cynics are more important. Diogenes is clearly a spurner of men as he is of their values. But Crates of Thebes who came to Athens and won golden opinions of all sorts of people was another man altogether. He went about visiting people, helping and exhorting. They called him θυρεπανοίκτης, the man who opens the door and looks in on the family. He gave up wealth, and when Hipparchia wanted to marry him agreed if she would share his way of life. She did. Some of Diogenes, but also some of Crates, clings to the Cynic way, which the Stoics called 'a short cut to goodness'. There were, of course, sham Cynics, but voluntary poverty was not unknown in the Hellenistic world.[2]

It remains for us to notice the actual ways in which the city-states in fact made some kind of 'welfare' provision. It might seem that this is all that needs to be done in this essay; but without the understanding of attitude and situation little can be learnt from the mere details. We are unfortunately very largely restricted to Athens and Rome in a brief summary like this; but at this point it is at least possible to mention the work of Professor A. H. M. Jones in making generally available evidence on the Greek cities, especially in Asia Minor, in Hellenistic times: his book *The Greek City from Alexander to Justinian*[3] throws a beam of light on these hidden places for which Christian scholars have particular reason to be thankful. Here only a brief classification is attempted, and illustration continues to be mainly literary. Professor A. H. M. Jones in his inaugural lecture deplored the use of Aristophanes's comedies as evidence for Athenian democracy. This is a fair objection on an historian's part (though even so some-

[1] See R. Hoistad, *Cynic Hero and Cynic King* (Uppsala, 1948). He finds language parallels with 2 Corinthians 6 (pp. 198 seqq.).

[2] The 'life' by Diogenes Laertius is in Book VI, ch. 85–93. See other material cited in D. R. Dudley, *A History of Cynicism* (London, 1937).

[3] Oxford, 1940. See especially chapters XIII and XIX.

what severe), but we may allow ourselves more freedom. It is perhaps like choosing Gilbert and Sullivan rather than Sidney and Beatrice Webb; but for some purposes they may reveal more. It is in the case of Rome that we are more at a loss. There is a mass of later literature which builds up a picture of the *mores antiqui*. This is nostalgic or Hellenized by turns, and it is a very distorting mirror of early Rome. It may therefore be best to reverse the usual order and deal summarily with the Roman evidence. After all, the *decemviri*, if their date can be trusted, are contemporary with Pericles. The basic social fact would seem to be that Rome remained more a place of clans than Athens. Solon achieved, or codified, the supremacy of the πόλις over family or other attachments and he could afford to allow θίασοι, guilds or voluntary societies, provided they did not offend public law. At Rome the great *gentes* were supreme. *Fato Metelli Romae fiunt consules*, Naevius wrote; and was jailed for it. But this was not the whole matter, for it seems that the relation of *patronus* and *cliens* grew within this early clan system. Again we have to work back from historical times; but it seems to be true that settlers who had lost or abandoned other citizenships and lacked legal status were the original *clientes*, and they attached themselves to leading Roman citizens. Freedmen came to form a large proportion of the *clientes* of later times. Descendants were involved on both sides of the relationship and duties attached to each party. The *patronus* was legal representative and defender from violence; he almost adopted the *cliens* into his *familia*—though not, of course, as any kind of heir. But he undertook responsibility for his burial. He exercised a *tutela*: the *cliens* was *in fide*, and any breach of patronal obligations was punishable with death: *patronus si clienti fraudem fecerit, sacer esto* is quoted as from the Twelve Tables from Servius.[1] This close and personal concern weakened as time went on and as whole communities became *clientes* during Rome's political and strategic advances. Yet even in classical times its reflection in the *salutationes* of the great and in the *sportulae*, the baskets containing food (and sometimes money), which he distributed we can see a debased but surviving sense of personal concern of the leading citizen as such for the underprivileged who attached themselves to him personally. Empty bellies were often filled by this means.

Trade guilds at Rome and even burial societies (*collegia funeraticia*) seem to belong rather to the empire than to the republic and may even be reflections back from the provinces of existing institutions there. But *collegia tenuiorum* (the *tenues* being the 'slight' people, neither senatorial nor equestrian) seem to have a longer history of mutual aid, and the degree of attachment of these to particular groups must remain uncertain in the absence of clearer evidence. There are, however, traditional Roman ways of 'public assistance'—land assignments and corn doles. The question of distribution of *ager publicus* was the cause of the murder of Tiberius Gracchus and so comes into political history. But Livy sees earlier colonies as designed to meet and forestall popular

[1] For a fuller (and perhaps less dogmatic) discussion, see E. Badian, *Foreign Clientelae* (Oxford, 1958), pp. 1–11.

agitation, and there may well be truth in this. As Bolkestein points out (op. cit., p. 351), he regards the planting of such colonies as made by the senate *ut beneficio praevenirent desiderium plebis* (VIII, 16, 13). Thus land grant, communal as then or in *assignationes viritanae* later, was a *beneficium*. The story of *frumentationes* also goes far back, to the establishment of the *cura annonae* and the responsibilities of the aediles. Special gifts or special emergencies produced corn distributions at various early dates, but after Gaius Gracchus (who knew about Greek σιτοδοσίαι) regular distributions were made in Rome to all citizens save during the brief Sullan 'reaction'. This is the *panis* of Juvenal's *panem et circenses*, no doubt; though there were also further public measures by that time. These were the imperial *alimenta*, which are contemporary with the early Church in Rome and Italy, but quite independent of it. These may have been modelled on earlier private generosity, but as public policy under the Flavians and Antonines they represent an advance on a mere policy of doles and show benevolence directed to need, and to need throughout Italy and not merely in Rome. The grant was specific in two respects: it was for children's maintenance and it was for children of the free-born *poor*. We do not know what the 'means test' was, but there were special magistrates for administration of the grants and elaborate machinery both for provision and distribution of the *alimenta*. One can say that this was in a sense a 'political' policy to stem the depopulation of Italy; but humane considerations undoubtedly moved Nerva and Trajan also.[1]

To return to the Greeks and to Solon, we find evidences for a great variety of voluntary associations within society aiming at mutual benefits of some kind. Aristotle says[2] that in any κοινωνία there are two elements, justice and friendship; and he cites 'old comrades' associations military or naval as examples. Burial societies and societies for common meals go back to the earliest reported form of Solon's enactment. These groups, together with the various trade guilds and associations, tend to repeat themselves in the evidences we have for the Greek and Hellenistic world. They tended to the benefit of the poorer members, as did many semi-public associations like that of the 'phratries' at Athens based on the tribes. The community itself took certain 'welfare' responsibilities also. These were partly restrictions on traders, especially in corn. Attempts were constantly made to prevent corn merchants holding the community to ransom.[3] This was especially important for economic and strategic reasons at Athens, but similar measures were taken in several Hellenistic cities.[4] These measures obviously helped the poorest most. They are more important than intermittent corn doles, which were in any case distributed to all citizens needy or not. Other measures taken in Athens were bitterly disputed by political groups, and we mostly have the case against them stated in extant writers. The pay for jurymen

[1] For detailed treatment see Alice M. Ashley, 'The *Alimenta* of Nerva and his Successors', *English Historical Review*, XXXVI (1921), pp. 5–16.
[2] *Ethica Nicomachea*, VIII, 9 init (1159b 25, 26). Bolkestein rightly notices this (op. cit., p. 235, n. 1).
[3] See, for example, Lysias, *Oratio XXII*.
[4] See A. H. M. Jones, op. cit., pp. 216–19.

and citizens attending assembly was intended to compensate for loss of earnings. The much-criticized 'theoric fund' also sought to free citizens from need to earn on the days of the festival. All these funds clearly helped the poorest most, though they were not confined to them. Many older citizens in Athens undoubtedly lived to a large measure on this State support, or at any rate had only this to keep them relatively 'independent' of family support on which they otherwise depended.

Two other institutions deserve special notice. 'Public doctors' existed as early as the sixth century, as we learn from the story of Democedes in Herodotus. Aristophanes implies (*Acharnians*, 1030, 1222; *Wasps*, 1432) that they did not always charge fees: Pittalus was consulted by rich and poor. Plato in the *Politicus* (259a; see my note in my translation, *Plato's Statesman* (London, 1952), p. 124, n.1) classes public and private doctors together in an analytical passage. A. H. M. Jones (op. cit., p. 219) indicates the extent to which such services developed in the Hellenistic and Roman periods, until Antoninus Pius actually limited the number of official doctors permitted. It may be true, however, that Aristophanes's patients had better chance of personal attention from the doctor than ordinary or needy people had in the Hellenistic cities.

The other interesting provision at Athens, of which we know from the Aristotelian *Constitution of Athens* and the very lively speech which is *Oratio XXIV*, of Lysias, was one said to go back to Peisistratus. A citizen too infirm to earn a livelihood had a small daily allowance: an obol in the early fourth century, but probably doubled later. There was a 'means test' for this (three *minae* when the grant was two obols—on a realistic modern valuation 1s. 6d. daily for incomes less than £67 10s.) and every recipient had to have his right to the grant checked annually by the Council. The Lysias speech, in which a recipient refutes a challenger to his rights at the annual check, is full of revealing asides. Only a well-to-do man, we are told, could be abusive of others: a poor man has to watch his words—so how could he have caused offence? Enough substance to enable one to be abusive was felt to be part of a free citizens's right at Athens!

This puts somewhat piquantly something basic to the Greek view of personal relations—that a man's self-respect must be maintained even under grinding economic conditions: he should still be able to be himself. Yet he cannot be himself unless he meets his due obligations. This comes out in two stories in Xenophon's *Memorabilia* with which we may conclude our study. Socrates is advising two friends who have lost wealth and estate in the recent revolution.[1]

Eutherus was elderly and had taken up heavy manual work, as being 'better than begging from anyone, seeing that I have no security to borrow on'. But he knew he could not keep it up long physically. 'Why not take work as a bailiff for

---

[1] The straitened conditions are reflected in the *Ecclesiazusae* and in the *Plutus* of Aristophanes. V. Ehrenbert in *The People of Aristophanes* (Blackwell, Oxford, 1943), pp. 169–80, deals with this situation. He may be a little severe on the Athenian view of beggars. Praxagoras' plans in the *Ecclesiazusae* of 'plenty for all' (587 seqq.) are made fun of; but from *Plutus*, 535, we learn that the ragged (and verminous) could warm themselves so closely by the furnaces at the baths that they got blisters in the process. They paid nothing for this privilege.

someone better off?' 'Because I don't wish to expose myself to another man's carping.' 'But all our magistrates have to do that: find a considerate man, keep off work you know you can't do physically and try hard at the work which you do get.'

Aristarchus looked very strained. Socrates asked if he could help. All his women relatives have landed at his home because of family problems—sisters, nieces, cousins. He can get no loan: it is hard to stand by and see his own folk dying, but how in these conditions can he feed so many? 'Ceramon seems to make a living.' 'Yes, but he has slaves and my folk are free.' 'Which is better, free or slave?' 'Free, of course; but slaves make things that sell. My ladies are gentlefolk.' 'What about cloaks, shirts, capes, smocks? Won't they sell?' 'No doubt.' 'Can't your ladies make these?' 'All of them.' So a woollen goods manufactory with free female labour is set up in Aristarchus's house, and he is teased as being the only idle mouth to feed. He is told he is the watch-dog and so earns his right to eat.[1]

The word for 'poor' (or rather for 'destitute') is πτωχός, and this is related to πτώσσειν, 'cower' or 'cringe'. Homer and Hesiod actually use it with a direct object to mean 'go begging from'. Cringing is hateful to the Greeks: they reject Oriental obeisances and demand that a man stand up on his feet.

Karl Barth has pointed to the divine factor standing outside the human bracket which transvaluates the values within the brackets. The Greeks are concerned to get the values within the bracket right; and they do so, at any rate for Western man. Therefore they cannot be ignored by anyone who is concerned with the profundity of the saying that it is more blessed to give than to receive.

[1] Xenophon, *Memorabilia*, II, 7, 8.

The Care of the Poor in the Old Testament

N. W. PORTEOUS

The subject with which this essay is concerned is that of the care of the poor in Israel in Old Testament times. The evidence which has to be taken into account is varied in character and not always easy to interpret. It is not surprising, therefore, that on quite important issues there can be the most radical differences of opinion. One thing, however, is quite certain. Poverty was felt to be a very real and pressing problem during the centuries which produced the Old Testament, and from what is said about it we obtain many a sidelight on the life that was being lived in the towns and villages of Palestine. The poor frequently figure in the stories which are told in its pages. The law codes take account of them and their needs. They have their champions among the prophets. In very many of the psalms we seem to be reading the authentic words of those who knew from personal experience what it means to be poor, though it is precisely in connexion with these psalms that one of the big cleavages of opinion occurs. There is clear evidence that in some quarters at least the worth of a man's character was judged in part at least by his attitude to the less fortunate among his brethren.

There is a great deal, on this as on many other subjects, in the Old Testament that we would like to know on which we cannot reach complete certainty. For one thing we are dealing with material much of which is anonymous and often of uncertain date. Yet there is no doubt at all that there was something about Israel's faith in God which prevented the problem of poverty from being ignored as something of no great consequence, and it is highly probable that we have to go right back to Israel's origins not only in Egypt and at Sinai but in Palestine itself for an explanation. There was exploitation in Canaan before the Conquest and that may very well have been carried over into the Israel which emerged. The complaint of the poor must always have been heard. This is not to say that there were not many Israelites who lived out their prosperous lives in supreme indifference to the plight of the less fortunate and indeed did not hesitate to add to their burdens. It is only too clear from the denunciations of the prophets and the laments of the psalmists that there were times when the brutalities of exploitation were such familiar features of Israelite society that the wonder is that anything survived of the precious thing that had been committed to this people. As one reads the tragic story of the decline and fall of the Hebrew kingdoms we may well marvel that there is an Old Testament at all.

What makes the subject of poverty in Israel and of the attitude taken to it so well worthy of study is that it leads us right into the heart of Israel's faith, and our study may help us to understand more fully why that faith has proved to be indestructible. The inequalities of human life, which are exhibited by almost every type of society, when they are brought about deliberately through certain individuals or classes taking unfair advantage, raise acutely the whole problem of human relationships. What made Israel unique in the ancient world was that its profoundest thinkers found themselves compelled to the belief that it was the object of the active, loving concern of a God who would not allow Himself to be worshipped in isolation from the relations which men ought to have to one another. It is this which gives its peculiar quality to the Old Testament; it bears witness to a God to whom the welfare of even the humblest of His creatures cannot be a matter of indifference and who rejects worship which leaves that out of account.

Now, a religious truth depends for its survival on its being acted upon. It has to be appropriated and lived. That almost inevitably involves a measure of institutionalization which brings its own danger. Yet in an imperfect world it is better to have institutions than nothing at all. It may well be, moreover, that there is a Utopian element in some of the rules for dealing with poverty in Israel. It seems unlikely, however, that they are purely ideal constructions and did not originate on the basis of some kind of actual practice. There must have been many men in Israel who tried to appropriate God's revelation of Himself and of His will in responsive action. Deuteronomy has indeed been described as 'a romantic dream' and there may be a sense in which that description is true. But it would never have been written at all if the way of life it advocates was merely a dream.

The three main Israelite codes, viz. the Book of the Covenant, the Code of Deuteronomy and the Law of Holiness (part of the Priestly Code) all legislate in the interests of the poor, and it is to these formulations that we must first direct our attention.

It is worthy of notice that in the Book of the Covenant the injunctions about the correct treatment of the poor do not occur among the *mišpaṭim* (which Albrecht Alt maintained to be akin to non-Israelite law) but in the paraenetic sections (which the same scholar regarded as characteristically Israelite). In the most recent commentary on the Book of Exodus, that by Martin Noth (A.T.D.,[1] 1959), the attempt is made by following approved form-critical methods to separate the original injunctions from later additions. This is supposed to be possible because of the curious alternation between singular and plural verbs and pronouns, and the suggestion is that the singular forms are original and the plural ones additional. For example, in Exodus 22[20] the alternation can be exhibited in English by retaining the old-fashioned words 'thou' and 'ye': 'Thou

[1] A.T.D. = *Das Alte Testament Deutsch*.

shalt not wrong an alien (*gēr*) nor oppress him: for ye were aliens in Egypt.' It is argued that the change in number implies that the last clause is an addition. The theory, however, runs into difficulties in the very next verse (v. 21), where we read: 'Ye shall not ill-use any widow or fatherless', where Noth gets out of the difficulty by suggesting that this verse must originally have been in the singular, but has become plural owing to the attraction of the plural in the second half of the preceding verse. We read on (vv. 23–23): 'If thou dost ill-use him ... for, if he cries to me, I will be sure to listen to his cry. I will blaze with anger and I will kill you with the sword, and your wives will be widows and your sons fatherless.' Noth supposes here that the first clause exhibits some kind of adaptation to the laws of casuistic type which are called the *mišpaṭim* and draws attention to the recurrence of the plural pronouns (presumably implying an addition) in what follows. One cannot help being a little suspicious of a theory which requires doctoring of the text to make it fit, especially as in v. 20 (*supra*) the change from singular to plural seems perfectly natural. It is not irrelevant to remember Steuernagel's grandiose but unsuccessful attempt to separate out two editions of Deuteronomy by using the clue of singular and plural verbs and pronouns. It is much more likely that in these curious alternations between singular and plural we have an illustration of the primitive oscillation between individual and group which has now been explained by the concept of corporate personality.

It seems to the present writer that in this type of injunction, which unlike the *mišpaṭim* is hortatory in character, the reason annexed is just as likely to be original as the injunction itself. Where there is no prescribed penalty which can be imposed by a court, it is not surprising that considerations should be added forthwith to make it likely that the injunctions will be taken seriously. In the present instances it is significant that the first appeal is to Israel's own experience of distress from which, as men well knew, they had been delivered by God, while the second appeal is to the certainty that God will intervene on the side of the wronged.

In what follows (in Exodus 22[24]ff.) there is the injunction not to exact interest on a loan made to a poor man, and, if a poor man's cloak has been taken as a pledge that he will repay a loan, to restore it to him before sundown. The explanation (v. 26) that the man needs the cloak to sleep in, since he has no other bedding, followed by the assertion that God will listen to him when he cries out, because He is compassionate, Noth merely asserts to be an addition. It may be submitted that the importance of the reason annexed to the injunction should not be lessened in this way. The explanation is really an essential part of the injunction without which it would presumably not have been made.

The early part of chapter 23 contains further injunctions which have the vulnerable classes in view. It is implied by vv. 3 and 6 taken together that the poor man is to receive strict justice like anybody else; he is neither to be favoured because of his poverty nor is advantage to be taken of him. The alien (*gēr*) is not to be ill-treated (v. 9), 'because ye know what it feels like to be an alien, for ye were aliens yourselves in Egypt'. Once again Noth claims these last words as an addition, but the same doubt of the correctness of this procedure may be permitted as before. In vv. 10 and 11 something new is introduced, the injunction about letting the land lie fallow in the seventh year. Nothing is said here to indicate whether this was to happen to the whole land at once, or whether, as is more probable, the process was staggered. The only reason for the practice given here is that it is a measure of poor relief, but Noth conjectures (with reference to a similar law in Leviticus 25) that originally the underlying idea was to let the land periodically return to its original state, what he calls a *restitutio in integrum*. This may well have been so, though there is the other explanation to which S. R. Driver alludes (I.C.C.,[1] *Exodus*, p. 177) that in this custom there may be a relic of communistic agriculture, whereby individuals were allotted land for limited periods only. However this may be, as the practice of letting land go fallow periodically is enjoined here, it has a definitely humanitarian motive. The same is true of the sabbath command inserted in v. 12. Once more, because of its plural formulation, v. 13 is treated by Noth as an addition.

How early these laws in the Book of the Covenant are cannot be certainly determined. The references to the alien (*gēr*) make it improbable that the so-called apodictic laws belong generally to a period earlier than the settlement in Canaan. Yet they need not be brought down later than the period of the settlement. There are widows and fatherless requiring help long before civilization becomes elaborate, while the problem of the alien (*gēr*), whether of another Israelite tribe or of the earlier Canaanite stock, living in an Israelite community would call for solution at an early stage. Alt believes (*Die Ursprünge des israelitischen Rechts*, p. 66, Kleine Schriften, vol. 1, p. 328) that the laws about the sabbatical year are early. In these laws, then, we get a glimpse of how social maladjustments were handled in Israel probably as early as the pre-monarchic period, though class distinctions became much more serious from the time of Solomon onwards, and we should take note of the combination of humanitarian and religious considerations which was already commended to the consciences of the people. No doubt that must have been done on the recurring occasions of the amphictyonic assembly.

It is not surprising that the Book of Deuteronomy, with its emphasis upon the gratitude due to God from Israel for the blessing bestowed upon them, that being the good land of promise and the good life which could be lived upon it, includes numerous provisions which have in view the needs of the defenceless, vulnerable folk, the widows and fatherless, the aliens (*gērim*) and the Levites who, being landless people, were dependent for their food on charity. Provision for the Levites seems to have been highly organized. They were to have their place at all the common meals at the sanctuary, provided for from the tithes and free-will offerings ($12^{18, 19}$; 14^{22-29}; $16^{11, 14}$), and the widows, fatherless, and aliens were to be included. Moreover, all these dependent people were to have the exclusive use of the tithes every three years. Emphasis is laid on the fact that

[1] I.C.C. = *International Critical Commentary*.

God had a concern in seeing that this was done and Israel would be blessed if He were obeyed. The lawgiver knows that men are all too ready to find plausible excuses for not observing these charitable customs, and so they are called upon to state publicly that all their duty in this respect has been honestly fulfilled (26^{12-15}).

The most interesting passage in the Book of Deuteronomy relevant to the present subject is the development of the custom of the sabbatical year (cf. Exodus 23^{10-11} *supra*) into a seven-yearly remission of debts (Heb. *šemiṭṭa*). This is referred to (15^{2b}) as a *šemiṭṭa laYahweh*, a remission for Yahweh or Yahweh's remission. Von Rad (A.T.D., Deuteronomium, p. 75) argues that here, as in the more elaborate law in Leviticus 25 (v. *infra*), there is a sacral basis for the injunction. It is, however, also possible that the phrase means a remission enjoined by Yahweh, though the parallel expression *šabbath laYahweh* (Leviticus 25^4) does lend support to von Rad's view. It is clear, however, that in Deuteronomy the emphasis is laid on the benefit the year of remission will bring to the poor who have fallen into debt.

It is generally agreed that this law had in view only charitable loans and not commercial loans and had, therefore, specifically to do with genuine poor relief. Loans to foreigners, which would be for commercial purposes, were excepted, and it is indicated that Israel had much to gain from such financial operations. It is not explained here how the poverty which the law was designed to relieve had come about, but it may be assumed that from the time of Solomon onwards with the rise of a commercial class the class of hand-workers in the various trades increasingly found its status lowered. The reference here (v. 7) is to the poor in the towns rather than to the depressed peasantry. At all events generosity was required of the rich and, in particular, the tendency on the part of some to be stingy in the matter of loans as the year of remission drew near was strongly disapproved. It is not made clear in this passage whether the remission which is enjoined is the suspension of interest for one year or the total cancellation of the debt. The more drastic interpretation is possible, as almost certainly purely charitable and not commercial loans are involved. Yet, on the other hand, the analogy of the fallow year might point in the other direction. What is certain is that obedience to the law will merit God's blessing, since God is concerned for the welfare of the poor. In v. 4 it is said that because of the greatness of God's blessing there will be no poor in Israel. In v. 11, however, expression is given to the realistic view that Israel will always have to reckon with a poor element in society and this means that there will always be need for generosity on the part of the rich towards their poorer brothers. Deuteronomy thinks of Israel as one big family and it is undoubted that this thought of a common brotherhood has a religious origin. It is worthy of note that Jesus (Mark 14^7) cites this same v. 11 when He is championing the woman who had lavished costly ointment upon Him. There is a καλόν which takes precedence even of acts of charity to the poor.

At v. 12 of this same chapter a new possibility is envisaged. A fellow Hebrew might be forced by his economic circumstances to sell himself into slavery to another Hebrew. The year of remission was to apply here, too, and the slave was not only to have his liberty restored to him but was to have liberal provision made him to enable him to make a new start in life. The reminder is given that Israel had been in slavery in Egypt and owed its liberty to God. The possibility is envisaged that a slave might actually for love of his master refuse his freedom, surely an indication that there must have been good men in Israel who treated their subordinates humanely and so even won their affection. This is surely more than a romantic fancy on the part of the law-giver.

Finally in Deuteronomy (unless we take into account the curse (27^{19}) pronounced on anyone who perverts the justice due to the alien, the fatherless, and the widow) there is a group of injunctions which are perhaps the most moving in the whole book. They are to be found in chapter 24. If a man has pledged some article of his possessions and has forfeited it, his creditor must not enter his house to seize the pledge, but must wait outside until the debtor brings the pledge out to him. Here we have a remarkable instance of respect for personality. A man's house is his castle. Furthermore, if a man, whether Israelite or alien, has been hired to do a job, he is to be given his wages before nightfall for no other reason than that he urgently needs the money. He is one of the vulnerable folk in whom Israel's God is specially interested. To treat him unfairly is to incur the guilt of sin in the eyes of God. Again the alien and the orphan are to receive just treatment and, in particular, the widow's cloak is not to be taken in pledge. That Israel had been in slavery in Egypt is to be borne in mind in this connexion also. The chapter closes with the injunction that the gleanings of harvest-field, olive-yard and vineyard are to be left for the alien, the fatherless, and the widow, and, like a refrain, the reference to slavery in Egypt is repeated. In v. 18 specific reference is made to Yahweh's act of deliverance from Egyptian bondage. The same God is now concerned for the unfortunates in Israel and it is implied that whoever opposes His will will have Him to reckon with.

How effective the Deuteronomic measures were in the relief of poverty and indeed to what extent they were actually enforced is a matter of conjecture. What is not in doubt is that there were those in Israel who thought kindly and generously about their unfortunate fellows, and such feelings do not exist among people who never trouble to translate them into action. One thing is clear, the Deuteronomic legislation seeks to solve the problem of poverty in as personal a way as possible. The poor are to share in the blessing of harvest, not apart from, but among, their more fortunate fellows. Israel is thought of as a community of brothers.

The Law of Holiness deals with the problem of poverty in two sections. In Leviticus 19 there is a brief reference (vv. 9 and 10) to gleaning. It is even more positive than the corresponding injunction in Deuteronomy; the gleanings are to be left deliberately for the benefit of the poor and the aliens (cf. 23^{22}). In v. 13 there is an injunction about paying the wages of a hired worker promptly which is also paralleled in Deuteronomy. In 19^{33-34} there is an injunction about the treatment of the alien which is couched in a curious mixture of singular and plural verbs and pronouns to which Noth draws attention (A.T.D., *Leviticus*, p. 124). With his preference for the singular formulation as the more original he underlines the words 'Thou shalt love him as thyself' (cf. v. 18, where the same is said of the neighbour (*rēaʻ*)). In this case these *are* the important words! All these injunctions are grounded in the pronouncements 'I am the Lord' or 'I am the Lord your God' which are repeated like a refrain. This is not merely humanitarian ethics. Moreover, it is important to notice how in this chapter the Law of Holiness is no less inward in its attitude to human relations than the Book of Deuteronomy itself. When it is a question of the treatment of the unfortunate there is a complete absence of legalism.

It is not necessary here to enter into all the details of Leviticus 25, but some of them are relevant. The chapter begins (vv. 1–7) with a law about the sabbatical year which is described as a sabbath of solemn rest, a sabbath of the Lord. As compared with Exodus 23^{10-11} there is less emphasis here on the needs of the poor. The aliens alone are mentioned as sharing with the rest of the household in whatever food is available in the seventh year.

At this point the question may again be raised whether the sabbatical year was observed. We are told that in Nehemiah's time (Nehemiah 10^{31}) both the injunction about leaving the land fallow in the seventh year and that regarding remission of debts were accepted, presumably to help solve the problem of poverty at that late period, while from 1 Maccabees $6^{49,53}$ it appears that the sabbatical law was observed so far as leaving the land fallow in the seventh year was concerned. In Leviticus 26^{34} *et passim* it is implied that the law of the sabbatical year had not been observed as it should have been and that the exilic period of seventy years (cf. 2 Chronicles 36^{21}) was to be regarded as a kind of compulsory Sabbath period to make up for preceding neglect. The account of the release and re-enslavement of the Hebrew slaves at a time of panic in Zedekiah's time (Jeremiah 34) implies that there had been a failure to keep the law (the reference seems to be to Deuteronomy 15^{12}ff. in this instance). A. Weiser A.T.D., *Der Prophet Jeremia*, p. 313) gets over the difficulty that, according to the Deuteronomic law, the slaves would not have to be released at one time by suggesting that in a moment of panic the Jews went beyond the letter of the law and released the slaves wholesale. The probability is that both Leviticus and Deuteronomy contain very old material and that regulations like those we have been considering may well have been put in force from time to time. It is difficult to believe that all this is mere Utopianism.

The complicated regulations about the year of jubilee in Leviticus 25 (vv. 8ff.) are designed to prevent the final alienation of land from the original owner, though the measures to prevent the alienation of houses in the towns give only limited protection. A special security for the Levites is, however, laid down. Whether the law of the jubilee was ever actually put in force we do not know. R. North in his very careful study of Leviticus 25 in his monograph *Sociology of the Biblical Jubilee* (1954) argues for a very early date and suggests that the jubilee was not intended to be repeated, but that the regulations were preserved as embodying a principle of permanent validity. It is probably wise to accept R. de Vaux's judgement (*Ancient Israel: its Life and Institutions*, pp. 175-7), who writes (p. 177) of the jubilee year: 'It was inspired by ancient ideas, and made use of the framework of an archaic calendar, which had not lost all its value in rural practice and in the religious sphere. But it was a Utopian law and it remained a dead letter.'

The remainder of Leviticus 25 contains regulations enjoining kindly treatment of the poor and the aliens which need not be detailed. Behind all these laws is a tremendous sense of the incongruity of injustice and slavery among a people which owed its freedom to God's deliverance of the forefathers from Egypt.

Now, of course, it would be wrong to suppose that Israel was unique in feeling concern for the poor and devising measures for their relief. In the Egyptian Wisdom literature, for example, the duty of care for the poor, the widow and the stranger, and God's concern for the poor are mentioned (J. B. Pritchard, A.N.E.T.,[1] p. 424). Or there is the negative confession 'I have not done violence to a poor man' in the Book of the Dead (op. cit., p. 34). In the Epilogue to the Code of Hammurabi (op. cit., p. 178) the king claims that his rule has been beneficent towards the unfortunate. In the Keret poem from Ugarit the king's son lets his father know that it is time he abdicated, because he can no longer look after the interests of defenceless folk (op. cit., p. 149). There is no parallel, however, to the elaborate concern which the Hebrew codes reveal or to the way in which this concern is related to the concern of the covenant God had laid upon the conscience of the covenant people, definite laws of poor relief being formulated.

It does not fall within the scope of this essay to go in detail into the elaborate denunciations of the prophets, which give a startling picture of the prevalence of inhumane treatment of the underprivileged both in the pre-exilic and in the post-exilic period. We can connect these denunciations with the development of class distinctions under the monarchy, the appearance of a commercial, moneyed class and the growth of a patriciate who lived a life of luxury and self-indulgence and gave not a thought to the miseries of the poor who toiled for them. We get vivid glimpses of what was going on especially in the pre-exilic prophets Amos, Micah, Isaiah, and Jeremiah, also in Ezekiel and in the great chapter which describes the fast which Yahweh chooses (Isaiah 58). One of the great social evils was the swallowing up of the crofts of the peasants into huge *latifundia*, because they were compelled to sell them and even their own persons to pay their debts (Micah 2^2 and Isaiah 5^8). There are frequent references to the ill-treatment and neglect of the vulnerable folk, the widows and fatherless and the aliens, and to the perversion of justice to the detriment of the poor and friendless. There were those who would stop at nothing provided they could make money. Injustice flourished among the highest in the land. Jeremiah (22^{13-17}) denounces Jehoiakim, who took advantage of his labourers to indulge his own craze for building fine palaces, and then contrasts him unfavourably

---

[1] A.N.E.T. = *Ancient Near Eastern Texts.*

with his father, the good king Josiah, who acted rightly by the poor and needy. 'Is not this to know me? says the Lord.' The connexion of charitable conduct with the concern of Israel's God could not be put more impressively. There is a telling summary in Ezekiel (18$^{5-9}$), who defines what it is to be a righteous man and among other characteristics describes him as one who 'does not oppress anyone, but returns his pledge to the debtor, does not commit robbery, gives his bread to the hungry, clothes the naked, does not lend at interest or exact increase'. One hears definite echoes of the law (cf. Ezekiel 22$^{7,\ 12,\ 29}$).

It may be said with some confidence that the denunciations of the prophets bear witness to a moral tradition which had been growing from the time of the early amphictyony. This tradition was taken over as representing the ideal for the Davidic monarchy (v., e.g., Psalm 72$^{1-4}$) and it appears in the picture of the ideal coming ruler (Isaiah 11^4). The prophets are not merely denouncing inhumanity; they are appealing to men's consciences and to their knowledge of what life in Israel was supposed to be like. We should at this point ask ourselves how this tradition had survived. In the instruction of the priests, no doubt, but surely also in the lives of many humble men and women who in their own quiet way did justice, loved kindness, and walked humbly with God (Micah 6^8). One has to account for the prophets themselves; they surely represent a living tradition of humane conduct.

Brief reference must be made to another line of evidence, namely to the remarkable way in which certain of the words for poor came in course of time to acquire a religious connotation. This subject has been exhaustively treated by scholars like A. Causse in his book *Les Pauvres d'Israël* and by A. Gelin in *Les Pauvres de Yahvé* (translated as *The Poor of Yahweh*). These writers supposed that a large number of the psalms are the work of poor men who, as Causse says, 'actually lived in the fields of ancient Palestine, in the unnamed village, the village on the hill-side, in the hollow of the valley . . . peasants, ploughmen and shepherds like their fathers. In the day-time they toiled, cultivated the rocky soil under the blazing sun; in the evening they returned home and under the eastern night they breathed out the lament of their souls; they summoned God to their aid' (Causse, op. cit., pp. 81–82). The description of the poor in those days is doubtless correct, but that here we have a correct account of the origin of many of the psalms is denied by S. Mowinckel (*The Psalms in Israel's Worship*, vol. II, pp. 91ff.), who argues cogently that the authors of these as of the other psalms were Levites attached to the Temple who, as it will be remembered, belonged to an order many of whom, especially in the countryside, were classed with the poor and needy and who would have deep sympathy with the underprivileged. The point, however, which must be made here is that it was the known concern of the God of Israel for the poor which made possible the subtle semantic change of these terms (*'āni, 'ānaw, 'ebyōn, dal*) from a social to a religious connotation, though the social connotation remains underlying the religious. Poverty was dignified by God's concern for the poor and the virtue of humility is exalted. This is not the place to trace the remarkable development of thought which leads right on into Christianity and to the beatitude pronounced on the poor.

There was, however, another attitude to poverty which is illustrated in the Old Testament, especially in the Wisdom literature, the view of poverty as something culpable and as an indication of idleness and misused opportunities. In a very interesting study of the Hebrew words for poor and rich (*'Arm und reich im Alten Testament mit besonderer Berücksichtigung der nachexilischen Zeit'* in Z.A.W., 1939, Heft 1/2, pp. 31ff.) A. Kuschke has pointed out that it is a different set of expressions for 'poor' that are characteristic of this attitude (e.g. *rāš*, *ḥāsēr*, and *miskēn*), not the words which acquired a religious nuance. Although in the proverbial literature there are words of sympathy with the poor, for the most part they are regarded with a cool, worldly-wise glance. The dominant note in the Old Testament, however, as we have seen, is of deep sympathy with the unfortunate, a sympathy which showed that men had understood something of the compassionate heart of God whose righteousness (*ṣᵉdaḳa*) included championship of the poor. It was not surprising that *ṣᵉdaḳa* should eventually come in certain contexts to acquire the connotation of 'almsgiving'.

It will not be unfitting to close this essay with a reference to the picture of Ruth among the alien corn at Bethlehem gleaning after the reapers, and of Boaz instructing his labourers not to interfere with her and even to pull out some of the stalks from the sheaves and leave them for her. This is not just an idyllic story; there were men like this in old Israel. And surely, too, the picture we get in Job 29 of the *Kalos k'agathos* is true to life, how he befriended the poor and fatherless, caused the widow's heart to sing for joy, was a father to the poor and took trouble to see that even a man he had not previously known got justice at the court. In chapter 31 we get Job's elaborate negative confession where he testifies to the common humanity of all men and declares that he has not failed to share what he had with the poor, the widow, and the fatherless, or to clothe the naked, warming him with the fleece of his sheep, and that he has not seized the chance to outwit him at court. Perhaps the author of this marvellous book is unconsciously giving us a self-portrait. The story of Israel has its dark shadows, but there are also sunlit spaces. Moreover, here in the Book of Job we get a certain universalizing of charity. Job is not an Israelite, though the author of the book is. Even in that most exclusive book, Deuteronomy, the *alien* (*gēr*) is to receive his share of the blessing, and is as it were an earnest of the great Gentile world outside, while Elijah was kind to a poor Phoenician widow (1 Kings 17[8]ff.), as a greater than Elijah reminded his audience in the synagogue at Nazareth. The Old Testament has its windows towards the future and one day the dominical word would be spoken: 'Inasmuch as you have done it unto one of the least of these my brethren you have done it unto me.'

Diakonia in the New Testament

C. E. B. CRANFIELD

I. THE USE OF DIAKONEIN AND ITS COGNATES[1]

In pagan Greek the verb *diakonein*[2] is used both in a narrow sense, with reference to waiting at table or attending to someone's bodily needs, and also in a broad sense, of service rendered to another person quite generally, while the cognates *diakonia* and *diakonos* are used to denote, respectively, the action of *diakonein* and the person who performs it. Further cognates, which are not found in the New Testament, also occur. In the eyes of the Greeks such service was undignified and menial (so, for example, in Plato's *Gorgias*[3] the adjective *diakonikos* appears in company with two other adjectives both of which mean 'servile'): the only *diakonia* regarded as honourable was that rendered to the State.

In the Septuagint *diakonein* never occurs, and *diakonia* and *diakonos* occur only a few times and then without any theological significance.

In the New Testament the word-group[4] is used non-theologically in both the narrow and the broad senses noted above for pagan Greek.[5] It is also used with theological significance in a variety of ways. It is used with reference to Christ's service of men: *diakonein* in Mark 10^{45} = Matthew 20^{28} ('the Son of man came . . . to minister') and Luke 22^{27} ('I am in the midst of you as he that serveth'); *diakonos* in Romans 15^8 (Christ in His earthly life is the minister of the Jewish people). *Diakonos* is used generally in connexion with service rendered to God (Romans 13^4; 2 Corinthians 6^4; (1 Thessalonians 3^2)), to Christ (John 12^{26}; 2 Corinthians 11^{23}; Colossians 1^7; 1 Timothy 4^6), to the new covenant (2 Corinthians 3^6), to the Gospel (Ephesians 3^7; Colossians 1^{23}), to the fellow disciple or to the Church as a whole (Mark 9^{35}; 10^{43} = Matthew 20^{26}; Matthew

---

[1] cf. (W. Bauer,) W. F. Arndt and F. W. Gingrich, *A Greek-English Lexicon of the New Testament and other Early Christian Literature* (Cambridge, 1957); H. W. Beyer, in G. Kittel (ed.), continued by G. Friedrich (ed.), *Theologisches Wörterbuch zum Neuen Testament* (Stuttgart, 1933—), II, pp. 81–93; H. G. Liddell and R. Scott, *A Greek-English Lexicon* (revised and augmented by H. Stuart Jones and R. McKenzie, Oxford, 1940); W. F. Moulton and A. S. Geden, *A Concordance to the Greek New Testament* (3rd ed., Edinburgh, 1926).

[2] Its earliest known occurrence is in Herodotus.

[3] 518 A.

[4] *Diakonein* occurs thirty-seven times in all in the New Testament, *diakonia* thirty-four times, and *diakonos* thirty times.

[5] e.g. in the narrow sense, Luke 17^8, 22^{27a}; John 2^5, and, in the broad sense, Mark 10^{45} = Matthew 20^{28} ('to be ministered unto'); Matthew 22^{13}.

23^{11}; Colossians 1^{25})—in this last connexion *diakonein* is also used in 1 Peter 1^{12}; 4^{10}, and *diakonia* in 2 Corinthians 11^8. *Diakonein* also occurs in Mark 1^{31} = Matthew 8^{15} = Luke 4^{39}; Mark 15^{41} = Matthew 27^{55}; Luke 8^3; 10^{40} (in this verse *diakonia* is used, too); John 12^2, where the reference is to such practical service as preparing a meal or waiting at table rendered to Jesus (or to Jesus and His disciples), and in Acts 19^{22}, where it denotes the assistance given to the apostle Paul by Timothy and Erastus. In the case of *diakonia* a technical use emerges, which we may call the *general technical use*—to denote a function or office within the Church or the activity of fulfilling it. Thus it is used of the ministry of apostles, evangelists, prophets, etc. (e.g. Acts $1^{17, 25}$; 20^{24}; 21^{19}; Romans 11^{13}; 1 Corinthians 12^5; 2 Corinthians 4^1; 5^{18}: cf. the use of *diakonos* in 1 Corinthians 3^5). It is not without significance that the technical term for functions in the Church which necessarily involve some measure of leadership has from the first been a word which signifies not pre-eminence or power but simply humble service, and, further, that it is the same word that was used of Christ's own service of men and also of the service owed by every Christian to God, to Christ, to his fellows.

But, side by side with this general technical use, there is to be seen what may be called the *specialized technical use* of the word-group. Thus *diakonein* is used in Matthew 25^{44} as a term covering the various services to the needy mentioned in vv. 42 and 43. In Romans 15^{25} it is used of the service Paul is rendering to the poor in Jerusalem by organizing the collection on their behalf. In Hebrews 6^{10} the reference is probably to the relief of the bodily and material needs of fellow Christians. In Acts 6^2 and 2 Corinthians $8^{19f.}$, while *diakonein* itself has some such sense as 'attend to', the combination of words of which it is a part refers, in each case, to service of the needy (in Acts 6^2 to the supervision of the communal meals, in 2 Corinthians $8^{19f.}$ to the collection for Jerusalem). Especially instructive is 1 Peter 4^{11}; for, while in the previous verse *diakonein* was used quite generally of the service rendered to one's fellow Christians by using to the full whatever spiritual gift one has received, it is here contrasted with *lalein* ('speak') and is most naturally understood to refer to the relief of physical and material needs contrasted with preaching, teaching, etc. In two other occurrences[1] it means 'discharge the duties pertaining to the office of a *diakonos*'.

Diakonia is used similarly of the daily distribution in the early days of the Jerusalem Church[2] and seven times[3] with reference to the collection for the brethren in Jerusalem. In Romans 12^7, where it occurs twice, while some scholars hold that it is used as a general term (our general technical use), which is then broken down into its various divisions ('he that teacheth', etc.), it is more probable that it is used in the specialized technical sense with reference to the practical service of the needy, since, if it were being used as a general term, it

---

[1] 1 Timothy $3^{10, 13}$.
[2] Acts 6^1.
[3] Acts 11^{29}; 12^{25}; Romans 15^{31}; 2 Corinthians 8^4; $9^{1, 12, 13}$.

would more naturally have been placed before, rather than after, the reference to prophecy. It is likely that in 1 Corinthians 16[15] also the word has the specialized sense.

With regard to *diakonos*, there are three occurrences in which it quite clearly denotes the holder of a particular office: Philippians 1[1]; 1 Timothy 3[8, 12]. In Philippians the *diakonoi* are coupled with, though mentioned after, the *episkopoi*; and similarly in 1 Timothy the section on *diakonoi* follows immediately that on *episkopoi*. But in neither passage are the functions of a *diakonos* indicated—though there is possibly some force in the suggestion that the two groups are mentioned in Philippians 1[1] because they have both had to do with the collection of the gifts for which Paul is thanking the Church, the *diakonoi* being mentioned after the *episkopoi*, as having acted as agents in the matter under their general supervision; and also in the suggestion that in 1 Timothy 3 the fact that, while aptness to teach (included in the section on *episkopoi*) is omitted from the requirements of a *diakonos*, the *diakonoi* are required to be 'not double-tongued, not given to much wine, not greedy of filthy lucre', might be a pointer to their office's having involved constant visitation of houses and the handling of material resources (though it is to be noted that the *episkopos* also is to be 'no lover of money'). The strongest argument—and it is a strong argument—in favour of the view that *diakonos* in these two passages denotes the holder of a particular office which had to do with the practical assistance of those who were in one way or another specially needy is the inherent probability that the specialized technical use of *diakonos* will have been parallel to the specialized technical use of its cognates *diakonein* and *diakonia*. What we know of the diaconate in the second century is, of course, further support.

There is one other occurrence of *diakonos* in the New Testament which must be mentioned. In Romans 16[1] Phoebe is described as '*diakonos* of the church that is at Cenchreae'. It is possible to understand the word here as a quite general reference to her service of the congregation; but the form in which Paul expresses himself (οὖσαν διάκονον τῆς ἐκκλησίας . . .) makes it more natural to take it as referring to a definite office. The latter part of v. 2, if it may be connected with her office, suggests that it had to do with affording practical assistance to those who stood in need of it.

We have now seen that there is in the New Testament a specialized technical use of *diakonein* and *diakonia* to denote the practical service of those who are specially needy 'in body, or estate', and that it is highly probable that the specialized technical use of *diakonos* also has the same reference. It is with *diakonia* in this special sense that we are here concerned.

II. THE THEOLOGICAL NECESSITY OF DIAKONIA

The necessity of *diakonia* as an essential function both of the Church as a body and of its individual members severally is so clear that we need not labour it. It is a theological necessity having its ground in the Gospel itself, in the grace of

God in Jesus Christ. It will be sufficient here merely to indicate some of the ways in which the New Testament brings it home to us.

It is clearly implied by the divine commandment so frequently repeated in the New Testament, 'Thou shalt love thy neighbour as thyself';[1] for to love one's neighbour as oneself certainly involves assisting him when he is in need, as our Lord's exposition of the law[2] made clear. A love which stopped short of such practical assistance could only be a love 'in word' or 'with the tongue' and not 'in deed and truth',[3] an empty and futile thing. A Church which was not zealous to succour the needy and afflicted would be a Church which flouted God's law.

It is brought home to us in the petition which Christ has placed on our lips: 'Give us this day our daily bread.'[4] For this is not just a petition for ourselves only, but intercession for others as well, prayer which embraces all who are our brothers in Christ, and not only those whom we can see and know to be such, but all men who are alive upon the earth.[5] And it is evident that to pray to God to give our fellow men their daily bread would be an insolent mockery, were our prayer not accompanied by action aimed at doing all that is within our power to bring about the answer to our prayer. For the Church to pray these words and yet not do what it can to feed the hungry and the starving would be to condemn itself as hypocritical and to insult Him to whom its prayer is addressed.

It is set forth in the example of Jesus Christ, whose ministry is the pattern of the Church's continuing ministry. His service of men was not limited to preaching and teaching, but included His service of the sick, the hungry, the afflicted, in His healing and other miracles. He had compassion on human distress, and His compassion issued in action for its relief.[6]

It is implicit in the Church's duty to bear witness to Christ.[7] For the witness required of the Church is not a witness of words only: its actions as well as its words are to be pointers to the reality and the nature of the grace of God in Jesus Christ. The witness of a Church which did not concern itself with the humble service of the needy and suffering would be an altogether incredible witness.

It is, above all, made inescapably clear in the Discourse on the Final Judgement in Matthew 25^{31-46}. For that discourse discloses a mystery—the mystery of the presence of the exalted Son of man in the persons of those who are needy and in distress. The theological necessity of *diakonia* as a function of the Church as a whole and of the individual Christian could not be more forcibly brought home to us; for when once it is apparent that 'Christ is either neglected or honoured in the persons of those who need our assistance',[8] there can be no

---

[1] Leviticus 19^{18}; Matthew 19^{19}; 22^{39} = Mark 12^{31}; Luke 10^{27}; Romans 13^9; Galatians 5^{14}; James 2^8.

[2] Matthew 7^{12}; Luke 10^{30-37}.

[3] 1 John 3^{18}.

[4] Matthew 6^{11} (cf. Luke 11^3).

[5] cf. Calvin, *Institutes of the Christian Religion*, III, xx, 38.

[6] Matthew 14^{14}; 15^{32} = Mark 8^2; Matthew 20^{34}; Luke 7^{13}.

[7] e.g. Luke 24^{48}; John 15^{27}; Acts 1^8; 4^{33}; 1 Corinthians 1^6; 2 Timothy 1^8; 1 John 1^2; 4^{14}.

[8] Calvin, in his comment on Matthew 25^{40}.

question about the Church's obligation to minister to the needy with loving practical service.

III. THE NATURE OF TRUE DIAKONIA

What has been said above about its theological necessity suggests clues which we may follow in our attempt to gain a deeper insight into the nature of true *diakonia* and to draw out some of the characteristics which the Church's, and the individual Christian's, practical service will exhibit, in so far as it really is the *diakonia* which the Gospel demands.

Our *diakonia* is part of our obedience to God's law. The New Testament makes it abundantly clear that the obedience God's law requires is not a legalistic obedience vainly aimed at putting God under an obligation but the true obedience which consists of faith and the attitudes and actions which are the expression of faith.[1] As part of this obedience our *diakonia* is a result of God's establishment of His law, by the ministry of His Son and the gift of His Spirit, in its true gracious and spiritual character as 'the law of the Spirit of life' which sets us free from the tyranny of sin and death.[2] It is an element of our calling God 'Father' in sincerity and truth which the Holy Spirit accomplishes.[3] As such it can only be an altogether free, grateful, and joyous activity.

It is the Church's enacted *amen* to its prayer of intercession for 'all those, who are any ways afflicted, or distressed, in mind, body, or estate', the deed which seals the sincerity of our words, the activity which marches side by side with our praying as its indispensable companion. But the indispensability is mutual; and *diakonia* in separation from prayer would as little be true Christian *diakonia* as would prayer in separation from *diakonia* be true Christian prayer. For Christian *diakonia* is not a self-reliant, self-sufficient human activity, but a human activity which is itself a humble waiting upon God's action. The Church remembers that the resources of its *diakonia* come not from its own independent generosity but from the generosity of God.[4]

It is a part of our following of Christ. His whole life was (in the general sense of the word) a *diakonia* of men, and the use in the New Testament of words of the *diakonein* group with reference to Christ[5] serves to indicate not only what His mission achieved but also the humble spirit in which He fulfilled it. True Christian *diakonia* (whether in the general or the special sense of the word) is always characterized by the meekness and humility of Christ. When those who give of their substance for the relief of the needy or those who organize and administer the Church's *diakonia* yield to the temptation to self-importance and lordliness, their service ceases to be authentic *diakonia*.

[1] cf. Romans 1^5 ('unto obedience of faith').
[2] cf. Romans 8^2. For an extraordinarily suggestive exposition of Romans 8 under the heading, 'The Gospel as the Establishment of God's Law', see K. Barth, *A Shorter Commentary on Romans* (London, 1959), pp. 88ff.
[3] cf. Romans $8^{15f.}$; Galatians 4^6.
[4] cf. I Peter 4^{11b}.
[5] Matthew 20^{28} = Mark 10^{45}; Luke 22^{27}; Romans 15^8.

It is a part of our witness to Christ. It is action so genuinely consistent with the message which the Church has to proclaim that it serves to illustrate and to confirm it. By its simplicity, its directness, and its adequacy for the particular human distress in question, it points to the simplicity, the directness, the adequacy of the grace of God in Jesus Christ. It is of the nature of witness that it should point beyond, and away from, itself to something or someone else. So the Church's *diakonia* points beyond the Church and its actions to Him who is, in the last resort, man's only Helper and Healer. And since it is witness to Jesus Christ it will abhor as altogether unworthy all ostentation and boastfulness. In this connexion it is important at all times, but especially in a day of ecclesiastical public relations officers, when the danger of the Church's *diakonia* being preceded by a trumpet is specially great, for the Church to remember that true *diakonia* is under the discipline of Matthew 6^{1-4} as well as of Matthew 5^{14-16}. At first sight the two passages might seem to be contradictory; for there seems to be little difference between 'before men, that they may see your good works' (5^{16}) and 'before men, to be seen of them' (6^1). But in each case the sequel makes the meaning plain. The Church is indeed to let its *diakonia* be seen so that men may have cause to glorify God; but that is something altogether different from every form of self-advertisement designed to make sure that the Church (or the individual Christian) 'may have glory of men'.

Finally, the mystery of the exalted Christ's presence in His suffering brothers and sisters means that *diakonia* is the Church's service of its Lord in person—the most intimate and personal service of Him that it is permitted to render. It is thus altogether free from the taint of patronizing. The Church knows well that, so far from there being any question of its being in a position to confer favours on the needy, it is the needy who are conferring a favour upon it, in that by their distress they present it with the opportunity to love and serve Him, to whom it owes more than it can ever repay. And, as the Church's *diakonia* is rendered without patronizing, so it can be accepted without any sense of humiliation. Moreover, it is unlimited, in the sense that the Church can never do enough, can never wish to set limits to the demands which the needy make upon it, can never be grudging in its service, because it knows that its indebtedness to Christ is infinite. So the Church, in so far as it is the true Church of Jesus Christ, delights to serve them unweariedly and always to be patient with them, and does not resent the fact that they are often ungrateful and difficult to help. Even in the most unresponsive, sullen and embittered, it discerns by faith the presence of its Lord, and so is enabled to minister 'with cheerfulness'.[1] And true *diakonia* always treats the needy and the suffering as persons. The very use of the word carries with it some suggestion of personal service to a person. But it is the recognition that Christ Himself, in His freedom and lordship, is personally—though hiddenly and mysteriously—present in the needy which makes it impossible for the believing Church ever to regard or treat them as merely so many cases of poverty, malnutrition or disease. For others they may perhaps be a

---

[1] Romans 12^8: ἐν ἱλαρότητι.

problem to be solved, a political, social or economic untidiness to be cleared up, a potential danger to be neutralized: for the Christian Church they must always remain persons, whose status as persons is guaranteed by the mystery disclosed in Matthew $25^{31ff.}$.

IV. THE SCOPE OF DIAKONIA

The question we are here concerned with is the question whether, according to the New Testament, the Church is under obligation to seek to relieve human distress as such wherever it is to be found, or only to succour the needy and afflicted within its own fellowship.

As far as the Synoptic Gospels are concerned, the position seems clear. According to Matthew 5^{43-48} = Luke $6^{27f., 32-36}$, the disciples of Jesus are to love their enemies, pray for their persecutors, and do good to them that hate them. In Matthew 7^{12} = Luke 6^{31} it is perhaps significant that the general term 'men' is used, and not 'your brethren'. Again, when Jesus is asked by the lawyer, 'And who is my neighbour?', He tells a parable in which it is a Samaritan who is the example of neighbourliness.[1] The implication is that in the commandment of Leviticus 19^{18}, which the lawyer has just quoted, 'neighbour' is to be understood in the broadest possible sense. And, finally, in Matthew 25^{31-46}, which is one of the most important New Testament passages for the theology of *diakonia*, it is hardly to be doubted—despite some opinions to the contrary—that 'these my brethren, even these least' in v. 40 and 'these least' in v. 45 denote the needy generally irrespective of whether they are disciples or not; for otherwise the having given help to them or withheld it could not be a universally applicable criterion, as v. 32 implies that it is (while all the individuals denoted by 'all the nations' would certainly have had an opportunity to assist a fellow man in need, it obviously could not be assumed that they would all have had an opportunity to assist a needy disciple).

But what of the rest of the New Testament? There is certainly a preponderance of references to loving and succouring fellow Christians;[2] and, as has often been pointed out,[3] it is not easy to find outside the Synoptic Gospels absolutely clear examples of *agapan* or *agape* used of the love owed by Christians with a wider reference than the fellowship of the Church. Perhaps the most explicit passage is 1 Thessalonians 3^{12} ('and the Lord make you to increase and abound in love one toward another, and toward all men . . .'). But there are others which make the wider obligation perfectly clear: Romans 12^{14} ('Bless them that persecute you; bless, and curse not'); Romans 12^{20} ('But if thine enemy hunger, feed him; if he thirst, give him to drink: for in so doing thou shalt heap coals of fire upon his head [i.e. inflict on him an inward sense of

---

[1] Luke 10^{25-37}.

[2] e.g. John $13^{34f.}$; Acts $2^{42, 44f.}$; 4^{32-37}; Romans 12^{10}; 1 Corinthians 16^{15}; Galatians 6^{2}; Colossians 1^4; 1 Thessalonians $4^{9f.}$; 2 Thessalonians 1^3; Hebrews 6^{10}; $10^{33f.}$; 13^{1-3}; James $2^{15f.}$; 1 Peter 4^{8-10}; 5^5; 1 John 3^{10-18}.

[3] e.g. in A. Richardson (ed.), *A Theological Word Book of the Bible* (London, 1950), p. 136.

shame]'); Galatians 6¹⁰ ('So then, as we have opportunity, let us work that which is good toward all men, and especially toward them that are of the household of the faith'); 1 Thessalonians 5¹⁵ ('. . . but alway follow after that which is good, one toward another, and toward all'); 1 Peter 2¹⁷ ('Honour all men. Love the brotherhood . . .'). In the last of these, while a different word is used for the more intimate relationship within the Christian community and thus a distinction is made, the word 'honour' certainly implies that Christians are to assist all men as they have need. It is probable that in Romans 12⁹ 'love' has a general reference: there is then added point in the words, 'In love of the brethren be tenderly affectioned one to another', in the following verse. Love toward all men seems also to be intended by 'love' in 1 Corinthians 16¹⁴ ('Let all that ye do be done in love').

These examples are enough to show that the second half of H. W. Montefiore's statement, 'It is probable (almost to the point of certainty) that Jesus had taught his disciples to show love to anyone in need, and that the early church narrowed the concept of neighbour until it was equivalent to church member',[1] is not justified by the New Testament evidence. There are a good many places in his article where New Testament passages are treated unfairly or where the argument is less than convincing. For instance, to infer from Paul's recognition that a fellow Christian has a special claim on one's support (e.g. Galatians 6¹⁰) that 'Paul did not regard it as a Christian duty to go out of his way to love a non-Christian'[2] is surely unfair.

In connexion with the relative fewness of explicit references to Christians assisting those outside the Church, it is important to remember the poverty of the primitive Church. In a situation in which it must have been difficult to support all the needy within the Church there will have been little opportunity for assistance on any large scale to the needy outside the household of faith. It was a situation altogether different from that of the Church in western Europe or the United States of America today.

There is, in any case, quite enough evidence in the New Testament—and it is not limited to the teaching of Jesus—to make it inescapably clear that churches and individual Christians, whether they are rich or poor, but especially when they are comparatively rich, are under an obligation to practise *diakonia* not only toward other Christians who are in need but toward the needy and afflicted wherever they are to be found.

V. THE DIAKONIA OF THE CONGREGATION AND OF ITS MEMBERS AND THE DIACONATE

We have now to ask what may be said, on the basis of the New Testament, about (i) the relation between the *diakonia* of the congregation as a whole and the

---

[1] 'Thou shalt love the [*sic*] neighbour as thyself', in *Novum Testamentum*, V (Leiden, 1962), p. 166.
[2] ibid., p. 162.

diakonia of the individual members, and (ii) the relation of both to the diaconate.

With regard to (i)—while it is true that every act of *diakonia* performed by a member of the congregation is a contribution to the *diakonia* of the whole, and that the *diakonia* of the congregation as a whole must anyway be carried out by its members, it is of vital importance that we should neither dissolve away the responsibility of the individual member, as though there were no room for *diakonia* by individual members on their own initiative and responsibility, but only for the carrying out of what is initiated by, and is the responsibility of, the congregation as a whole; nor dissolve away the responsibility of the congregation, as though its *diakonia* were simply the sum total of the acts of service undertaken by the several members on their own initiative and responsibility. For the New Testament clearly envisages both a *diakonia* which is undertaken by the congregation as a whole (though it is necessarily carried out by particular members), as may be seen, for example, in Acts 6^1 and in passages referring to the collection for the poor in Jerusalem (Acts $11^{28f.}$; 24^{17}; Romans 15^{25-27}; 1 Corinthians 16^{1-4}; 2 Corinthians 8^{1-15}; 9^{1-15}) and also a *diakonia* which is a matter of the individual Christian's responsibility and initiative (though it is also, of course, a contribution to the *diakonia* of the congregation), as is clear from such passages as Matthew 25^{31-46}; Romans 12^{20}; Galatians 6^2. While the individual is loyally to join in the *diakonia* undertaken by the community, he is not thereby released from the responsibility to minister, on his own initiative and in his own name as a Christian man, as the opportunity for such ministering occurs; and, on the other hand, the congregation in its corporate life cannot escape its corporate responsibility on the pretext that *diakonia* is the private responsibility of its members. The responsibility for ministering to Christ, as He comes to us under the veil of the suffering humanity of His brothers and sisters whether inside or outside the fellowship of the Church, rests squarely both on the congregation as a whole and on every individual member severally.

With regard to (ii)—we have already seen that there are only two passages in the New Testament[1] which both use the word *diakonos* and make it absolutely clear that the reference is to the bearer of a specific office in the Church, and that, while it is very highly probable that the *diakonoi* referred to in these two passages had special responsibility in connexion with the *diakonia* of the congregation, like the deacons of the second century, this is not expressly stated in either passage. But the fact that there is thus some uncertainty in connexion with the diaconate in New Testament times is much less of an embarrassment than one might at first be inclined to expect. For the really important question is not whether there is absolutely clear evidence in the New Testament of the existence of a diaconate similar to that of the second century, but whether it affords unambiguous evidence of the perpetual necessity of *diakonia* as a function of the Church on earth. And of this there is no doubt at all. Even if there had been no mention of deacons in the New Testament, we should still have been obliged, in

[1] Philippians 1^1; 1 Timothy 3^{8-13}. cf. p. 39.

loyalty to the New Testament, to explore the possibility that the twentieth-century Church might fulfil its function of *diakonia* more effectively with an order of ministers having special responsibility in this field than without one.

But the element of uncertainty which we have noticed ought not to be exaggerated. It is certainly the present writer's conviction that, when all the relevant New Testament material, and not just the two passages referred to above[1] (backed perhaps by the much more problematical evidence of Acts 6),[2] is considered, the image of a primitive diaconate becomes tolerably distinct. That the diaconate did not free either the congregation as a whole or the individual members severally from their responsibility for *diakonia* is clear from evidence already considered. Rather it must have served to stimulate and to organize, to lead and to focus, the *diakonia* of the whole Christian community.

VI. DIAKONIA AND CHURCH FINANCE

It is obvious that between the Church's *diakonia* and its finance, that vast ecclesiastical hinterland seldom explored theologically, there is an intimate and extensive mutual involvement. What light does the New Testament throw upon this complicated relationship?

The principle that those who are whole-time workers for the Gospel are entitled to support from the Church's resources has good New Testament authority.[3] But, at the same time, the fact that the apostle Paul refused to claim this right for himself and preferred to work with his hands to support himself[4]—

---

[1] A verse, not yet mentioned, which is particularly interesting in this connexion, is Romans 12^8; for it seems very probable that in ὁ προϊστάμενος (R.V.: 'he that ruleth') and ὁ ἐλεῶν (R.V.: 'he that sheweth mercy') we catch a glimpse of the primitive diaconate at work, the former being probably either the person whose function it was to organize and preside over the congregation's charitable work or else someone to whom the congregation looked (perhaps partly on account of his social position) for support for those, such as widows and orphans, who were in a weak position in society, and the latter someone recognized by the congregation as having gifts which made him specially suited to concentrate on direct and personal contact with the needy, tending the sick, caring for the aged, relieving the poor, etc. (See, further, the present writer's *A Commentary on Romans 12–13* (Edinburgh, 1965), pp. 35–37.)

[2] The difficulties of Acts 6$^{1-6}$ are well known. The word *diakonos* is not used here; after verse 3 nothing more is said of the involvement of the Seven in the Church's welfare work (it is noticeable that in 11^{30} it is 'to the elders' that the gifts from Antioch are sent); one of them (Stephen) is depicted in the latter part of the same chapter as teaching and disputing, while another (Philip) is shown in chapter eight proclaiming Christ and in 21^8 is referred to as 'the evangelist'; the others are never mentioned again in Acts. The questions raised by these verses are such that the proper discussion of them requires a whole paper to itself. But it may be said here that Acts 6$^{1-6}$ implies: (i) that the author regarded it as something to be taken for granted that the Church had an obligation to care for the poor among its members; (ii) that at the time when Acts was written it seemed natural to think of the Church's charitable work as a function separate from that of preaching and oversight; (iii) that, separated though they were in his own time, the author of Acts thought of these two functions as having been originally united in the ministry of the apostles.

[3] We may refer to 1 Corinthians 9$^{1-14}$; Galatians 6^6; 1 Timothy 5$^{17f.}$, and also to Matthew 10^{10b}; Luke 10^7.

[4] Acts 18^3; 20$^{34f.}$; 1 Corinthians 9$^{12, 15-18}$; 2 Corinthians 11$^{7-12}$; 12$^{13f.}$; 1 Thessalonians 2$^{6, 9}$; 2 Thessalonians 3$^{8f.}$

though he did apparently accept material help from the Church in Philippi[1]—is something which in this connexion should certainly not be entirely forgotten. And Mark 6^{7-12} = Matthew 10^1, $^{9-14}$ = Luke 9^{1-6} and Luke 10^{1-16}, passages containing sayings-material which was no doubt specially preserved because of its relevance to the situation of later missionaries, should certainly be remembered. While full allowance must be made for changing conditions and circumstances (as a matter of fact, some modifications are already to be seen in Mark $6^{8f.}$ as against Matthew 10^{10} and Luke 9^3), the Lord's instructions still hold in principle for the continuing ministry of the Church; and they certainly give no encouragement at all to the idea that the clergy have a right to be supported in luxury. There is no evidence in the New Testament to suggest that apostles normally travelled first class.

When we turn to the subject of church buildings and their maintenance, upon which such a large proportion of the modern Church's resources is spent, there is not unnaturally a sparsity of relevant material. It is probably not unfair to say that, since the need for the Church in a particular place to gather together regularly is clearly recognized,[2] and since the use of private houses could hardly be expected to continue indefinitely, the Church's possession of buildings for its own special purposes is justified in principle.[3] According to Acts 19^9, Paul, when he was no longer able to use the synagogue in Ephesus, had resort to the lecture-room of Tyrannus for his teaching. On what terms he had the use of it we are not informed. But there is nothing in the New Testament to encourage the notion that God regards unnecessarily expensive buildings or furnishings as contributing in any way to His glory; and to appeal to the Old Testament in this connexion is perhaps a questionable procedure. At any rate, Mark 13^{1-4} may serve as a warning against assuming that the mere fact that multitudes of the curious come to admire an expensive new church is a proof that all the expenditure involved in its erection and adornment is justified.

But when we come to question the New Testament on the use of the Church's resources for the relief of human distress and need we get an altogether unambiguous answer. According to Matthew 25^{31-46}, Christ has specially chosen the suffering humanity of His needy brothers and sisters as the place where He will receive our gratitude and service. To set against this Mark 14^{3-9} and parallels is beside the point; for the circumstances of the incident there recorded were altogether unique.

We conclude that, while a large proportion of the Church's money is rightly spent on the training of the clergy and their support in modest comfort, on the erection and maintenance of necessary buildings, and on a good many other things which contribute to the efficient fulfilment of its mission, the relief of human suffering and wretchedness has a special claim upon the Church's

---

[1] 2 Corinthians 11^9; Philippians $4^{15f.}$

[2] e.g. 1 Corinthians 11^{20}; Hebrews 10^{25}.

[3] It is quite another matter whether in modern Britain the Church's possession of church buildings for the exclusive use of any one denomination can possibly be justified.

material resources, and every proposed ecclesiastical expenditure ought to be responsibly and critically scrutinized in the light of this claim, lest the Church be guilty of using sacrilegiously for its own, and its ministers', worldly prestige and status, and for other selfish and frivolous purposes, that which by right belongs to Christ in the persons of His needy brethren.

Diakonia in the Early Church

G. W. H. LAMPE

'In the form of an altar a table served to express at one and the same time the love of God and the love of our neighbour.'[1] In the early Church the two great commandments were united at the focal point of Christian worship; for service to the brotherhood was not a merely secondary activity proceeding from the primary duty of service to God. It was not simply a practical working out in daily life of ethical obligations that were inculcated by the preacher and implied in the liturgy. *Diakonia* was itself enshrined at the heart of worship. *Diakonia* and *leitourgia* were so indissolubly linked with one another as to be, in effect, two aspects of one and the same Godward act on the part of the Christian community; for service to man was an expression of the worship of God and was itself in turn embodied in the divine service of the liturgy. The Christians' sacrificial offering to God was made both in prayer, thanksgiving and the Eucharistic liturgy and also in charitable work for the needy;[2] the same ministers were entrusted with the administration of the Communion bread and the distribution of the Church's resources to the poor; and the interchangeability of the words *diakonia* and *leitourgia*, so that the former could be used of congregational worship in church[3] and the latter of service to one's neighbour,[4] reflects the inseparable connexion of the two forms of ministry to God.

This intimate and constant relationship between the cult and practical service, together with the fact that the latter was not only a matter of individual and sporadic acts of charity but a highly organized activity of the Church as ·a corporate body, afforded an immense advantage to Christianity over its rivals. Paganism could not match its concern for the relief of the sick and needy. Distress and calamities multiplied during the very period (the third century) of the Church's rapid growth in membership, organization and resources. Even at the best of times, however, life tended to be hard for those artisans, small traders and people of the lower middle class who seem to have formed the bulk of the Church's membership; and despite the proliferation up and down the empire of

---

[1] Harnack, quoted by Troeltsch, *The Social Teaching of the Christian Churches*, p. 92.
[2] cf. Justin, *1 Apol*. 13: in contrast to the pagan sacrifices, Christian worship consists in offering the Creator's gifts to ourselves and those in need, together with thanksgivings to him in prayers and hymns.
[3] As in the Liturgy of St James.
[4] e.g. Eusebius, *h.e.* 5.1.9.

collegia tenuiorum religionis causa, which testified to a universal need for mutual support through friendly societies and burial clubs, it was only the Church which could supply the motive and the means for meeting that need on a large scale. Its operations were not limited to one locality nor confined to those who shared one particular occupation. Unlike the extensive charitable work carried on within Judaism, from which the Church inherited much of its theory and practice of *diakonia*, the Christian social ministry was not tied to membership of an exclusive racial minority; and, unlike pagan clubs, the Church did not merely take a god for its patron, but believed that its *diakonia* was both directed towards Christ, in the persons of His needy brethren, as its object and performed by Christ acting through His servants.

The superiority of the Church in this respect is strikingly illustrated by the emperor Julian's desperate attempt to inject a similar spirit of philanthropy into 'Hellenism' and to persuade that synthetic religion to imitate the Church by turning its priests into a combination of cultic officials and welfare officers.[1] Priests must be tested by two criteria which recall the injunctions of the Pastoral Epistles: they must convert their own dependents to piety towards the gods, and they must be willing, even though they may be poor men, to share their property with the needy, striving to the best of their ability to do good to others. The latter duty, according to Julian, required the more urgent attention; for he recognized that paganism's neglect of the poor had given 'the impious Galilaeans' their opportunity. These had enticed faithful people away into atheism by means of their ἀγάπη, ὑποδοχή, and διακονία τραπεζῶν: and Julian adds the comment that these technical terms are characteristic of Christianity because the activities which they denote are so prominent in that religion.[2]

The emperor's letter to Arsacius, the high priest of Galatia, is equally revealing. Hospices must be built in every town for the care of strangers; there must be organized poor relief throughout the province, with distributions to poor travellers and beggars; for it is disgraceful that in the Jewish community no one needs to beg, and that the 'impious Galilaeans' look after pagans as well as their own people, while no aid is available to 'Hellenists' from their co-religionists. 'Hellenists' must therefore be instructed to contribute to this *leitourgia*, and be taught that the practice of benevolence belongs to the traditions of Hellenism itself: for Homer inculcated the duty of charity (Od., 5.56).[3] Julian was optimistic in his belief that it was still possible in the fourth century for the pagan world to compete with Christian *diakonia*, but his rather pathetic attempt to create a rival combination of *leitourgia* and *diakonia* is strong evidence of the powerful attractiveness of the Christians' service to God through man and to man in God. There are many causes for the triumph of the Christian Church over its rivals, but one of the most potent was undoubtedly the central place which it gave to *diakonia* in its life and worship.

---

[1] The priest must possess two essential qualities: τὸ φιλόθεον and τὸ φιλάνθρωπον (Galatians 305D).
[2] ibid. (305B, D).   [3] Julian, *ep.* 49.

To say this is not to deny either that the Christians' service to their fellow men was limited in its scope or that disinterested and self-sacrificial love was in any way the only motive for its exercise. In the vastly more complex society of the industrial world, where the State fulfils a ministry to human need in a manner and on a scale undreamed of by the imperial government and impossible of achievement even in the recent past, it is proper for Christians to practise *diakonia* along secular rather than ecclesiastical lines. Provided that Christian people are willing to find a sphere of ministry in the agencies of the State, it is unnecessary and often harmful for the Church to maintain its own parallel organs of *diakonia*. Nor, in these conditions, need Christian *diakonia* be envisaged merely as an ambulance service for social and economic casualties. Christians can seek, individually and corporately, to guide and utilize the political and economic institutions of secular society in order to effect radical improvements in the social structure. The long-term object of *diakonia*, in the broadest sense of the term, can become the abolition, or at least the universal alleviation, of distress, rather than only the consolation and relief of the afflicted. The sphere of Christian service can be seen to be the world itself, without limitation or distinction. Its purpose is realized to be service to God in and through ministry to the world of His creation, since it is for the sake of God's world that the Church exists.

In the early centuries such a conception of Christian ministry would have been impossible to put into practice, and largely unacceptable in theory. The world stood over against the Church. It was from and out of the world that Christians trusted that they were being saved. Its institutions had, indeed, a certain function to fulfil in the divine purposes. The emperor, so long as he did not usurp the place of God, was entitled to loyalty and respect; for the State provided a defence against chaos; it maintained order and justice, and thus, if it were willing to acknowledge its proper role, it ought to enable the Church to discharge its own task in a more important field. At best, under Christian rulers, it could encourage the Church, assist it materially, and restrain its pagan and heretical enemies. Yet the Church's attitude to worldly institutions during the pre-Constantinian period was scarcely more positive than that of tolerance. At best the Church could do no more than coexist with the secular system, serving it from outside, as it were,[1] by prayer, rather than from within it by practical participation in its affairs.[2] Christians 'know of the existence in each city of another sort of country, created by the Logos of God', and they 'call upon those who are competent to take office' not to serve the State but 'to rule over the churches'. Hence Christians avoid civic responsibility in order to 'keep themselves for a more divine and necessary service in the Church of God for the sake

---

[1] cf. *Diogn.*, 5–6: Christians live in Greek or barbarian cities, but they have 'the constitution of their own citizenship'. They inhabit their respective countries as though they were temporary sojourners. Though their relation to the world may be likened to that of the soul to the body, this analogy is conceived dualistically: although the soul holds the body together, it does not belong to it, but is temporarily imprisoned in it. Its true interests are elsewhere.

[2] Tert., *apol.*, 30ff.; Or., *Cels.*, 8.73–74.

of the salvation of men'.[1] The Christian's duty to the world was to convert it, or, if need be, to offer passive resistance to it, rather than to minister to it. Even when the empire had become Christian, the best laymen tended to withdraw to the monastery rather than to serve the State.

Julian does, indeed, imply that Christian *diakonia* was directed towards pagans as well as Church members, without discrimination; but by his time the Church was in a dominant position in society and the confrontation of the Church with the world had become less sharp. It is true, also, that in the preceding century Christian charity towards the heathen was sometimes an object of admiration to the general public and a powerful factor in dispelling ignorant prejudice against the movement. This occurred particularly in the great plagues. At Carthage in 252 under Cyprian's leadership *ministeria* were allotted to the Church's members according to their status and resources: some to give financial aid and some personal service to the plague-stricken; and in obedience to the commandment, 'Love your enemies', they extended their good works to all men and not only to those who were of the household of faith.[2] The same may have been true, though this is not explicitly recorded, of the devoted conduct of the Alexandrian Christians in the plague of 263, which won them much respect by contrast with the selfish cowardice of their heathen neighbours (certain presbyters and deacons, and some of the laity, giving their lives in caring for the sick and attending to the dead).[3]

Generally speaking, however, the object, or at least the primary object, of *diakonia* certainly was the household of faith. *Diakonia* was a function of the Church in respect of its own members, an expression of Christian love within the brotherhood, directed either towards individuals or towards the corporate institution itself. On the level of individual philanthropy it maintained the traditions of Judaism, in which almsgiving played so prominent a part and was inculcated in texts, especially in the Wisdom literature, which were constantly on the lips of Christian preachers. Almsgiving is, indeed, a regular theme for sermons. Upright conduct and charity towards the needy are the two essential requirements demanded of all Church members in their daily life. That the poor must be always with us was taken for granted, just as was the institution of slavery. In fact, it was the existence of riches rather than poverty which presented a problem and a challenge to Christian thought. Clement of Alexandria in his *Quis dives salvetur?* and many other writers established the compatibility of Christianity with the possession of wealth, but only on certain strict conditions. These included spiritual detachment, recognition of the duty of stewardship (riches being a divine gift held in trust), and benevolence to the needy. The Fathers, however, generally assume that the poor have an advantage in the spiritual life, whereas the rich are inevitably handicapped. The primitive community of possessions described in Acts was constantly held up as an ideal, how-

---

[1] ibid., 8.75 (tr. H. Chadwick).
[2] Pontianus, *v. Cypr.*, 9–10.
[3] Dionysius of Alexandria ap. Eus., *h.e.*, 7.22.7–10.

ever unattainable in practice, so that it played a part in Christian social teaching something like the role of a mythical golden age in Stoicism.

Hence, although the Church certainly strove to encourage almsgiving as an expression of spontaneous love, it inculcated that duty for other reasons as well. These concern the spiritual good of the giver rather than the benefit of the receiver. Cyprian's exhortation to works of charity[1] makes the following main points. Alms are gifts to God, and to Christ in the persons of the poor; to renounce one's possessions is to reap spiritual gain; the great example to be borne in mind is the total sacrifice of private property made by the primitive Christians at Jerusalem; almsgiving ensures a heavenly reward; to give away temporal possessions is therefore to make certain of acquiring spiritual riches, and almsgiving establishes a claim upon God, making God one's debtor (Cyprian here echoes Tertullian); it is a way of recompensing Christ for his self-denying love;[2] on a less exalted plane, it is a way of defeating the tax-collector, who may raid one's earthly property, but cannot touch the heavenly riches which one may gain in exchange for it; and no prudential motives should restrain one from giving away one's money, since God can be trusted to provide for oneself and one's family.

Countless preachers made the same points, sometimes with the additional reflection that in Christian society rich and poor have reciprocal obligations: the rich supply the material needs of the poor, and the poor in their turn contribute to the rich from their own more abundant spiritual resources, by praying for their benefactors.[3] This principle was expressed in a more formal way in the duty of prayer assigned to widows maintained by the Church. Despite this last idea, however, the ministry of individual almsgiving is too often viewed in terms of the moral and spiritual self-improvement of the benefactor: almost, indeed, his material enrichment in the future life (cf. Pseudo-Cyprian's exhortation to remove one's estates and villas to paradise through doing good deeds).[4] Thus the idea of *diakonia* too readily passes over into that of the merit of good works, and of giving to the poor in order that God may not withhold the heavenly reward.[5] Charity, therefore, tends to be viewed as a spiritual exercise. On the other hand, by an opposite process, a spiritual exercise can sometimes be practised in an outward-looking way and made a ministry for the benefit of others. This is naturally the case with fasting. Hermas is told to live on bread and water, to reckon the cost of a full meal, and to give a corresponding amount to a widow, orphan or poor person.[6] Many preachers urge the need to combine almsgiving with fasting, and Chrysostom and Eusebius of Alexandria assert that without the former the latter is useless as an act of devotion.[7] It is interesting that *2 Clement*

---

[1] *de opere et eleemosynis.*   [2] cf. *2 Clem.*, 1.3 (ἀντιμισθία).
[3] e.g. Herm., *sim.*, 2.5–8; Chrys., *hom. 34.4 in 1 Cor.*
[4] *de aleatoribus*, 11.
[5] cf. Chrys., *hom. 3.2 in Phmn*: 'You approach God asking for the kingdom of Heaven, yet when you have been asked for money you have not given it.'
[6] *sim.*, 5.3.7.
[7] Chrys., *hom. 57.6 in Mt.*; Eus. Al., *serm. 1* (*PG.* 86.316A).

ranks almsgiving above fasting, though this seems to be in respect of its meritoriousness as a good work.

All this private ministry found its focus in corporate worship, for gifts to the needy were directly related to the liturgical oblations; so that almsgiving passes over at this point into organized charitable work undertaken by the Church. Justin's description of the Eucharist includes the statement, καὶ οἱ ἔχοντες τοῖς λειπομένοις πᾶσιν ἐπικουροῦμεν, καὶ σύνεσμεν ἀλλήλοις ἀεί.[1] This refers to the offerings brought by the congregation, for, after mentioning the distribution of the eucharistic elements to those present, and, by the ministry of the deacons, to those unable to attend the service, Justin explains that everyone contributes according to his means, of his own free will; and the collection is deposited with the 'president', who uses it to succour orphans, widows, the sick, prisoners, strangers, and all who are in need.[2] Thus the administration of the sacrament is set in the context of a eucharistic sacrifice offered to God by the whole Church through the medium of service to mankind.[3] Tertullian similarly gives a central place to this form of ministry in his account of Christian worship. He offers a striking picture of the organized relief work undertaken by the Church with resources contributed by the worshippers, and he points out that it is this brotherly service which so impresses non-Christians as to make them exclaim, 'See how they love one another.'[4]

The connexion between ministry and worship is again emphasized by Cyprian, when he castigates the behaviour of a rich worshipper who comes to the liturgy without bringing a sacrifice and yet partakes of a sacrifice which has been contributed by a poor man;[5] and it is therefore not a wholly fanciful metaphor which the author of *de aleatoribus* uses when he says, 'Pecuniam tuam adsidente Christo, spectantibus angelis et martyribus praesentibus, super mensam dominicam sparge';[6] for it was the offerings that were brought to the Lord's table in the presence of the bishop and his clergy which constituted the Church's resources for its corporate *diakonia*. Thus the deacon's biddings at the end of the synaxis in the liturgy of the *Apostolic Constitutions*[7] include intercession 'for those who make offerings in the holy church and provide alms for the poor, and those who offer sacrifices and first-fruits to the Lord our God'. The former class contribute to poor relief, the latter to the maintenance of the clergy.

---

[1] *1 apol.*, 67.
[2] ibid.
[3] Irenaeus cites Proverbs 19^{17} and Matthew 25$^{34ff.}$ (stock texts about almsgiving) in the context of an exposition of the Eucharist.
[4] *apol.*, 39: 'modicam unusquisque stipem menstrua die, vel cum velit, et si modo velit et si modo possit, apponit. . . . Haec quasi deposita pietatis sunt. Nam inde non epulis . . . sed egenis alendis humandisque, et pueris ac puellis re ac parentibus destitutis, iamque domesticis senibus, item naufragis, et si qui in metallis, et si qui in insulis, vel in custodiis, dumtaxat ex causa Dei sectae alumni confessionis suae fiunt'; cf. Arist., *apol.*, 15.
[5] *de op. et eleem.*, 15.
[6] *de aleator.*, 11.
[7] 8.10.12.

The relation between charitable work and liturgy was thus extremely intimate. The agape was, indeed, a separate observance from the Eucharist; nevertheless it was closely related to it, and in itself it was a rite which combined worship and edification with service to the needy. To this meal of fellowship the poor were invited, or a distribution was made to them from the food provided. It was held under the authority of the bishop,[1] who presided if he were present, a presbyter or deacon deputizing for him in his absence.[2] It may be to the agape, in this sense of the word, that Ignatius alludes when he accuses heretics of ignoring 'agape', widow, orphan, the afflicted, the prisoner, the hungry and the thirsty.[3] As a common meal for the members of a church, the agape was often liable to be abused by the greedy (as in St Paul's time at Corinth),[4] or as a means of providing maintenance for the clergy,[5] a practice forbidden in the fourth century by the twenty-seventh canon of Laodicea. Yet it was an occasion for prayer, praise, exhortation and Scripture reading (this is an aspect of the agape which is given prominence by Clement of Alexandria and Tertullian),[6] and with it there was associated the traditional evening service when the lamp was lit.[7] Its primary object, however, was poor relief,[8] and, at a time when it was tending, outside monastic circles, to fall into disrepute (as canons 27 and 28 of Laodicea suggest), it was commended by the eleventh canon of Gangra, which anathematizes any who despise those who give agapes and invite the brethren in honour of the Lord. The apocalyptic *Visio Pauli* even portrays extreme torments in hell for those who were restrained by worldly hindrances from giving agapes, caring for widows and orphans, entertaining strangers and travellers, offering their oblation, and taking pity on their neighbour.[9]

The donor was usually a private individual. It might take place in the church, though this was forbidden by canon 28 of Laodicea and by later councils, or in a private house. The widows maintained by the Church were often the invited guests, and a general distribution to the poor, under the supervision of a presbyter or a deacon, might be made afterwards from the surplus provisions.[10] The same charitable object was pursued in the agape that was held on the anniversary of the death of a member of the Church;[11] and Paulinus of Nola is extravagantly enthusiastic about the huge agape given by Pammachius at the time of the funeral of his wife, Paulina, at Rome. This reminded him of the Feeding of the Five Thousand; it was an acceptable sacrifice to Christ, providing refreshment

---

[1] Ign., *Smyrn.*, 8.2.
[2] Hipp., *trad. ap.*, 26; *Can. Hipp.*, 180.
[3] *Smyrn.*, 6.2.
[4] cf. Clem. *paed.*, 2.1.4.
[5] *Didasc.*, 2.28: although the agape is given for the benefit of aged women, the lion's share goes to the clergy.
[6] Clem., *paed.*, 2.7.53; Tert., *apol.*, 39.
[7] Hipp., *trad. ap.*, 26.
[8] Tert., *apol.*, 39: quantiscunque sumptibus constet, lucrum est pietatis nomine facere sumptum, siquidem inopes quosque refrigerio isto iuvamus; cf. Eus., *orat. Const.*, 12.4
[9] *Vis. Paul.*, 40.
[10] Hipp., *trad. ap.*, 26.
[11] Tert., *coron.*, 3, *de exhort cast.*, 11; *Lit. ap. Const. App.*, 8.42, 44.

so that the recipients, in their turn, might offer their sacrifice of praise to God. To have fed the hungry and clothed the shivering would bring the benefactor a heavenly reward, and, through the prayers of the beneficiaries, to Paulina in the life after death. Pammachius could be described as 'lacrymas corpori fundens, eleemosynam animae infundens'.[1]

The agape is closely related to the ministry of Christians to their brethren in prison. Tertullian sends an exhortation to the martyrs 'inter carnis alimenta quae vobis et domina mater ecclesia de uberibus suis, et singuli fratres de opibus suis propriis, in carcerem subministrant'.[2] It may be to an agape celebrated in prison that Lucian refers when he describes how, when Peregrinus had been imprisoned as a Christian and the brethren had tried in vain to rescue him, old women, widows and orphans gathered at the jail, and the leaders of the Church, having bribed the warders, passed the night inside with him; meals were brought in and sacred words were said.[3] This might, however, be a garbled idea of a Eucharist in prison, such as Cyprian indicates when he instructs the clergy not to allow the brethren to go *en masse* to visit the imprisoned confessors, lest the authorities should refuse admission to anyone; presbyters are to visit them singly, each accompanied by a deacon, and 'offer' with them, taking care that the same person does not go more than once.[4]

Care for the victims of persecution was, in fact, one of the most highly organized and effective forms of practical service undertaken by the Church. Lucian imagines visitors coming from as far as Asia to aid and cheer Peregrinus in prison in Palestine ('for their first lawgiver persuaded them that they were all brethren to one another'); and his picture is not exaggerated, for the Christian sources are full of allusions to the organization of relief and comfort for those in prison or condemned to the mines. It was one of the most telling points in the Donatist propaganda against Caecilian of Carthage that when he was the bishop's senior deacon he had discouraged the faithful from frequenting the confessors in prison. Special care had to be taken of the poor, too, in time of persecution, and Cyprian, in his instructions about this to his presbyters and deacons, commends those who 'nec paupertate adacti nec persecutionis tempestate prostrati, dum Domino fideliter serviunt, ceteris quoque pauperibus exemplum fidei praebuerunt'.[5]

Cyprian's presbyters are here doing duty for the bishop in his absence, for it was the officers of the Church, and particularly the bishop and his deacons, who bore the responsibility for organizing the corporate *diakonia* of the community and supervising the many forms of private ministry which its members undertook. Their special functions are only to be understood properly in the context of the whole Church's service of God through ministry to the brethren: in the yet wider setting, indeed, of the *diakonia* of Christ as mediator between the

[1] *ep.*, 13.11–14.
[2] *ad martyres*, 1.
[3] *de mort. Peregr.*, 12–13.
[4] *ep.*, 5.2.
[5] *ep.*, 12.2.

Father and man,[1] and of the angels who minister God's benefits to his people.[2] Every kind of ministerial function in the Church is described as *diakonia*; but the administration of relief to the needy is specially the task of the official *diakonos*, as the bishop's assistant and right-hand man.

Episkopos and *diakonos* always stand in the closest relationship to each other, whether in a dual ministry of presbyters (who were, at least in some churches, called *episkopoi* in respect of their function of oversight) and deacons[3] or in the developed threefold Ministry of bishops, with their deacons and presbyters. They may be listed in this order, for although in status the presbyters, as well as the bishop, rank above the deacons, in function the deacon is connected more closely with the bishop than with the presbyters. The later history of the ministry is to some extent the story of how the more numerous presbyterate gradually took over liturgical and administrative functions which in earlier times belonged to the bishop and deacons, especially when the presbyters ceased to be the bishop's *consilium* of elders (whose duties, apart from sitting by the bishop, are somewhat obscure), and became relatively independent overseers of parishes, responsible for the *leitourgia* and *diakonia* within them.

At first the term *diakonos* denotes the function performed by some member of the community rather than his possession of a definite title as one who belongs to a defined order of ministry. It is probably in this sense that *1 Clement*, 42.4, pictures the apostles, as pioneer missionaries, appointing their senior converts to discharge the ministries of oversight and administration in the congregations which were to grow on the scene of their own labours (εἰς ἐπισκόπους καὶ διακόνους τῶν μελλόντων πιστεύειν). The very nature of Christian *diakonia* in its relation to worship meant that the officer who presided at the latter would be responsible for organizing the former. Thus *episkope* and *diakonia* are inseparable aspects of one and the same ministerial function. Indeed, Chrysostom supposed that in the apostolic age the terms *episkopos* and *diakonos* could be applied interchangeably, so that the 'bishop' could then be referred to as a 'deacon'.[4]

When we encounter *diakonos* as the title of a special class of minister it is always in the closest connexion with 'bishop' (or 'presbyter' in churches which do not yet possess a bishop distinct from the rest of the presbyterate). The deacon is the bishop's assistant in discharging their common task of leading worship, receiving the offerings and arranging their distribution. Hence in the threefold ministry they are subordinate in status to the presbyters, but are the bishop's 'fellow servants'.[5] As an assistant, the *Apostolic Tradition* emphasizes, the deacon is not appointed for priesthood, but for the service of the bishop, to do the things commanded by him. He does not receive the Spirit which is common to the presbyterate, but receives that which is entrusted to him under

---

[1] cf. Eus., *h.e.*, 5.10; Ps. Ath., *orat. c. Ar.*, 4.6.
[2] cf. Or., *Cels.*, 5.4.
[3] e.g. at Rome and Corinth in the time of *1 Clem.*, at Philippi in Polycarp's time, and in the church order described in the *Didache*.
[4] *hom. 1.1 in Phil.*
[5] Ign., *Smyrn.*, 12.2.

the bishop's authority. Hence he is ordained with the imposition of the bishop's hands alone and not those of the presbyters.[1] He is a subordinate assistant (and therefore is very often called a 'levite'), although Cyprian's correspondence shows that a bishop's deacon might at times prove presumptuous.[2] On the other hand, his relation with the bishop was such that the senior of a bishop's deacons (later known as 'archdeacon' and appointed to be such without regard for his actual seniority in years) tended to be the natural successor in the see. From the apocryphal Acts, which supposed that the apostles had attendant deacons, in the manner of the contemporary bishops, it is clear that the deacon's position was rather like that of a modern bishop's chaplain or personal secretary.[3]

The duty of assisting the bishop extended in some measure to the episcopal function of teaching. The *Didache*[4] urges the congregation to appoint *episkopoi* and *diakonoi* (both of whom must possess the same virtues of gentleness, in exercising authority, and honesty and truth, in discharging administrative responsibility), as substitutes for the ministry of prophets and teachers. The prophet had been the liturgical celebrant and the recipient of offerings, as well as a teacher by virtue of his charisma. The deacon is presumably meant to assist the *episkopos* in the discharge of all these functions, including teaching. A duty of giving instruction seems to fall to the deacons, with the bishop and presbyters, according to the *Apostolic Tradition*,[5] but the sense of the passage is not clear. Hermas certainly links deacons with teachers;[6] and deacons are not infrequently mentioned in connexion with catechetical teaching. This part of their duty extended also to preaching, for the second canon of Ancyra (314) suspends lapsed deacons from their liturgical functions and from preaching; but this privilege seems to have been withdrawn and confined to the bishop and presbyters, for in the fourth century the permission given to Aetius as a deacon to preach was regarded as unusual and censured.[7]

Principally, however, the deacon's assistance to the bishop was centred upon liturgy and poor relief. At the Eucharist the deacons bring the offerings to the celebrant,[8] and the prayer at a deacon's ordination asks that he may receive grace to bring into the holy of holies that which is offered by the high priests.[9] This duty, rather than any right of the deacon himself to celebrate, is probably indicated by the second canon of Ancyra when it suspends lapsed deacons from 'offering the bread and the cup'. The deacons minister the Communion to the people, and hence are called by Ignatius '*diakonoi* of the mysteries of Christ'.[10] Justin describes how 'those who among us are called "deacons" give to each of

[1] Hipp., *trad ap.*, 9.
[2] Cypr., *ep.*, 3.
[3] *A. Thom.*, 65; *Hom. Clem.*, 16.1.
[4] *Did.*, 15.1.
[5] 33.
[6] *vis.*, 3.5.1.
[7] Philostorgius, *h.e.*, 3.17; Thdt., *h.e.*, 2.24.6.
[8] Hipp., *trad. ap.*, 4, 23; *Const. App.*, 8.12.3.
[9] Hipp., *trad. ap.*, 9.
[10] *Trall.*, 2.3.

those present a share of the bread over which thanksgiving has been said, and wine and water, and take some away to those who are absent' (the sick and others prevented from attending the service being thus united with the congregation in eucharistic fellowship).[1] Hippolytus, however, in his directions for the Communion of the newly baptized, assigns the distribution of the bread to the bishop, and only the administration of the cups to the deacons (and then only if there are not enough presbyters to do this);[2] and a similar procedure seems to be implied in Cyprian's account of the portents which happened when lapsed Christians presented themselves for Communion.[3] Canon 18 of Nicaea forbids deacons to administer Communion to priests.

Similar to his task in administering Communion (or at least the chalice) is the deacon's task of distributing blessed bread at the agape.[4] He had other duties at the Eucharist as well. According to the *Acts of Thomas*, which suppose that the apostle, like a bishop, had an attendant deacon, the latter prepared the table: 'The apostle bade his deacon to set forth a table; and he set forth a stool . . . and spread a linen cloth upon it, and set on the bread of blessing'.[5] He might read a psalm,[6] or, according to the *Apostolic Constitutions*,[7] either a presbyter or a deacon might read the Gospel. At Alexandria, according to Sozomen,[8] this was read by the archdeacon, whereas elsewhere it was assigned to deacons.

Next in importance, however, to the deacons' duties of presenting the offerings and administering Communion, is their function as links between the celebrant and the congregation. They give instructions to the people so as to enable them to take their full part in the liturgy. Thus before the service a deacon warns those who are at variance to reconcile their differences and be at peace with one another.[9] Deacons instruct the 'hearers' to withdraw before the prayer for the catechumens,[10] and all who are not baptized before the liturgy of the faithful.[11] They announce the biddings for prayer, and thus lead the intercessions of the congregation;[12] they call for silence and attention at the Scripture readings,[13] announce the kiss of peace,[14] and dismiss the congregation at the end of the service.[15] They arrange the placing of the congregation, and maintain order, to prevent whispering, laughter or other unseemliness.[16] One of the deacons

---

[1] *1 apol.*, 65, 67.
[2] Hipp., *trad. ap.*, 23.
[3] *de laps.*, 25, 26.
[4] ibid., 26.
[5] *A. Thom.*, 49.
[6] Ath. *fug.*, 24 (*PG.*, 25.676A).
[7] 2.57.7.
[8] *h.e.*, 7.19.6.
[9] *Const. App.*, 2.54.1.
[10] *Lit. ap. Const. App.*, 8.6.2.
[11] ibid., 8.10.2; cf. *Liturgy of St James* and other liturgies.
[12] e.g. Chrys., *hom.*, 2.5 in 2 Cor., hom. 21.4 in Ac., and the rubrics in the liturgies.
[13] e.g. Chrys., *hom. 3.4 in 2 Thess.*
[14] Cyr. Hier., *catech.*, 23.3.
[15] e.g. *Lit ap. Const. App.*, 8.15.10.
[16] *Const. App.*, 2.57.13.

stands by the eucharistic oblations, one keeps the doors; they act together at the offertory.[1]

At baptisms the deacon descends with the candidate into the water,[2] having prepared him for baptism. Whether a deacon might actually baptize was a disputed matter. According to Tertullian the chief minister of baptism is the bishop, but presbyters or deacons may baptize with the bishop's authorization.[3] The *De Rebaptismate* envisages baptism by 'minor clerus' in an emergency,[4] and Canon 77 of Elvira allows baptism by deacons, provided that it is completed later by the bishop's blessing. Cyril of Jerusalem also recognizes the deacon as a minister of baptism,[5] as does Chrysostom,[6] though the latter realizes that this is a scandal to many people. On the other hand, the *Apostolic Constitutions* allow only the bishop and presbyters to baptize, the deacon's part being merely to assist.[7] On this view the deacon's part in baptism is parallel to his role in the Eucharist: 'it is unlawful for a deacon to offer sacrifice or baptize; this would subvert Church order'.[8]

The deacon also assists the bishop in his pastoral work. Deacons are responsible for looking after any who have been excommunicated,[9] and in cases of necessity Cyprian allows a deacon to receive the confession of a lapsed Christian and reconcile him to the Church with the laying-on of hands.[10]

Primarily, however, and as an extension of his ministry of Communion to the brethren, the deacon's work is concerned with administering resources for the supply of the wants of the needy. In this respect, too, he is an assistant. In the time of Polycarp it was the presbyters at Philippi who had the oversight there of widows, orphans and the poor, and, as being in charge of the funds, they were warned against favouritism and avarice.[11] With the rise of 'monepiscopacy' the ultimate responsibility devolved on the bishop. His agents, however, for this purpose were the deacons. They have the care of widows and orphans.[12] They are appointed to administer, and to report to the bishop what is necessary:[13] not, says Hippolytus, to take part in the counsels of the clergy (the *Testamentum Domini* rather curiously contradicts this last statement; Hippolytus tends to stress the subordinate role of deacons, whereas the *Testamentum* exalts their status). They are to notify the bishop of brethren who are ill, so that he may visit them.[14] They also visit the sick themselves,[15] and minister to the brethren in

[1] *Didasc.*, 2.57.6.
[2] Hipp., *trad. ap.*, 21.
[3] *bapt.*, 17.
[4] 10.
[5] *catech.*, 17.35.
[6] *hom. 46.3 in Ac.*
[7] 3.11.1.
[8] 8.46.11.
[9] *Const. App.*, 2.16.1.
[10] *ep.*, 18.1.   [11] *ep.*, 6.1.
[12] e.g. Herm., *sim.*, 9.26.2.
[13] Hipp., *trad ap.*, 9.
[14] ibid., 30, and frequently in the Church Orders.
[15] *Didasc.*, 3.13.

prison in times of persecution.[1] The deacon's administration of Church funds occasionally produced scandals,[2] and these, together with the many warnings against self-seeking that were given to deacons, indicate that they exercised a good deal of independence in their control of the community's money. Generally speaking, however, they are subordinate assistants of the bishop whose work they share, and act under his direction.[3] They report to him;[4] they bear his messages, and they may act as envoys, rather like the 'apostles of churches' in the time of St Paul.[5] The deacon, in fact, and later the archdeacon, had good reason to be called 'the bishop's eye'.[6]

In all this work the deacon, as was often pointed out, typifies Christ who 'came not to be ministered to, but to minister'.[7] Polycarp tells the Philippians to be submissive to the presbyters and deacons, as to God and Christ.[8] Ignatius says that the deacons have been entrusted with Jesus Christ's *diakonia*: they are to be reverenced as Christ, whereas the bishop typifies God the Father;[9] and in the *Didascalia* the deacon is said to be a type of Christ.[10]

The deacon appears to have been elected to his office,[11] possibly after public scrutiny.[12] He was ordained with the imposition of the hands (or hand: the Church orders vary) of the bishop alone, with a prayer which makes little mention of his duties, though the *Apostolic Tradition*[13] speaks of his presentation of the eucharistic offerings, Serapion's prayer[14] alludes to the appointment of the Seven, who were believed by the Fathers to have been the first deacons, and the *Apostolic Constitutions* include in the prayer a reference to St Stephen.[15]

The last of these prayers includes a petition that the deacon may come to merit promotion to higher rank. This marks a very significant change in the whole idea of the diaconate. Instead of being a highly important office in its own right, directly linked with that of the bishop, it gradually becomes a lower rung in a ladder of preferment, so that the deacon comes in time to be no more than an apprentice priest. It is hard to trace the beginning of this development, but it is already indicated in the *Apostolic Church Order*,[16] and by the fourth century it is becoming generally accepted. Scriptural warrant was found for this idea in 1 Timothy 3[13], interpreted as meaning that a meritorious deacon ought normally

---

[1] e.g. Dion. Al. ap. Eus., *h.e.*, 7.11.24, and Cyprian's correspondence.
[2] e.g. Cypr., *ep.*, 52.1.
[3] *Didasc.*, 3.13; 'diaconi sint in actibus similes episcopis suis, sed exercitationes'.
[4] e.g., *Hom. Clem.*, 3.67.
[5] Ign., *Philad.*, 10.1.
[6] *Clem. ep.*, 12; *Const. App.*, 2.44.4.
[7] e.g. *Const. App.*, 3.19.3.
[8] *ep.*, 5.3.
[9] *Magn.*, 6.1; *Trall.*, 3.1.
[10] 2.26.5.
[11] Hipp., *trad. ap.*, 9 (but the versions differ, some stating that he is appointed by the bishop); cf. *Const. App.*, 8.18.2.
[12] cf. Cypr., *ep.*, 67.4.
[13] 9.
[14] *euchol.*, 26.
[15] 8.18.2.
[16] 22.

to receive promotion to the presbyterate. This depreciation of the deacon's office, together with the transformation of the presbyterate into a parochial priesthood, brought a great change in the relation of deacon to bishop in the organization of the Church's *diakonia*. Like the minor orders, the diaconate came to be used as a sphere of training for the priesthood, and only the archdeacon maintained for a time (until his office was also assigned to presbyters) the old association between bishop and deacon.

This change may be connected with an increase in the numbers of the deacons. In the third and early fourth centuries this is limited to seven in any one church, on the analogy of the Seven in Acts 6,[1] however large the population might be.[2] But the number became larger in the fourth century at Alexandria, and by the time of Justinian there were a hundred deacons in the Great Church at Constantinople. In the earlier period the deacons were greatly outnumbered by the presbyters; and these few men, exercising great influence and financial power, in the closest relation to the bishop, must have been highly important members of the community, despite the fact that their order held the third place in the hierarchy. It is not surprising that some of the Church Orders were evidently disposed never to let the deacon forget that he belonged only to the third order.

According to the *Liber Pontificalis*, the assignment to deacons of the ecclesiastical administration of the civic regions of Rome was effected by Fabian. This bishop used each of his seven deacons to look after two of the fourteen regions into which Rome was divided for the purpose of civil administration. The origin of the number seven, however, seems to lie in the text of Acts rather than in the local administrative situation in the capital.

The duties of these few deacons could, however, be shared by assistants. The Eastern versions of the *Apostolic Tradition*[3] provide for the appointment of subdeacons, who are not ordained but simply nominated to serve the deacons. In the middle of the third century each Roman deacon had a subdeacon.[4] Cyprian's correspondence shows subdeacons acting as messengers.[5] Canon 10 of Neocaesarea and the *Apostolic Constitutions*[6] refer to them as ὑπηρέται.

The word *diakonos* may be feminine as well as masculine, and there is also the corresponding term *diakonissa*. Whether or not Phoebe at Cenchreae held a recognized office in the Church, Pliny's mention of two women servants 'quae ministrae dicebantur'[7] (cf. Justin's 'those who among us are called "deacons" ') indicates that in the early second century in Bithynia there were women ministers with an official title which in Greek would have been either *diakonos* or *diakonissa*. Clement speaks of διάκονοι γυναῖκες who undertake the instruction of women

---

[1] Cornelius ap. Eus., *h.e.*, 6.43.11; Prudentius, *peristeph.*, 2, 5 (*PL.*, 60.293, 380).
[2] Canon 15 of Neocaesarea.
[3] 14.
[4] Cornelius ap. Eus., *h.e.*, 6.43.11.
[5] *ep.*, 9.1.
[6] 3.11.1, 6.17.2.
[7] *ep.*, 96.

(he supposes that the wives of the apostles acted in this capacity as συνδιάκονοι with their husbands);[1] and the *Didascalia* says much about their office and its importance. They are to be honoured as a type of the Holy Spirit.[2] Their special task is ministry to women, visiting them in their homes, caring for them in sickness, and, in particular, attending upon them at baptism.[3] Epiphanius contrasts the Church's deaconesses with the Collyridian priestesses, saying that the former are restricted to assistance at the baptism of women and sick visiting,[4] to which the *Apostolic Constitutions* add the duty of keeping the doors[5] (i.e. probably at baptisms). The *Testamentum Domini* mentions the taking by deaconesses of Easter Communion to women who are unable through illness to attend the liturgy.[6]

These ministers, who are very often mentioned by Eastern writers, were ordained, according to the *Apostolic Constitutions*,[7] with the laying-on of the bishop's hands in the presence of the presbyters, deacons and existing deaconesses, and with a prayer that alludes to the prophetesses of the Old Testament, but says little about their duties. Canon 15 of Chalcedon also mentions their ordination; canon 19 of Nicaea, which has sometimes been understood as prohibiting the ordination of deaconesses, probably refers to Paulianist deaconesses and is not relevant, but later Western councils do forbid it.

In the West deaconesses as such appear late on the scene, and do not play the same prominent part as in the East. Some of their work, however, was performed by the widows. Widows everywhere formed a large proportion of the poor people who were maintained by the Church. At Rome in the middle of the third century there were 1,500 widows and others 'on the books' of the Church.[8] They were not, however, merely the objects of charity. They had corresponding obligations. They formed an *ordo* into which they were duly enrolled, but not ordained.[9] Their duty, according to the *Apostolic Tradition*, was prayer, this being the return expected of them for their maintenance.[10] The Didascalia adds that they should accept gifts of wool in order to be able to make garments to give, in their turn, to other poor people.[11] The *Testamentum Domini* gives them a rank in the hierarchy, a place in the sanctuary, and the duty of visiting the sick.

As recipients, as well as promoters, of charitable service, the widows are in some degree in a similar position to that of the clergy themselves. The ministry of Christians to their brethren included the contribution of maintenance for the

---

[1] *str.*, 3.6.54.
[2] 2.26.6.
[3] 3.12.
[4] *haer.*, 79.3.
[5] 8.28.6.
[6] 2.20.
[7] 8.19.2.
[8] Cornelius ap. Eus., *h.e.*, 6.43.11.
[9] Tert., *ad uxor.*, 1.7; cf. Or., *Jo.*, 32.12.
[10] Hipp., *trad. ap.*, 11; cf. *Didasc.*, 3.5.2.
[11] *Didasc.*, 3.7.8.

clergy, whether it were the prophet of the *Didache*,[1] who received firstfruits, or the bishop with the presbyters and deacons. These are listed in the *Didascalia* along with the widows and orphans as proper recipients of offerings by the people,[2] and in the *Apostolic Constitutions* with orphans, widows, strangers and the poor as people to whom firstfruits and tithes should be devoted.[3] The *Apostolic Constitutions* elsewhere direct that firstfruits shall go to the maintenance of the bishop, presbyters and deacons, and tithes to the lower clergy, virgins, widows and the poor. Thus the mutual service of the brethren to one another comprehended those who themselves had the oversight and administration of the charitable work which was centred in worship and the offerings made in it to God.

[1] *Did.*, 13.3.
[2] *Didasc.*, 2.26.3.
[3] 7.29, enlarging on the *Didache*.

On Mediaeval Charities

G. BARROIS

I shall confine myself to the Western area. This artificial limitation, which still does not save me from feeling cramped, will not, I hope, be damageable to my subject. There was in Byzantium a statute of public charities with elaborate rules for the various categories of establishments: *xenodochium, ptochotrophium, gerontocomium, orphanotrophium, brephotrophium*. Early Roman foundations kept using those names, which gradually lost their originally precise meaning, while the legal provisions for the administration of charity were no longer heeded, due to the collapse of imperial power in Rome.

The mediaeval West, and the Westerners in their oversea possessions during the era of the Crusades, had to make a fresh start in these matters, and their institutions in favour of the poor and the sick can hardly be considered as mere copies of Byzantine models, or as the natural outcome of the early Roman *diaconiae*.

There are references to the institutions known as *diaconiae* in the letters of Gregory the Great. One of these letters is addressed to a certain Iohannes, a subdeacon of Ravenna, to the effect that the administration of moneys received by him or spent for the subsistence of the poor and the service of the *diaconia*, would not be subject to audit by any man, in any way, or under any pretext.[1] Another letter, written in the same year, rebukes a prefect who had retained grain and moneys marked for delivery to the Neapolitan *diaconia*.[2]

In the latter part of the eighth century Pope Hadrian reorganized the Roman *diaconiae*. There were sixteen of them at the beginning of his pontificate. Their number was increased to eighteen. They were administered centrally from the Lateran, the actual 'fieldwork' being entrusted to monks and religious persons. The same Pope also made a donation in order that 'the poor of Christ might from time to time enjoy the solace of a bath',[3] and he commanded that 'each week on Thursday, one would walk in procession, to the singing of the Psalms, from the siege of the *diaconia* to the bath-house, where orderly distributions would be made to the poor, and where alms would be given'.[4] At Naples, the

---

[1] *Migne, P.L. 77*, col. 1137.
[2] *Migne, P.L. 77*, col. 1080.
[3] *Liber Pontificalis*, ed. Duchesne, I, pp. 509f.
[4] *Liber Pontificalis*, ed. Duchesne, I, p. 506.

diaconia of S. Ianuarius even dispensed some soap twice a year, at Christmas and Easter.[1]

These details, the existence of *diaconiae* in areas open to the influence of the East, such as Ravenna or Naples, and actual parallels in various Eastern Churches, give support to the thesis of Henri Marrou,[2] that the Roman *diaconiae* were foreign importations, rather than a homogeneous development of the *septem regiones* set up by Pope Fabian in the third century for the ecclesiastical government of the city, including the administration of relief by seven deacons, while 'seven subdeacons would gather the acts of the martyrs from the records of the seven notaries'.[3]

The eventual combination of the *regiones* with the *diaconiae* around A.D. 1100, according to Marrou, resulted in the institution of the Cardinal deacons as a distinct class of the Roman clergy. But one may well wonder whether the poor and the sick fared any better, now that the organization of relief had become just one item among many on the general agenda of the Church.

The exercise of charity during the Middle Ages was mostly the fruit of private initiative: generous donors of every rank and station, monasteries and religious orders, commons, and lay brotherhoods. This is not to say that rulers, civil or ecclesiastical, defaulted with regard to the endeavours of Christian charity. But relief to the poor and the suffering members of the society was not deemed an essential part of government. It belonged rather in the personal charities of the prince or of the prelate, moved as they were by much the same motives as their own subjects, but also by considerations proper to their rank, since general distributions were meet to ensure their popularity, and to keep the masses reasonably quiet.

The functions of the Grand Almoner of France, a charge created formally by Charles VII, were to assist the king in his private charities and in the nomination of ecclesiastical beneficiaries as well, rather than actually centralizing relief work or administering the kingdom's hospitals and institutions. Similar offices at the English court finally turned into sinecures, and it seems that mediaeval Christendom had much to learn from the early Islamic institution of the *awqāf*, with its competent keepers of deeds and curators of charitable foundations. It originated after the death of Muhammad as early as the first century of the hegira, and was formally organized in the second century.[4] It provided an effective outlet for the charitable aspirations of the Arabs, and it may have been shaped, at least partly, after the imperial institutions found in the conquered lands.

---

[1] cf. H. I. Marrou, 'L'origine orientale des diaconies romaines', in *Ecole Française de Rome: Mélanges d'Archéologie et d'Histoire*, LVII (1940), p. 118. The soap was probably a contribution of the corporation of the *saponarii*, which Gregory the Great had taken under his protection; cf. *Migne, P.L.* 77, col. 1084.

[2] 'L'origine orientale des diaconies romaines', in *Ecole Française de Rome: Mélanges d'Archéologie et d'Histoire*, LVII (1940), pp. 95-142.

[3] *Breviarium Romanum*, in Nocturno SS. Fabiani et Sebastiani.

[4] *The Encyclopaedia of Islām*, s.v. 'wakf'.

Let us, for the sake of concreteness, sample the varieties of charitable houses and foundations of the Middle Ages. First, the hospitals. Here, a word of caution is in order: our information is unavoidably lopsided, based as it is on the hospital records of large urban centres; but we know precious little about lesser establishments, or about the care of the sick and the poor in the countryside.

The *Hôtel-Dieu de Paris* began as a refuge and nursing home under the episcopacy of S. Landry in the first half of the seventh century. A community of religious women was in charge, and, some two hundred years later, the priests of Notre-Dame made it their custom to visit the house and wash the feet of the poor on Maundy Thursday. Enriched with royal privileges and private donations, the original 'Maison-Dieu', rebuilt several times and modernized—to a measure—is still in operation.[1]

The *Hôtel-Dieu de Beaune*, founded in 1443 by Nicolas Rolin, Chancellor of Burgundy under Philippe le Bon, has for us the added interest that the ancient buildings have been preserved with a minimum of alterations. The central ward, the pharmacy, the kitchen, which were still in use after the First World War, are kept as a memorial, the actual services having been transferred to more suitable quarters.

In Rome, Pope Innocent III ordered the erection of a hospital of three hundred beds, with facilities for feeding a thousand poor daily. The direction of the hospital was entrusted to the religious of the Holy Spirit, recently founded in southern France by a certain Guy de Montpellier, who died in 1208. It is not immaterial that his birthplace was the seat of an influential school of medicine. The hospital, located in the Borgo, was known as the *Ospedale di S. Spirito in Sassia*, presumably because of an older hospice for Saxon pilgrims. The activities of the hospital are described in great detail in a fourteenth-century codex, the *Liber Regulae S. Spiritus*.[2] Once a week teams of religious toured the streets of Rome in horse-drawn chariots and brought the sick to the hospital, where they were registered, bathed, deloused and put to bed. In addition to the wards for poor patients, the hospital had also rooms for the 'nobles' and for women in childbirth, which appears somewhat exceptional for the time, since well-to-do people preferred to be treated in their homes, and since child-bearing was not regarded a case for medical attention. But the affluence of foreigners and pilgrims of both sexes in Rome, where they had no regular quarters, made special accommodations necessary.

Similar causes explain the unusual extension taken by the Hospital of S. John the Baptist in Jerusalem.[3] It developed out of a hospice for pilgrims built in 1063 by merchants of Amalfi. It had replaced an earlier house founded by Charlemagne, and destroyed by the mad Caliph in 1010. The Benedictine monks of S. Maria Latina were in charge of the hostelry of the Amalfitans, while the nuns

---

[1] *La Grande Encyclopédie*, s.v. 'Hôtel-dieu'.
[2] *Enciclopedia Italiana*, s.v. 'Ospedale', p. 677.
[3] H. Vincent and F. M. Abel, *Jérusalem: Recherches de Topographie, d'Archéologie et d'Histoire*, II, pp. 646ff.

of S. Mary Magdalen cared for the women. Destitute pilgrims, overcome by fatigue or by illness, were received in a third establishment, the *xenodochium* or hospital proper. The Hospitallers of S. John obtained from Pope Paschal II a bull of exemption in 1113, and, five years later, their first Grand Master, Raymond du Puy, gave the new order its statutes, which added to the service of the hospital the mission of protecting the pilgrims and the local Christians, and of defending the Holy Places against the attacks of the infidels. John of Würtzburg, who visited Jerusalem in 1160, admiringly described the hospital, 'wherein in various rooms is collected together an enormous multitude of sick people, both men and women, who are tended and restored to health at very great expense. When I was there, I learned that the whole number of those sick people amounted to two thousand, of whom sometimes in the course of one day and night more than fifty are carried out dead, while other fresh ones keep continually arriving.'[1] According to the thirteenth-century description of *La Citez de Jérusalem*, those dead were taken 'to the charnel-house called Chaudemar—a popular corruption for Akeldama—where they threw the pilgrims who had died in the house of the Hospital. This piece of land, where the charnel was, had been bought with the *denarii* received by Judas when he sold the body of Jesus Christ, just as the Gospel witnesseth.'[2] Theodoric, writing toward 1172, had mentioned a funeral chapel in connexion with the burial-ground, 'where, on Palm Sunday, we laid our deceased brother, Adolf by name, of Cologne'.[3]

Special establishments were created for patients requiring a lifetime attention, rather than a medical cure deemed impossible in their case. Such are the hospices for the blind, as, in Paris, the 'Quinze-Vingts', founded and endowed by S. Louis, and further enriched with gifts and privileges, especially by John XXII and Philip IV the Fair, who decreed that the inmates would bear the royal fleur-de-lis as a distinctive mark. The 'Quinze-Vingts' sheltered three hundred destitute blind persons, and not, as a romantic legend has it, which had already been exploded by the end of the thirteenth century, three hundred knights whose eyes would have been gouged by the Saracens.[4] Less famous, but older than the 'Quinze-Vingts', was the hospice for the blind established at Rouen by the Dukes of Normandy.

In the wake of the Crusades lepers and bearers of communicable diseases—allegedly a foreign import—were secluded in isolated houses in the suburbs or in the country, not in the hope of a cure, since only by a miracle of God could a minority of these unfortunates be made whole or 'clean', but rather as a means of preventing the contagion from spreading. Some of the major hospices for lepers in Europe and in the Levant were administered by the Knights of S. Lazarus, whose institution is attributed to Baldwin IV of Jerusalem, toward the middle of the twelfth century. The care of patients suffering from the

[1] Tobler, *Descriptiones Terrae Sanctae*, p. 159; cf. E. J. King, *The Knights Hospitallers in the Holy Land*, p. 67.
[2] Text quoted by De Vogüé, *Les Eglises de la Terre Sainte*, p. 442.
[3] Tobler, *Theodorici Libellus de Locis Sanctis*, p. 50.
[4] *La Grande Encyclopédie*, s.v. 'Quinze-vingts, Hospice des'.

so-called 'Mal des Ardents', alias 'Feu Saint Antoine', an inflammatory skin disease producing gangrenous phenomena, was the speciality of the *Antoniani*, originally an eleventh-century congregation of friars who, by a bizarre turn of circumstances, became ordinary attendants to the papal curia in its peripatetic wanderings through Italian cities besides Rome: at Assisi, Perugia, Todi, Viterbo, Orvieto, and also in Avignon.[1] Lazarets in the principal seaports and special hospitals for the contagious and the incurables became increasingly numerous in the fourteenth and the fifteenth centuries, endowed as a public service by princes and communal authorities.

In hospitals not owned or regularly operated by a religious order nursing services were performed by male or female attendants invited by the patrons or municipal bodies from local congregations. The rapid growth of the middle class and the rise of spontaneous religious and social movements from the latter part of the twelfth century onward had as one of their results the increasing participation of lay brotherhoods and sororities in the voluntary assistance to the poor and the sick in hospitals and hospices. Some fraternities assumed responsibility for a given establishment, or even owned their hospital, where their members tended the patients in a spirit of Christian charity, and for the expiation of their own sins. Thus most of the companies of penitents known in northern and central Italy as the *battuti* added the support and service of some hospital or some house of refuge to their ascetic practices, their periods of fasting and their processions of scourgers.

The fraternity of the *Misericordia* of Florence deserves a special mention.[2] There is no agreement as to its origins. It may have been founded by a certain Pier Luca Borsi, head of the *facchini* of the *Arte della Lana*, the clothiers' guild, some time between 1240 and 1244, for gathering sick persons deserted by their kin, and giving the dead a decent burial. The work of the fraternity is said to have been subsidized with fines levied on the brothers every time they used blasphemous language. According to another hypothesis, the *Misericordia* originated as a special project of the *disciplinati* of S. John the Baptist, who were recruited among street porters. It had its own statutes and its hospital already in the first two decades of the fourteenth century. It seems less probable that the *Misericordia* would have been founded by Peter of Verona, who has been already credited, on debatable grounds, with the paternity of a *Societas fidei* for the active defence of Catholic orthodoxy against the heretics, transformed at a later date into an association of charity called the *Compagnia del Bigallo*. The fact is, however, that Cosimo de' Medici ordered the fusion of the *Misericordia* and of the *Bigallo* in 1425. Whatever its origins and early vicissitudes, the *Misericordia* was completely reorganized in 1475 by popular demand, after a corpse had been found lying for some time in a street near the church of Santa Croce. The brotherhood, whose statutes were revised from time to time, is still in full activity, not only at Florence, but in many Italian cities, where its

[1] *Enciclopedia Italiana*, s.v. 'Ospedale', pp. 675f.
[2] *Enciclopedia Italiana*, s.v. 'Misericordia, La Compagnia della', p. 436.

members provide first aid and ambulance service, escort the priests on their way to administer the sacraments to the dying, and prepare the dead for burial. They continue wearing their medieval attire, complete with black cowl and rosary, for which they substitute crisp hospital whites during the summer months, and they drive their modern ambulances to the sound of screaming sirens.

Our information concerning medical service is scanty. The statutes of the Hospital and the *Liber Regulae Sancti Spiritus* mention or imply that a small number of physicians and surgeons was permanently attached to major houses, but we may assume that outsiders were summoned and paid for their services whenever the situation demanded it.

Ancient bidding prayers come to mind as one is enumerating the various ways in which medieval men helped one another: 'Pray for the poor and the sick . . . for the captives . . . for the travellers by land and sea.' Foremost among the captives are those who had been reduced to slavery by the Moors in the course of the Crusades or of the Spanish wars. There were hardships to be alleviated, ransoms to be paid, and the return to Christian lands to be arranged. To further these aims, religious orders had been instituted,[1] such as the *Ordo Sanctissimae Trinitatis*, founded by John of Matha and Felix of Valois, confirmed by Innocent III in 1198, and nicknamed the *Ordo Asinorum*, because its members were not allowed other mounts than asses. They were called also the 'Maturines', from the titular Saint of their Parisian church. The revenues of the Order were divided into three parts: two for current expenses and general charities, the third part being kept in reserve for the paying of ransoms.

In 1228, the *Ordo Beatae Mariae de Mercede Redemptionis Captivorum*, in short 'la Merced', was founded by Peter Nolasco, and approved by Gregory IX. Its members added to the traditional vows of religion the pledge to give themselves as personal surety for the liberation of Christians in grave danger of apostasy.

Somewhat similar occasions occurred in the fight of the Church against heresy and during the so-called Albigensian crusade. Converts and particularly widows and daughters of heretics had to be sheltered, supported and given instruction. The foundation of the monastery of Prouille by S. Dominic in 1206 aimed at meeting these needs.[2] It is only one relatively late example of several medieval attempts at giving a regular status to unattached despondent women. One might mention here the picturesque Order of Fontevrault founded in Brittany by Robert d'Arbrissel and confirmed by Paschal II in 1106, with its contingent of monks ministering to the nuns, the widows and the virgins, the magdalens, and eventually the lepers, all under the matriarchal government of the Abbess.[3]

And now, the travellers: as early as the Carolingian era, hospices had been

---

[1] *Enciclopedia Cattolica*, s.v. 'Ordine della S.ma Trinità', 'Mercedari'.
[2] R. Loenertz, 'Archives de Prouille', in *Archivum Fratrum Praedicatorum*, XXIV (1954), pp. 5–49.
[3] *Enciclopedia Cattolica*, s.v. 'Fontevrault'.

established at the high Alpine passes for their convenience and safety.[1] Here was the Christian version of the ancient *castella* or *burgi*, from which detachments of auxiliaries policed the mountainous tracts of the imperial roads. Most of the Alpine hospices were built and maintained by order and at the expense of local princes or prelates, and were manned by monks or members of religious congregations. The hospice at the Mont Genèvre was founded by a Bishop of Turin in the course of the eleventh century, and was assigned regular revenues by Guillaume Taillefer, Count of Vienne, in 1179. The goods of those travellers who died intestate in the limits of the hospice accrued to its treasury. The hospice at the Mont Cenis originated in the Carolingian period. The ancient pass of the *Mons Iovis* became associated with the name of S. Bernard of Menthon, and the hospice, whatever be the date of the original foundation, was mentioned in the twelfth century as the *Domus hospitalis SS. Nicolai et Bernardi Montis Iovis*. The hospice of the Johannites at the Simplon pass goes back to the thirteenth century, and is due to the initiative of local authorities. The hospice at the Saint Gotthard was built in 1171 by Galdino, Archbishop of Milan, and the church was consecrated in 1230. With the Alpine hospices we come probably the closest to a conception of a public service undertaken as a charge of the State.

Hagiographic legends and local traditions suggest that the building of bridges over important rivers was regarded during the Middle Ages a singular act of devotion. The construction of the most sung 'Pont d'Avignon', toward the end of the twelfth century, is attributed to S. Bénezet, of whom we otherwise know very little, and the Dominican Gunzalo of Amaranth is credited with the building of a stone bridge spanning the Tagus. Multiple references to brotherhoods in connexion with the construction or operation of bridges, especially in the Rhône valley, from the twelfth to the fourteenth century, has led some scholars to assume the existence of a medieval order, the so-called *Fratres pontis*. A recent study by Marjorie Boyer has clearly shown that the 'Brothers of the bridge' were not a centralized religious order, but lay fraternities independent from each other, and engaged in a variety of tasks.[2] While their primary objective was to provide for the building and maintenance of bridges, as at Lyons and in Avignon, local circumstances rather than a uniform policy determined the nature and extent of their activities, such as levying tolls, collecting funds, and running hospices and hospitals, not necessarily for the benefit of travellers or pilgrims, but, at Pont Saint Esprit, for the poor of the locality. The brothers seem to have had in view their spiritual advantage at least as much as the welfare of the users of the bridge.

On the surface, the charitable record of Christians during the Middle Ages looks impressive. But we wish further to explore their motives and eventually their rationalizations. A logion of Jesus, according to Matthew 25^{36-40}, had

---

[1] *Enciclopedia Italiana*, s.v. 'Moncenisio', 'Monginevro', 'San Bernardo', 'San Gottardo', 'Sempione'.

[2] 'The Bridgebuilding Brotherhoods', in *Speculum*, XXXIX (1964), pp. 635-50.

proved most effective in moving them to action: 'I was hungry and you gave me food, I was a stranger and you welcomed me, I was naked and you clothed me, I was sick and you visited me, I was in prison and you came to me . . . I say unto you, as you did it to one of the least of these my brethren, you did it to me.' These words were preached, referred to, commented upon, and interpreted realistically. They offered suitable themes for legendary amplifications and tempting motifs for sculptors and painters. Gregory the Great tells the story of a certain monk Martyrius, on his way to visit the abbot of a neighbouring monastery, when he came upon a traveller suffering from elephantiasis, *elephantinus morbus*, lying, exhausted, by the roadside. Martyrius, moved of compassion, wrapped the man in his mantle, loaded him on his back, and took him to the monastery. The abbot, who watched them drawing near, called on his monks with a loud voice: 'Make haste! Fling open the gates of the monastery, for our brother Martyrius is coming; 'tis the Lord he is bearing.'[1] The point is this: a Christian who gives to the needy is not only helping a naked poor, a pathetic wretch, a fellow man sick in body and in soul, but he stands in front of Christ Himself. It is the shoulders of Christ that S. Martin, still a catechumen, covers with his cloak, and it is the Christ child whom S. Christopher carries across the river. Thus the record of Christian deeds becomes the story of men meeting God face to face.

The assimilation of the poor and the sick with Christ, in the eyes of a devoted Christian, has important consequences. When a man gives alms to a beggar he does not really give of his own, but he gives what he himself has received from God in trust. Since Christ is in the beggar, then the man who refuses to help is, in fact, defrauding the beggar, and appropriating to himself that which is God's. S. Peter Damian, in the eleventh century, tells of a certain Waldericus, who was going to visit his aged mother. He met a poor man gathering wild herbs, who complained bitterly that the lady, out of stinginess, had refused to give him a pinch of salt to season his meagre fare. Upon entering the house, Waldericus discovered some salt left in a box. Flaring in anger, he threw the salt away, for, said he, 'a Christian has no right to eat that which he has denied Christ'.[2] The narrator adds that a few days later, the empty salt box was miraculously refilled, which shows that it pays to be generous—somehow an anticlimax to the story and a discordant note, upon which we shall comment later. Disregarding the last point, the principle involved is formulated by Peter Damian in these words: 'The rich are commanded to be dispensators rather than possessors, nor shall they dispose of their properties just as they please, since they were granted those perishable riches, not that they would seek their own delight nor use them for their private convenience; they ought rather to act as administrators, as long as they continue in the trust, *villicatu*, committed unto them.'[3] S. Basil had already said the same in a sentence as nervous as Peter Damian's speech is verbose:

[1] *Migne, P.L. 76*, col. 1300.
[2] *De Eleemosyna, Migne, P.L. 145*, col. 217.
[3] ibid., col. 210.

"Tis the bread of the hungry you are holding, the shirt of the naked you put away in your chest, the shoe of the barefooted which rots in your closet, the buried silver of the poor on which you sit!'[1]

Since Christ is in the poor and the sick, they must be treated like one would treat Christ himself. S. Benedict of Nursia orders that 'the care of the sick is to be put before anything else; they are to be treated as Christ himself who tells us: I was sick and you visited me . . . The sick on their side are to reflect that the attention paid to them is for the honour of God, and they are not to be a grievance to those that tend them, by demanding too much. Yet even if they ask too much, they are to be borne with, for thereby they are means to a greater reward.'[2]

The rules for the 'Maison-Dieu' of Vernon in Normandy prescribe that the patients be treated with great kindness as the 'lords of the house', *comme li sires de la maison*. According to the statutes of the Hospital, the patients are described as 'Our lords the sick', in the prayers recited every evening. Their sufferings confer upon them the dignity of Christlikeness, and the assumption is that their intercession is, on that account, singularly pleasing to God: '*Seignors malades*, pray for peace, which God grant us from Heaven here on earth! *Seignors malades*, pray for the fruits of the earth, which God may increase, that he be served here, and Christendom be maintained! Pray for the pilgrims who journey by sea and land! God guide them and bring them safely home in health of body and soul! Pray for those who beg for alms, and for the captive of the Saracens! May God set them free through your prayers! *Seignors malades*, pray for yourselves and for the sick in the whole world! The Lord give them health of soul and body as he knows best! *Seignors malades*, pray for all the brothers and sisters of the Hospital, and all who serve in the office of charity in the holy house of the Hospital! And may our Lord grant unto all a good end!'[3]

In addition to Matthew 25$^{35-36}$, other *loci* from Scripture and from the Apocrypha have undoubtedly influenced the traditional catalogue of the works of mercy. Such as James 1^{27}: 'Religion that is pure and undefiled before God and the Father is this: to visit orphans and widows in their affliction, and to keep oneself unstained from the world.' Also Tobit 12^2, a mediaeval favourite: 'When you prayed with tears, and buried the dead, and left your meal, and when you hid the dead in your house by day and buried them by night, I presented your prayer to the Lord.' Of course, the lists of the so-called acts of mercy did not merely derive from the texts by deductive process, but, at least for an equal part, from actual practice.

Already S. Benedict had listed several of the traditional works of mercy among other precepts of his monastic rule: 'Relieve the poor, clothe the naked, visit the sick, bury the dead, help those that are in trouble, comfort the afflicted!'[4]

---

[1] *Migne, P.G. 31*, col. 1752.
[2] *Regula*, ch. 36, transl. Owen Chadwick.
[3] Léon Lallemand, *Histoire de la Charité*, III, pp. 198ff.
[4] *Regula*, ch. 4, transl. Owen Chadwick.

But it is not until the twelfth or early thirteenth century that the enumeration of the works of mercy became definitive and stereotyped and that scholastic theologians ponderously commented upon their number, their significance, and their symmetrical distribution into corporal and spiritual works of mercy.

Mnemotechnic verses are quoted by Alexander de Hales, Albertus Magnus, Bonaventura, and Aquinas:

visito, poto, cibo, redimo, tego, colligo, condo,
consule, castiga, solare, remitte, fer, ora,

corresponding respectively to: visit the sick, refresh the thirsty, feed the hungry, redeem the prisoner, clothe the naked, take the stranger in, bury the dead; and, for the second verse: counsel the perplexed, correct the sinner, comfort him who is sad, forgive the offender, bear with him who is burdensome, and pray for all men. This enumeration limps: seven and six are thirteen, an odd number. To make it even, Aquinas splits the *consule* at the beginning of the second verse in two, and distinguishes 'teach the ignorant' and 'counsel the perplexed' as two specific acts of spiritual mercy.

Commenting upon Matthew 25^{35-36}, Aquinas remarks that the burial of the dead is not mentioned by Christ, nor, for that matter, by James, and he imagines for this omission an odd reason: the formulation of the *logion* precludes 'the error of those who say that the soul is not at rest until the body is laid in the tomb, but that is not true, since the soul does not receive anything from the body as long as they are separated from each other'.[1] Whether or not supported by the authority of the Gospel, the burial of the dead and the solemn observance of funeral customs were regarded during the Middle Ages as a singular act of devotion, appropriately reckoned among the works of mercy. We are not speaking here of the *suffragia mortuorum*, that is, the prayers for the dead, the psalters, vigils, and anniversary masses; these belong in the category of the spiritual works of mercy, but we speak of the last duties paid to the body of a Christian as it is laid out for burial and sealed in the tomb. The hymn for the first Vespers of the feast of S. Francis of Assisi beseeches him to visit 'the house, the door, and the tomb', *domum, portam et tumulum*. Among his sons, the Capuchins have been particularly mindful of this part of their inheritance, to be watchmen over the tombs, whether those in a village cemetery, or the catacombs of the Piazza Barberini, or the Imperial sepulchres in the *Kapuzinergruft*. There is a Shakespearian note about a similar survival of the Middle Ages at Florence: the Olivetans of San Miniato al Monte, standing perpetual guard over the city of the dead, and officiating at an interminable line of Sunday weddings, which conclude with much picture-taking on the terraces of the nearby Piazzale Michelangelo.

The corporal works of mercy have been a familiar subject for mediaeval artists. The care of the sick is, as one would expect, the theme of miniatures such as those of the *Liber Regulae Sancti Spiritus*, or of mural decorations in

---

[1] *Commentarium in Matthaeum*, Parm. X, p. 238.

churches and hospital buildings. The popular devotion to SS. Cosmas and Damian, 'unmercenary healers of men and beasts', whose names were written on the diptychs of the Roman Mass, materialized in a score of paintings, ranging from the Italian Primitives to Fra Angelico to Ambrose Francken of Antwerp. The two brothers, in the attire of mediaeval physicians, are shown amputating the gangrenous leg of a patient and replacing it by a sound, but very black leg severed from the corpse of a very black Moor, who had been freshly buried; of course, they would not have thought of disintering a Christian and of mutilating his remains, even for medical purposes. As a series, the corporal works of mercy begin to appear in the Romanesque sculpture of the twelfth century, as, for instance, at the baptistery of Parma. However, the seventh work, namely 'burying the dead', does not occur in art prior to the fourteenth century. The traditional series appears complete, perhaps for the first time, at the church of S. Maria della Salute, Viterbo.

From what was said above, it seems that the Scriptural record as a whole might call for a theological elaboration which would make the care of the poor and the sick a cult to God and a service to mankind, in either case an observance of justice. In the Old Testament the Deuteronomic context of what looks at first like humanitarian precepts is the worship which the Holy One claims for Himself, and the Prophets never tire from repeating that mercy is the most excellent form of sacrifice. The New Testament witness also is unambiguous. The bread we eat, the bread we throw away, is not ours; it is the bread of Christ and of His poor, and we make ourselves guilty of theft every time we forget this. S. Basil, whom we have quoted earlier in this essay, said it, and he meant it. Early Western writers have echoed his voice, with unfortunate rhetorical overtones and accessory motives which blur the message.

The theological systems of the twelfth and the thirteenth century move in quite another direction. Of course, the precept of doing mercifully is not forgotten, but it is tied up with the commandment: 'Love thy neighbour!' It spells not an obligation of justice, but an office of love. Our works of mercy arise not from our acknowledging that the poor have a right to seek and to obtain help; they are a free *exhibitio caritatis*. S. Thomas regards the virtues of *beneficentia*, *misericordia*, and their derivatives, as varieties and manifestations of *caritas*, which is basic. Religion, on the opposite, he places in the category of justice. The equation of the works of mercy with 'religion pure and undefiled' of James 1[27], is to be so understood that the external acts of charity indeed are 'ordered' by the virtue of religion, but not 'elicited' by it.[1] This piece of scholastic jargon means that the works of mercy originate immediately and spontaneously in the effect of Christian love. Secondarily and indirectly, they contribute to the worship of God, to which they are further ordained, and they establish a relationship of equity between the one who gives and the one who receives. But in the absolute propriety of terms, we cannot say 'mercy = sacrifice'; this is a metaphor.

[1] *Summa Theologiae*, IIa, IIae, qu. 81, art. 1, ad 1m.

The perspective opened by this kind of theology, at least in its positive aspect, is unquestionably broad. It may even attain to a universal amplitude. S. Thomas probably never doubted that right acts of charity can be found in the case of a man who, through no fault of his own, has not been touched by the Gospel—*anima naturaliter christiana*. Be it as it may, S. Thomas saw the works of charity as having their natural climate among those Christians who are in a 'state of grace'. Charity, then, is the live principle which ought to animate all our activities, and moralists like Gregory the Great took a dim view of works of mercy not actually inspired by it: they do not benefit our souls.[1] Still, the stomach of the hungry is being filled, something which should not wait until after we deserve their gratitude.

Flowing, as they are seen by S. Thomas, from the hidden springs of Christian charity, the works of mercy partake of the dignity and all-embracing dimensions of the so-called theological virtues, viz. faith, hope, and love, before and independently from any determination of positive law, divine or human. But this seems too broad a conception to be fully effective, and effectiveness is of the essence of a right system of ethics. If the exercise of charity is everybody's business, is there not a danger that it may end by being nobody's business? We know that it has been historically the business of a few, but it did suffer greatly from being optional, left to private initiatives, insufficiently guided, guarded, and co-ordinated.

To give cohesion to the random development of charitable institutions, it would have been necessary for society as a whole, acting through its responsible leaders or officers, to acknowledge the right of its suffering members to obtain assistance, and to make this assistance an essential obligation of government. But this supposes a sharply defined conception of social justice, which was generally foreign to the mediaeval way of thinking. S. Thomas, it is true, recognizes a general function of the virtue of justice, inasmuch as it ordains the entire activity of man toward the common good.[2] But this *iustitia generalis*, without further determination, is bound to remain theoretical. It is as broad as the effect of charity, which at least has the advantage of being concretely motivated, whereas general justice calls upon a cold abstraction, the *bonum commune*. Modern attempts at identifying the *iustitia generalis* with what we call 'social justice' are fallacious, because of anachronism: one cannot possibly read Lyndon Johnson's *Great Society* back into Aquinas!

The Middle Ages knew only two kinds of justice in the strict sense, neither of which could serve as a foundation for a policy of assistance to the needy: the *iustitia commutativa*, which balances private claims and obligations resulting from contracts or pursuant to a statute, and the *iustitia distributiva*, which prompts the ruler to treat his subjects according to merit. The former has nothing much to contribute to the organization of relief. The latter is perhaps more relevant, but it involves a measure of arbitrariness. Assistance may be

---

[1] *Moralia*, Migne, P.L. 76, col. 122.
[2] *Summa Theologiae*, IIa, IIae, qu. 58, art. 5.

'granted' by the prince, freely or grudgingly; we insist that it must be a vital function of the human community, and that it must be meted according to fixed rules.

The order of charity is not enforceable by law: one does not love people by decree, and some people one does not like also need help. Meanwhile a working pattern is needed for the ordering of charitable activities. That is why S. Thomas engaged into a system of casuistry, in order to answer such questions as: How much shall we give to charities, a sacrificial gift, or a token gift? And the perennial problem: Who, after all, is my neighbour? The not-too-subtle answer to the first question is that one must contribute to charities from his surplus, *de superfluo*. Whether one may give from his necessary, *de necessario*, is a matter of personal choice.[1]

S. Bonaventura, in a different context, explains what 'necessary' means. It may be understood as the bare minimum for keeping soul and body together, *secundum naturae arctitudinem*, or as the amount of goods required by a man in a given situation, judging from common standards, *secundum communem usum vivendi*.[2] It is, of course, in the latter sense, that we may be moved to give from our necessary.

The Schoolmen bring here another distinction, equally slippery: that which we must do, according to what was just said, falls under the precept: 'Thou shalt love!' That which we may do is of supererogation, and belongs in the counsels of perfection. Thus a barrister is not to be ordered *ex officio* to defend the cause of an indigent. Nor is he under any moral obligation freely to offer his help, except perhaps in an extreme emergency. For that matter, says S. Thomas, he is in about the same situation as his neighbour the physician.[3]

The second question seeks to determine an order of urgency in caring for the sick and the poor. S. Thomas launches into a chain of pedestrian considerations: we must follow the *ordo caritatis*:[4] first ourselves, then our parents, then our relatives, then the neighbours, then the strangers, and finally, the enemies. But accidental occurrences play havoc with this beautiful order. Shall we give priority to a kinsman, who may be a not too lovable character, or to a stranger who is more deserving, the need being supposed equal? These problems are scrutinized ... in the professorial chair, and the ultimate conclusion of all that casuistry—a conclusion which remains unformulated—might very well be that we are left to rely on our common sense and our good heart. But it certainly does not make for efficiency in the organization of relief, or of medical or legal assistance. Whatever organization there was, was due, among other things, to the rules of the Hospitallers, born out of experience, and which became a model for other institutions, and to the private statutes of brotherhoods engaged in charitable activities.

[1] ibid., qu. 32, art. 6.
[2] *In IV Sent.*, dist. 15, pars 2, art. 2, qu. 1.
[3] *Summa Theologiae*, IIa, IIae, qu. 71, art. 1.
[4] ibid., qu. 26.

The separate listing of the spiritual works of mercy had its counterpart in the actual provisions made for the spiritual care of the poor and the sick admitted in mediaeval houses of charity. This ministry, originally performed by the clergy of the parish under the territorial jurisdiction of which the hospice was located, soon became entrusted to resident chaplains on call day and night for the administration of the sacraments to the dying. Thus in 1272 the chapter of Notre-Dame decided that two priests would be permanently attached to the Maison-Dieu of Paris, which was thus far under the care of the Curés of S. Christopher.[1] In the houses of the Hospital, patients upon arrival confessed to the chaplain and received Holy Communion, their condition permitting. On Sundays the wards would be sprinkled with Holy Water, and the Epistle and Gospel of the Mass would be chanted solemnly. [2]At Florence, the hospital of S. Maria Nuova, founded in 1287 by Folco Portinari, the father of Dante's Beatrice, had a staff of priests able to receive the confessions of pilgrims and travellers in their own tongue, and a tablet divided into four columns would inform the chaplains of the patients whose confessions they were to hear, of those who were to receive communion, of those whose condition called for the office of the *commendatio animae*, and of those to whom the Extreme Unction was to be administered.[3]

In all establishments of charity, and in all fraternities, prayers, the recitation, of the Psalter by monks, clerics and nuns, and the celebration of Vespers, Vigils and Masses of *Requiem*, as a supreme work of mercy, constituted the *suffragia mortuorum*, the multiplication of which was rightly criticized, since it competed unwarrantedly with the common prayer and praise of the Church.

As might be expected, mediaeval theologians appraised the spiritual works of mercy higher than the corporal, seeing that the spirit is more noble than the flesh. Even S. Thomas, in spite of his insistence upon the essential unity of the 'human composite', accepts the traditional dichotomy. In principle, what benefits the soul is more excellent than what benefits the body, *donum spirituale praeeminet corporali*. But he hastens to add that, from the point of view of the needy, the priority may be reversed, and then he quotes Aristotle: substantial alms are better for the beggar than a discourse—which is common sense.[4]

We have no documentation concerning the admission of non-Christians in the mediaeval establishments of charity. The case may have been unfrequent in the West. In the Crusaders' states the statutes of the Hospital do not seem to make any special provision for Moslems in need of medical assistance. However, there is sporadic evidence that a *modus vivendi* had gained acceptance by the time of the late Crusades, and under the influence of such liberals as Frederick II, particularly in Western cities engaged in the Levantine trade. As for the Jews, they had always taken care of their own. They had even provided the

---

[1] Léon Lallemand, *Histoire de la Charité*, III, p. 197, n. 14.
[2] Rule of Raymond du Puy, ch. 16; cf. E. J. King, *The Knights Hospitallers in the Holy Land*, p. 327.
[3] Léon Lallemand, *Histoire de la Charité*, III, p. 197, n. 21.
[4] *Summa Theologiae*, IIa, IIae, qu. 32, art. 3.

Christians with physicians infinitely superior to the majority of Western quacks.

The growing importance ascribed to funeral rituals, which we mentioned above, is a characteristic feature of the Middle Ages. It manifests a general obsession, verging on hysteria, with what comes after death: Heaven or Hell? Participation in the works of mercy gave everyone some kind of assurance. One would refer to a medley of quotations from Scripture or the Apocrypha, truncated or out of context. Translating from the Vulgate:'Redeem your sins with alms, and your iniquities with acts of mercy' (Daniel 4^{24}); 'Give alms from your surplus, and behold, all things shall be pure unto you' (Luke 11^{41}; 'Alms deliver from death and purge sin away, and make one receive mercy and eternal life' (Tobit 12^9). Thus the personal advantage obtained from almsgiving or showing mercy was in the way to being considered first, the interest of the poor and the sick coming only second best. This is certainly not in line with Paul's idea of charity, which 'seeketh not its own', and we shall let Professor Nygren decide whether it is subchristian or not. The Schoolmen do not seem to have been much disturbed by this self-interested motivation of their contemporaries. Only they wanted to make it clear that do-gooding was not a free pass to wanton living. S. Thomas explained that if a man would repent and desist from sinning, only then would his works absolve him, *sic potest esse quod aliquis abstinet et poenitet, et sic per eleemosynam potest liberari.*[1]

S. Bonaventura painstakingly sought in which circumstances did the works of mercy constitute a satisfaction for sin or a credit toward Heaven, and he concluded with a cry from the heart: 'I believe that so great is God's mercy, that he accepts everything we offer, and that he saves us, so to speak, for nothing.[2]

There is no reason for making mediaeval theologians responsible for the shortcomings of mediaeval charities, for it was not the purpose of the theologians to work out a rationale for ways of helping the poor and the sick. What they attempted was a more or less conscious rationalization: how to justify the practice of their age at its best, and reconcile it in a measure with the demands of the Gospel. Should we be inclined loudly to deplore their failure to grasp the nature of what we recognize as a social duty, then we had better realize that our actual achievements are not equal to our insights. We have not progressed as much as we like to think, when live minorities and active lobbies too often delay or defeat the voting of much-needed provisions for public welfare, through prejudice or sordid interest.

[1] *Commentarium in Matthaeum*, Parm. X, p. 238.
[2] *In IV Sent.*, dist. 15, pars 2, art. 2, qu. 1.

Diakonia at the time of the Reformation

JAMES ATKINSON

LUTHER

1. *Diakonia as Luther inherited it*

The noble art of beggary was a legacy the sixteenth century inherited from the fifteenth. In Luther's day it had developed into a recognized trade, even an art, judging by contemporary accounts of their practices. Beggars were recognized in many cities to the extent of being taxed like any other citizen, and in 1477 in Erfurt they took tickets in the town lottery along with other citizens. Beggars stood at every church door, beggars walked the streets, beggars roamed the lanes: beggars were everywhere. They had even crept into contemporary literature as 'characters' of everyday life. Beggary was the plague of Europe.

This state of affairs had arisen partly owing to social and political causes, partly religious. Luther attributed much poverty to the rising class of rich merchants, supported by the landed gentry and monied class, who wasted the country's wealth on frivolous dress, luxury goods and exotic food and drink, as well as to the papal curia which treated Germany as a milch-cow. Both of these criticisms stand examination. Other contemporary observers blamed the German people for not working hard enough, and used to instance towns and communities where, when all the priests, nuns, mendicants, beggars and loafers were added up only about one in fifteen was working seriously and producing food and goods. They argued that the economy could not stand so many idle hands. Further, now that the trade routes to the East had been opened up, the glorious prosperity both of the rich cities of southern Germany with their transit trade, as well as of the great northern Hanseatic ports, was beginning to decline. That was not all. Gold had become a means of exchange, there developed a shortage of silver, and people experienced a mysterious and uncontrollable rise in prices. A shortage of land caused everywhere acute hardship and a paucity of food before a rising population. It was the peasant who found it hardest. Luther knew all this at first hand. His father had been compelled to move owing to land shortage, found farming impossible, and turned to metal mining. Not all had the ability, resources, or determination of old Hans Luther. Armies of people succumbed to the poverty and hardship, and simply gave in.

The gap between the rich and the poor grew wider. Butzer in Strassburg complained that nobody wanted to work at the traditional tasks, but everybody was rushing to trade and business in order to make money. Contemporary observers were unable to diagnose these problems; even present-day historians and sociologists are in little better position to understand and interpret these events. All that the sixteenth-century man knew was the tightening grip of worsening poverty.

There was another cause of the pernicious beggary of the early sixteenth century. The Church had long taught beggary as an ideal of the full contemplative life, and poverty as Christian perfection. For example, Prince Alexius chose to lie at his father's gate as a beggar rather than live in the castle rightly his own, and for this earned a universal reputation for piety. Or again, Luther tells the remarkable story that as a boy he saw the saintly Prince of Anhalt, a wretched skinful of bones, begging in the streets. The almsgiving and works of mercy of the Church of Luther's day needed this vast sink of human misery in order to exercise its charity and earn merit, and the very charity of the Church maintained this beggary. Every monastery, every hospital, gave freely and liberally without question to every person who knocked at its door: none was denied. Every Christian man felt obliged to give; not necessarily for the sake of the suffering poor, but for the sake of the giver. The impulse and the necessity lay with the giver, generally without concern for the result of his giving. The giver had given, he had earned merit: that was his life, and his religion.

2. *Diakonia as Luther conceived it*

Luther severed the very tap-root of this unwholesome growth, and it perished overnight like Jonah's gourd, at least in those territories where Luther was heeded.

It is important to bear in mind that Luther's teaching on *diakonia* was the sequel of a precise theological reformation and not a mere reformation of Church order or discipline or social practice. It was neither a return to the ways of the primitive Church of Acts, nor was it an attempt to cope with the immense social problem of beggary maintained by catholic merit-earning practice. In effect it did restore primitive convictions and practice, and it also, by its teaching on justification by faith, caused works as a means of grace to wither away and work as a means of grace to rehabilitate itself. Nevertheless these were only fruits of a profound theological revolution.

Luther's interpretation of Christianity was wholly different from that of the Church of his day, and may be seen most clearly perhaps in his controversy with Erasmus on the bondage of the will. Luther recognized that Erasmus, alone of all his contemporary opponents, had perceived Luther's real evangelical concern and did not confound the issue with discussion of indulgences and immorality and scandals. Erasmus opposed Luther in the belief that man was essentially good, would respond to the good, and by appropriate effort could attain some fellowship with God. Luther argued, on the contrary, that man's salvation lay not with man and his works but with God and His Work: it lay wholly, utterly and only in the sovereign grace of God, free and unmerited, and that the natural man lay fast bound in sin, and was raised out of this death-dealing paralysis by the effectual calling of God in Christ. He described the error of Erasmus as *hominem praedicare*, and saw this error as both the ruin of the Church as well as the breeding-ground of all abuses and scandals. Faith to Erasmus meant, in the main, belief in man and assent to the Church's doctrines. To Luther it was a living and known assurance of a God who had shown His hand in Christ: a total recognition of man's fraility, his creatureliness, his finitude, his sin; in answer to which God of His free mercy had given Christ 'for us men and for our salvation', and had elected us to certain salvation and unwavering faith in Him.

It was Luther's Christology that made the Reformation. He argued that a man cannot talk of God until God has talked to him and declared His promise of salvation in Christ. 'When it pleased God . . . to reveal His Son in me . . . (Galatians 1^{15}f.) was Paul's beginning and Luther's. The heart of Europe was strangely warmed when it turned from seeking salvation in merit to heed salvation offered in Christ only.

This first principle of salvation in Christ alone stunned Luther when it first dawned into his searching mind. The entire New Testament lit up for him, and with that the Old. He knew that it was not of him that willeth, nor of him that runneth, but of God that showeth mercy (Romans 9^{16}). He trembled in the realization that it had been revealed to him that the Church had lost by and large her doctrine of salvation, and with that her *raison d'être*. He grew painfully aware of the futility of monasticism, fastings, vigils, pilgrimages, expiations, ascetic practices, 'good works'. . . .

It was this conviction that spelt death to a mediatorial priesthood. Mediaeval Christians were taught that the life of the soul was created, nourished, perfected through sacramental grace of which the priest was the sole purveyor. Pardon was forgiveness pronounced by the priest, grace a medicine he dispensed: the keys of heaven and hell were on the girdle of the priest. But with the doctrine of salvation in Christ alone the priest lost his role as mediator between God and man. That place could be filled only by a minister of the Word of God preaching and offering salvation in Christ only.

With the collapse of the mediatorial priesthood there collapsed the entire diaconate, deacons and subdeacons alike. Luther had no room for these minor orders, responsible for reading the Epistle and the Gospel and for being in attendance at mass. In fact, he described them as a plague in the Church. To Luther all clergy, archbishop and parish priest alike, were ministers and servants. They were called to minister the Word of God and to serve the people of God given to their charge; to nourish them with prayer and sacrament, to give general pastoral and personal oversight; to minister Christ and the things of Christ:

Therefore, the man upon whom the preaching office has been bestowed has had committed to him the highest office in Christendom. This man may, in addition, baptise, say mass, and bear all responsibility for the cure of souls. Or, if he does not want to do all these, he may keep to the preaching alone and leave baptism and all the other lesser offices to others. This is what Christ did, and Paul too, and all the apostles (Acts 4). In the light of this we see that the bishops we now have and our spiritual leaders are just painted images and no bishops at all. For they leave the highest office of the ministry of the Word, which is their only proper function, to the very lowest orders, namely, chaplains and monks, mere alms-collectors! They even leave them to do the minor offices as well, such as baptism and pastoral work. On the other hand they administer confirmation; they dedicate bells, altars and churches, none of which are Christian or episcopal tasks. They are invented out of their own heads. These men are just blind play actors. They are playing at bishops like children.

(Dass eine christliche Versammlung 1523, WA.11.415.30–416.10. See also: De captivitate Babylonica 1520. WA.6.564.15ff.; Von weltliche Obrigkeit 1523. WA.11.271.11ff.; Vermahnung an die Geistlichen 1530. WA.30.2.335ff.; and in many places throughout Luther's writings. Luther held to this view to the end, e.g. Hauspostille 1544, WA.52.587–98.)

The deacons, referred to in the quotation given, were to Luther the pastor's assistants, who in ministering to the sick, the poor, the lonely, the suffering, the workless, were doing the second great task of the Church, and further were actually freeing the true ministers for their real task:

The diaconate . . . is a ministry, not for reading the Gospel and the Epistle, as the practice is nowadays, but for distributing the Church's bounty to the poor, in order that the priests might be relieved of the burden of temporal concerns and give themselves more freely to prayer and the Word. This was the purpose of the institution of the diaconate, as we read in Acts 6. Therefore, whoever does not know or does not preach the Gospel is not only not a priest or a bishop but is a plague of the Church. Under the false title of priest or bishop he is a wolf in sheep's clothing. Such men oppress the Gospel. They are wolves in the fold.

(De captivitate Babylonica 1520, WA.6.566.34–567.5.)

It was this vital first principle of justification in Christ alone that at once caused both the collapse of the mediatorial priesthood and with it the mediaeval practices in relation to the sick and poor; and also founded the evangelical ministry with its first task the ministry of the Word and its second the care of all in need. It is essential to make one further point in this context. Justification by faith is often set against justification by works. This contradistinction is, of course, true in the relation of Christianity to Judaism, and rightly occupied the prime place in the New Testament. In Luther's day, although the Church taught meritorious works (as Judaism had done before it), the real divergence lay not in a justification by faith on the one hand and a justification by works on the other, for the word justification carries a different meaning in each case. The justification experienced by the believing sinner elected in Christ is wholly different from that kind of 'justification' which a man feels who has performed works. Justification meant two different things to a Paul and a Gamaliel. Our conflict lies elsewhere. The counterpart of justification by faith is priestly absolution. This was why the mediatorial priesthood collapsed and in its stead stepped in a ministry of the Word. Good works were henceforth seen as a fruit of faith, as the New Testament teaches; not only the doling out of alms but in the whole giving of one's life to the well-being and welfare of one's neighbour. As Luther carefully taught in his Freedom of a Christian Man (1520), a man lives in Christ through faith and in his neighbour through love.

Luther therefore set the whole matter on the high plane of Christian love as the expression work of a man justified by faith. He sought to intensify and to regularize it. Already at the Leipzig Disputation, 1519, he disapproved of mendicant orders. In his Treatise on the Blessed Sacrament and the Guilds (1519) he advocated the establishment of a common parish chest for the aid of craftsmen when in need. In his Address to the German Nobility (1520) he strongly disapproved of any and every kind of mendicancy and beggary and advised every town to assume responsibility for its own poor and needy by appointing an official to advise the pastor.

Once Luther had established evangelical theology, society realized that beggary must go. A strong conscience on work had developed once Luther had demolished the idea of a 'higher' morality of 'spiritual' folk (monks, nuns, priests) and a 'lower' morality of 'secular' folk (princes, merchants, soldiers, artisans, parents). If a person was justified by faith in Christ, then in that status or relationship to God any work was God's work, whether it was ploughing the field, milling the corn, sweeping the house, or bringing up children. If that relationship were absent, then any work, even the so-called meritorious good works such as pilgrimages, endowments, etc., were futile, purposeless, unwanted by God. With this theology there was reborn a sound doctrine of work, and professional beggary, no matter how 'holy' the beggar, was disapproved, on the grounds of bad theology and harmful social practice. It was later to be severely punished.[1] Nevertheless, this treatment was meted out only to a vagrant. The evangelicals took a personal care in the sick and poor and needy who lived in their parish confines.

It was during Luther's absence at the Wartburg that Karlstadt put these principles into practice at Wittenberg in his *Beutelordnung* (1521) (Common Purse), as part of the new Church order. Unfortunately, Karlstadt was the wrong man, for all his religious work was wrecked by his 'socialism' and 'enthusiasm'. Within a year the *Kastenordnung* (common chest) followed. Influenced by this, the congregation at Leisnig, which had deposed its priest and gone

---

[1] There was an interesting development of this in Elizabethan poor law. The Beggars' Litany which ran 'From Hell, Hull and Halifax, Good Lord deliver us', arose from the fact that it was at both Hull and Halifax that vagrants were rigorously punished. In Halifax they were summarily put into a machine which decapitated them and at Hull publicly flogged. Vagrants did what they could to avoid Hull and Halifax and hoped God might deliver them from the third place. Chroniclers say vagrants were afraid of Hull and Halifax, but not of Hell.

evangelical, drew up an *Ordinance for a Common Chest* and submitted this for Luther's criticism. It delighted Luther and he wrote a Preface to the document in 1523.

The essence of the Ordinance was as follows. All the parish solemnly agree to choose their own pastor in accordance with Scripture. Every householder was to hear the exposition of the Word of God, and to see that all servants and children in his care were to do likewise. The whole parish was resolved to put down all sin, vice, drunkenness and immorality. Then the care of the common chest was regulated. All churchly incomes had to go into this chest. Over it ten wardens were to be appointed, representative of the nobility down to the peasantry. Three times a year the parish meeting was to be held, to hear the report of the wardens, transact business and elect officers. Out of the chest were to be paid the salaries of the clergy, sexton and school teachers, and their expenses of office; all care of the church property; support of the poor and needy of all classes. There was also to be a girls' school maintained (very advanced thinking). Only non-residents were expected to pay fees. The common chest should always be administered to leave some reserve for an emergency such as plague, famine or storm. If the regular income proved inadequate, powers were given to levy or tax to supplement resources.

Luther's preface approved of all this, and further advised on what to do with declining monasteries. (The whole affair compares most favourably with what happened in England under Henry VIII and Cromwell, and under Edward VI and his advisers.) Luther counselled the taking over of these properties by the temporal authorities. Remaining inmates, no matter for what reason they chose to stay, were to be generously supported for life. Those who chose to leave were to be given the means of making a fresh start in life. Needy heirs of the original benefactors were to have their needs met first. Only the remainder was to go into the common chest for the benefit of nobility and commonalty alike. Where profit had accrued from usury, that wrongful interest had to be restored. Mendicant houses were to be converted into schools for boys and girls, and sometimes into ordinary dwelling-houses. The whole programme was to be carried out in a spirit of evangelical love.

Luther was realist enough to know that his advice was a counsel of perfection. Neither the temporal authorities nor the churchmen rose to the needs of the hour: where they did, they were quickly to fall back into old ways. Luther realized here (as elsewhere) he would have to wait 'until our Lord God makes some Christians'. It was to administer this common chest in evangelical love that the Diaconate was called. So Luther determined, but we must now turn to consider how it all worked out in practice in the Reformation Church of the sixteenth century.

3. *Diakonia in the sixteenth-century Lutheran Church*

Luther's criticisms of the Church and her ways occasioned a great deal of ferment, even confusion in places. The evangelical ethic which Luther taught needed the proper theological convictions for it to develop and grow. All too often the picture is one where the old ways and virtues had collapsed owing to reformed criticism, but the evangelical convictions had not taken their place and the last state was worse than the first. Complaints and attacks against the Church for its wealth, its buildings and its consuming interest in money had been on lips other than Luther's; for instance, Karsthans, Eckard, and Westerburg had all spoken. Particular feeling was expressed against the pressure to coup endowments for the Church from the dying. There was also the scandal of indulgences. For instance, reformers were quick to point out that in Nürnberg in 1484 indulgences costing 20,000 gulden had been drained from the city without a pfennig left for the Nürnbergers. In 1490, 6,500 gulden had been filched, leaving this time a paltry 600 gulden for the city's needs. By 1516 the corporation had plucked up enough courage to send the indulgence-seller packing with ten gulden for travelling expenses. Complaint was now rife, and very bitter; in England, Strassburg, Germany, everywhere, the documents tell the same sad story. In 1521 students at Wittenberg rough-handled a mendicant. Their days were now over.

It should be remembered that the Church had always cared for its poor before Luther, even though it were an exercise in merit earning. The Nominalists had been more realistic, but in their case it was a political-social movement within the context of the independence of Church and State. For Luther it was a religious and ethical concern. Nevertheless, it was precisely those places which had taken the Nominalist teaching seriously which took most readily to Luther's new emphases.

For instance, Augsburg in 1522 under Oecolampadius made a firm beginning to the evangelical care of the poor. Similarly in Nürnberg in 1522 we find weekly allowances of quite surprising worth allowed to the various grades of the poor, people known as individuals to the Church, not just poor people. In Strassburg we find as early as 1523 a thorough evangelical organization under the care of a director, four assistant directors, nine church workers with twenty-one helpers. Here it was stipulated that the poor were not only to be helped materially but to be visited as persons at least four times in a year. Money, too, was collected at church services (in those familiar bags on long poles!). Similar arrangements were carried on in Breslau (1523), Regensburg (1523), Magdeburg (1524) all directly owing to the new evangelical theology. In all this Luther emphasized the necessity of the prior work of preaching the Word of God, and leaving all details and plans to the operation of the Spirit in the hearts of converted men. Nevertheless, he knew the necessity of organization, and as indicated earlier wrote his Preface for the Leisniger Kastenordnung while in the Wartburg.

As the old pattern was breaking up, a new pattern independent of the churches began to emerge, again owing to Luther's theology, when society itself in the form of princes and magistrates assumed some social responsibility. Luther preached the responsibility of a Christian *Obrigkeit*, and consequently much of the work began to be assumed by princes and town councillors. Nevertheless, as far as the Church was concerned, the care of the poor had now taken on the form of early Church practice based on Acts 6. One needs to remind oneself that in those days the community was essentially a churchly unity. Modifications were made. Bugenhagen found one common chest unpractical and in 1528 ordered one for the Church and her needs and another for the poor and their needs, with deacons to manage both. *Kastenordnungen* are now general; we find them the practice in Hesse (1532) and Würtemberg (1536).

The common chest was the inheritor of all the resources of the Middle Ages—everything went into it, proceeds of masses, vigils, guilds, endowments. The congregation subscribed in the *Klingelbeutel* after the sermon (as today), and this the deacons publicly put into the chest uncounted. Collections at church doors were infrequent (as today), though sometimes the deacons collected from house to house, generally in kind (fruit, vegetables, food, wine) rather than cash, and took these to the needy. Sometimes collections were taken at weddings, baptisms and funerals. Pressure to bring in a compulsory poor tax was resisted strongly by the reformers: all gifts had to be freely given from a glad heart.

The managers of the common chest were at first called deacons (on the pattern of Acts 6 and 1 Timothy 3), but later *Kastenherren*. They were not in holy orders. Their duties varied, but Luther insisted that their election was the responsibility of the congregation. Most careful safeguards were made in the collection and administration of these funds. Audits were annual. No capital sum could be lent without the approval of the council. Deacons were to meet regularly and apportion the money collected. Most chests had three keys, so that the chest could only be opened collectively. (Magdeburg's chest had ten keys!)

In administering the resources of the chest the first claim was the 'deserving' poor. These people comprised unemployed or sick bread-winners, widows, orphans, spinsters, aged faithful servants, and generally meant known worthy folk fallen on hard times, age, or sickness. Vagrant scroungers, the workshy, and ne'er-do-wells were treated with firmness: help was given, but only at minimum levels with the maximum of good counsel! The deacons were always predisposed to help or even to re-establish a genuine worker. There was always a remedial touch to their activities, and where a man was the victim of his own sin, careful consideration was given as to the reformation of his character and habits. Deacons were expected to know all their needy personally, and the unknown poor needed very respectable credentials to be helped. Poor folk genuinely travelling were helped (as residents), and were not classed as vagrants. It was generally accepted as normal practice that relatives should help their own, and each had a Christian responsibility to his own neighbour, apart from the official responsibility of the deacons.

What is particularly impressive about this work is the real concern for the genuinely sick, particularly to women in childbirth. Careful allowances are given to midwives and to home help for the mother. Genuine solicitude is shown for the young, especially the neglected or orphaned. These children were schooled and trained for a trade. There is evidence of deacons asking the wealthy to pay school fees or further education fees for bright boys, and of this being considered an honourable and Christian request. The deacons helped the girls to an honourable marriage. Prisoners and delinquents, too, were given special care, and were visited and helped by the clergy: condemned prisoners were to be given spiritual comfort and the sacrament offered them.

Deacons had to keep records in books, and the poor on the books were helped weekly (in money or kind), mostly by personal visit, sometimes in the church. Certain towns developed the practice of issuing a badge to these regular poor, but Bugenhagen thought this stigma a mark of officialdom and insisted that all help should be given from love and in utter confidence.

Efforts were made to bring the hospitals under the control of the parish deacons, but this did not work everywhere. In any case, deacons were to visit and help every parishioner in hospital and administer spiritual comfort. Bugenhagen had fine ideas on infirmaries: he organized private wards and devoted spiritual nursing, not only in the interests of the patient but to limit infection. One result of this was the founding of establishments in many cities for orphans, poor, aged seamen, unmarried women and similar groups.

Nevertheless when all this is recounted, the last word is sad. The great ideas of the Reformation were never fully appropriated by the ordinary people. Social change worked against religious change and religious enthusiasm waned. The south German towns were declining, as were the great Hanseatic cities. The Peasants' War had impoverished the land: one hundred thousand peasants had been massacred, and whole villages laid waste. The survivors were heavily fined, and those unable to pay the cruel fines were thrown out on to the streets. A succession of bad harvests from 1529 to 1536 made life desperate, and contemporary chroniclers record pathetic necessity everywhere. On this ground evangelical charity could not blossom. Further, the necessary payment of the prior claims of providing for the parson and his church, the schoolmaster and his school, and the infirm and needy poor were now beginning to strain all the resources available. There began a steady falling off, even a failing of personnel, and in times of plague or stress, the shortage was desperate and paid help had to be called in. The early zeal was cooling. And then, too, many established hospitals, brotherhoods and stifts were reluctant to sacrifice their independence to the deacons and clung to former ways. There grew a generation of reluctant rather than zealous deacons, and as early as 1536 in Württemberg we find deacons fined for refusing to fulfil their duties or attend deacons' meetings.

By the end of the sixteenth century Reformation *diakonia* had lost its soul, though when the century turned we find many 'stifts' being founded for orphans, sick, poor, widows, spinsters and others in need. Nevertheless, by the seventeenth century the Reformation Church had sunk back into the plainest pre-Reformation casuistry. The Reformation did not achieve what it set out to achieve. Yet it left stamped upon Christendom its idea of a properly co-ordinated and managed care of the poor and needy as the concern of the Church and as the responsibility of the Christian community.

Diakonia in Martin Butzer

BASIL HALL

Luther, indignant at Butzer's developing talent for trying to talk theological opponents into the appearance of agreement, called him a *Klappermaul*. Moreover, Calvin wrote once of Butzer that his pen could not keep pace with the fluency of his ideas and language and grace them with clarity;[1] and Butzer himself confessed as much, describing his own writing as '. . . perplexa, indigesta, obscura omnia . . .'[2] But on the theme of the Church's service of mankind Butzer is clear, forceful and consistent; he has more to say to the point here than any of his contemporaries—and he wrote of this service more urgently than most theologians since his time. He could well deserve the name of 'the theologian of diakonia'.

Dr Barth has written what could serve as an admirable epigraph for this study of Butzer as the theologian of the ministering community: 'Diaconate means quite simply and generally the rendering of service. Hence it does not denote only a specific action of the community but the whole breadth and depth of its action.' Then after referring to the deacons of Acts VI, he goes on to write 'In the rest of the New Testament the word διακονία usually indicates quite generally the relationship of service in which especially the apostles stand, but also all other Christians, and Jesus Christ Himself at their head (Romans 15⁸).'[3] Nevertheless, this theme of the ministering community has not been heavily stressed in the Church's long history; not even during the Reformation, when the purpose of the Church was fundamentally re-examined. It is hardly surprising that the questions, among so many other important questions raised during the Reformation, What is the Church of Christ, What does He intend it to do, and How does it set about doing this? received answers in the sixteenth century which often were unavoidably controlled by the social and political needs of the time, and by the dogmatic requirements of the theological controversy with Roman Catholicism. While the Reformers, in this difficult situation, did not overlook the theme of the Church rendering service to mankind, Butzer alone among them gave this theme a fundamental place. From his first appearance in print at Strassburg in 1523 to the year of his death in exile from that city when

---

[1] Calvin, *Calvini Opera Omnia* (C.R.) vol. X Pars posterior, 402, Epistle No. 191.
[2] Gustav Anrich, *Martin Bucer* (Strassburg, 1914), p. 70.
[3] Karl Barth, *Church Dogmatics*, vol. IV, Part III, pp. 889-90.

SC-G

he completed his last important work *De Regno Christi* at Cambridge in 1550,[1] Butzer strove to show how the Christian community should serve God in serving its neighbours—'his end was in his beginning'. He alone of all the theologians of his time gave intense concern to putting in the foreground of Christian faith and practice the διακονία of the Church to mankind. His emphasis on discipline (unlike Calvin he made it a *nota* of the Church), reflects precisely his concern that Christians because of their holiness in Christ the head of the Church, must serve their neighbours in love. For this emphasis Butzer has been called, misleadingly, the first Pietist, and this is not the only way in which he has been misunderstood. Unless we discern his motives and his theological principles, we shall continue to misunderstand him, not least in failing to grasp what he intended in his discussions of both aspects of διακονία; the ministering by Christians to their neighbours, and the special ministry of deacons in the Church.

All his life Butzer differed from the great theologians who were his contemporaries in avoiding definitive theological formulations marked by a precision tending to exclusiveness.[2] But Butzer in his ecumenical zeal wished, as we say nowadays, to be 'open-ended' in church relations; he desired fluidity and not doctrinal hardness in describing the great truths of the faith, that faith which is supremely manifested in love. It is not easy for the authors of *Dogmengeschichte* to give an account of Butzer's theology, not because he was incoherent, or self-contradictory or lacked theological acumen; but because he wished to turn away from formulations that might become 'scholastic'. Butzer wished to point instead to the dynamic life of the Christian community fulfilling by faith in Christ through the Holy Spirit the works of love—and, therefore, he emphasized this fundamental theme and its Christological reference in his discussion of the Church and its ministry.

No significant theologian fails to reflect the influences which formed his mind at the onset of his own creative powers—if he did not reflect them at that period, he would not be a significant theologian. Butzer was not the only man of his generation to owe a great debt to both Luther and to Erasmus, but none went to their writings with such simplicity and directness and found there two major themes which were to become rapidly fused and developed as the ground bass of a theology. He makes the source of his debt plain for us when we read his letter to Luther in 1520: 'You and Erasmus are our great hope.'[3] And two years earlier Butzer had used words to become characteristic of him when he described to his friend Beatus Rhenanus the joy, release and freedom he found, which

---

[1] *Censura super libro sacrorum* and *De vi et usu sacri ministerii* are probably Butzer's last writings.

[2] Butzer's attitude is well seen in these words from the preface to his commentary on the Psalms: 'Usu compertum habeo praecipuas tam apud priscos quam recentes, dissensiones, tantum in verbis, non in resitasa: quibus tamen interim caelum terrae, et terra caelo miscetur . . . salus in sola concordia, mutuaque charitate consistit.' *Psalmorum libri quinque ad hebraicam veritatem traducti, et summa fide, parique diligentia a Martino Bucero enarrati.* Stephanus, Geneva, 1554.

[3] Enders, *Luthers Briefwechsel* (1884) Vol. IV, p. 375.

were 'pious and holy', in hearing Luther and talking to him at Heidelberg.[1] When Butzer wrote in the Preface to the first edition of his Commentary on the Gospels, 1527, *sua fide justus vivit, non aliena* he shows his debt to Luther, but he owed him more than this. He heard Luther's twenty-eighth thesis at the Heidelberg Disputation in 1518, 'Man's love is aroused by what man likes, but God's love finds nothing lovable in man. God excites in man what God loves': and he also heard Luther's explanation, 'the love of the Cross, born of the Cross, is this: it transfers itself not where it finds some good to be enjoyed, but there where it may confer some good to a sinner or to an unfortunate'.[2] Further, Butzer read and appropriated for his own theological creativity such themes as these from Luther's *Treatise on Christian Liberty*: that our works are to be given over to the welfare of others, and that every Christian must give himself as a Christ to his neighbour, just as Christ offered Himself for us; and that what we do in this life should be necessary, profitable and salutary to our neighbour, since through faith we have an abundance of all good things in Christ.[3] Again, Luther's *Commentary on Galatians*, in the edition of 1519, had a powerful and liberating effect on the developing theology of Butzer wearied, as he said, using an old and plodding joke of his student years, by 'den verführerischen unchristlichen Büchern ihres Thomas von Wasserburg, den sie von Aquino nennen'.[4]

But an earlier influence than that of Luther had also been at work, Erasmus, who was for Butzer *tantum numen*. J-B. Pineau sums up the ethic of Erasmus as 'the double commandment of the Gospel, love of God and love of the neighbour'.[5] From the writings of Erasmus issued prior to 1520, Butzer would learn of the innocence and joy to be found in that obedience to Christ so clearly shown in the New Testament when its interpretation was shorn of dogmatic and scholastic presuppositions. Erasmus's letter to the Archbishop of Palermo in 1523, to be printed as a preface to his own edition of the writings of St Hilary, contains, among other matters of which Butzer would have approved, these words: 'true theological science consists in defining nothing which is not prescribed in Scripture, and these instructions should be set forth in simplicity and in good faith . . . One will not be condemned for being ignorant of whether the procession of the Holy Spirit is single or double, but one will not avoid damnation if one does not try to possess the fruits of the Spirit, which are love, joy, patience, goodness, sweetness, faith, modesty, continence. . .'[6] This

---

[1] J. W. Baum, *Capito und Butzer*, 1860, p. 99.
[2] D. Martin, *Luthers Werke, Kritische Gesammtausgabe* (Weimar, 1897), Band 7.
[3] ibid., Band 7, pp. 65, 66.
[4] J. W. Baum, op. cit., p. 95.
[5] J.-B. Pineau, *Érasme, sa pensée religieuse* (Paris, 1924), p. 248.
[6] 'Imo hoc demum est eruditionis theologicae, nihil ultra quam sacris literis proditum est, definire; verum id quod proditum est, bona fide dispensare.' *Opus Epistolarum Des. Erasmi Roteradami*, P. S. and H. M. Allen, tom. V, p. 178. This letter addressed by Erasmus to John Caronselet and published as the preface to the edition of the works of Hilary, which Erasmus issued at Basle in 1523, is of fundamental importance for Erasmus's views on theological renewal against traditionalist scholasticism through biblical studies.

non-doctrinaire approach to theology stayed with Butzer to the end.

After his transformation from a Dominican made restless with 'Thomas von Wasserburg' by his Erasmian reading, to a 'Martinian', a devotee of Luther, Butzer was comparatively inactive, seeking an outlet for his considerable energies, until he appeared as a chaplain under the patronage of Von Sickingen. Fortunately, he had no need to follow so dubiously ruthless a representative of *obrigkeit* again. Then briefly he was parish priest at Wissenburg until he was excommunicated by the Archbishop of Speier for marrying a wife. When he came thereafter to claim the protection of Strassburg where his father had citizen's rights, and where according to Gerbel two years before 'our preachers are lukewarm and cold',[1] Butzer had to defend his preaching at Wissenburg, about which malicious reports were spreading—and the complaint was not that this preaching was 'cold'. Butzer's defence issued in 1523 shows that from the first he was preaching on that dominant theme which stayed with him all his life. 'The whole law is fulfilled in loving thy neighbour as thyself.'[2] Here he claims too that Christian freedom delivers men from the elaborate laws of the Church concerning fasting, of eating and drinking; but the *christlicher fryheit* is also freedom for the service of others.[3]

Also in 1523 appeared at Strassburg a much more important book than his apology for his first sermons, this was issued with the cumbersome but self-explanatory title *Everyone should live not for himself but for others, and how men may fulfil this*, words which show his simple theme and its practical application. 'One must make no difference between men but have the same love and desire to procure for each all the good to which he is responsive. From this it follows that the best, the most perfect and blessed condition on earth is that in which a man can most usefully and profitably serve his neighbour... The ministry [of the pastors of the Church] serves not some particular men, but the community, it deals not with material but only spiritual things, and leads to eternal blessedness'.[4] He goes on to state that although all must show 'love' to one another, this especially is true of the ministry proper; and next to this office is that of the secular authority which has a duty and responsibility reaching out to the whole community. Here Butzer first brings forward what is going to be characteristic of his later activity, and was going to dominate his last great work *De Regno Christi*, the mutual relationship of Church and State for the service of the whole of society. Butzer then ends the first part of his little treatise: 'To conclude ... according to the order and commandment of the Creator, no one should live for himself but each man should out of love for God live for his neighbour

---

[1] 'Unsere Prediger sind lau und kalt . . .', N. Gerbel to J. Schwebel, 20 December 1521, cited in J. W. Baum, *Capito und Butzer*, p. 199.

[2] *Martin Butzers an ein christlich Rath und Gemeyn der stat Weissenburg Summary seiner Predig daselbst gethon* (1523, reprinted Strassburg, 1891, ed. A. Erichson), p. 20. 'Dann so alles gesatz erfullt wurt in disem einigen Wort. Hab dein nechsten also lieb als dich selb, und der Herr Mat. VII sagt.'

[3] op. cit., p. 18.

[4] *Das ym selbs niemant sonder anderen leben soll undwie der mensch dahyn kummen mög.*

and by all means be of service to him in matters pertaining to both the spirit and the body; that this obligation rests above all on those who were called and established to promote public usefulness, both spiritual and secular . . .'[1] Butzer was clear from the beginning—where his colleague at Strassburg, Capito, was not—that there should be no sympathetic collaboration with Anabaptist ideas of withdrawing from the corruptions of the world into separately organized communities of saints. In this, as in other ways, Butzer does not suit the description of being a Pietist. His whole concern is for an outgoing service within the full range of men's social existence to transform it. This transformation must not be construed as an early version of the *Syllogismus practicus*: his doctrine of Predestination, as he will develop it later, is not set down in terms that lead to that trap of later Puritanism. In his other works the activity of the elect in the loving service of mankind is seen by Butzer not as a proof of election but as a consequence of it;[2] and at this stage of his thought, the first theological writing, he states: '. . . Faith, finally, takes away from us love for the present life—its honours, fortunes and pleasures—love which hinders so many from exercising a true love and service to their neighbour. Faith brings . . . living wholly for others for the glory of God. . . . If faith is not such, then it is not true and legitimate faith, it is a dead faith, it is no faith at all.'[3]

Citations from several of his works at different periods of his life show the same theme recurring until its final reassertion in Butzer's last full-scale work *De Regno Christi*. In 1527 appeared Butzer's first open attack on Anabaptism in his *Getrewe Warnung gegen Jakob Kautz* (an Anabaptist preacher at Worms), and here again comes the characteristic theme that good works must follow upon faith in Christ, love must reach out through good works: 'that love which is described in the first epistle to the Corinthians is the fulfilling of the law, and the sum of all good works which derive only from faith in our Lord Jesus Christ'.[4] Again in the sermon he preached at Bern during the Disputation there in 1528 Butzer said: 'In all works we must practise brotherly love unremittingly, in them all we shall . . . please our God and father, praise His honour, and improve our neighbour.'[5] In his commentary on the gospels at Matthew 5, Butzer has a long section headed *De Proximo* where he makes it plain that our neighbour is whoever God places us next to to help him and to aid him even if he should be an enemy; and on Matthew 25, 1536 edition (a chapter frequently used by Butzer), he begins: 'Nemo est piorum qui nesciat ut aegre vigilemus in opere Domini . . .'; and on the two parables of the chapter he concludes by emphasizing selfless love of our neighbour.[6]

[1] op. cit. *Deutsche Schriften* (1962), Band 1 (Das ym selbs . . .).
[2] Several places, e.g. Commentary on Ephesians (1562), pp. 26f. Again in his commentary on Gospel of St John (1553), p. 260. [To the elect] . . . nihil aeque illos ad amorem Dei aeque inde ad omne opum bonum que at excitari.
[3] op. cit. *Deutsche Schriften*, Band 1 (1962) (Das ym selbs . . .).
[4] Butzer: *Deutsche Schriften*, Band 2 (1962) (*Schriften der Jahre*, 1524-8), p. 251.
[5] op. cit. *Martin Butzers Predig gethon zü Bern*.
[6] 'Duabus itaque his parabolis tota pietatis ratio tradita est; priore fides . . . hac vero, syncera dilectio, qua nihil nostri quaerentes, toti in hoc incumbimus ut iis quae a Deo accepimus,

In his *Ein summarischer Vergriff der Christlichen lehre* . . ., 1548, which was a defence of the Strassburg Reformers against the charge of Anabaptism, presented to the Emperor shortly before the Interim was declared which led to Butzer's exile, he wrote: 'Love fulfils the divine law in such a way that a man is led to learn to do and suffer . . . as the eternal and temporal salvation of his neighbour requires him . . . Without this love of God and men which leads to a constant zeal for good works, there is no true faith in Christ, and those who lack it do not belong to Him.'[1] Two years later in England in his *De Regno Christi* prepared for Edward VI in 1550 (though it was not published until 1557, at Basel), Butzer renews the theme: 'Christ our governor and master lives and labours in all the faithful, He seeks in all by the ministry of all, those who are lost and leads them to salvation. It is necessary then that all those who are of Christ should have the care of their brothers in His name and in His authority . . . and exhort them by all means possible to do their duty.'[2] This general statement—which he has made so frequently before—Butzer now expands and particularizes on the following lines: the Church must improve men's moral and intellectual education beginning especially through catechizing the young; there must be in the 'Christian Republic' a thorough organization of poor relief and assistance to the sick (it is here that he expands for the first time the work of 'Deacons'); for the fulfilment of these ends discipline is essential, and so there must be a thorough organization of labour and leisure. As derivatives of these principles he showed the need for a better professional training through the improvement of schools and universities; improved technological efficiency in mining, the wool industry, and farming, all of which he found to be economically inferior to Imperial German methods. (Like Erasmus—they were both proud citizens of the empire—he also 'thought imperially' in urging on another occasion his need of one of the great tiled German stoves for central heating in cold, damp Cambridge.) At several points in these prescriptions he showed that such matters are important, not in themselves alone, but because of their consequences for one's neighbour: for example, if the rich show luxury in dress or manners, then there is lack of love for their neighbour. Again in writing of reform of the civil laws, Butzer added: 'It is necessary that all laws both divine and human should be related to these two points (the love of God and of the neighbour, citing Luke 10[17]), and that those who ordain . . . the laws . . . should look above all to command only the things which agree with the purity and integrity

---

sive spiritualia sint, sive temporalia proximis inserviamus: in primis tamen, hoc dantes operam, ut Deo ipsos lucremur.' *In sacra quatuor Evangelia Enarrationes perpetuae*. In his commentary on the Psalms, Butzer also has this same emphasis: 'Deus praecepto dilectionis proximi summavit omnia. Nihil igitur indecens vel dicet vel aget imo ne cogitabit quidem, dilectione semper profictura proximis, hoc est vere sancta, Deoque grata suggerente.' op. cit. (Geneva, 1554), pp. 17, 18.

[1] Reprinted with introduction and notes by F. Wendel in *Revue d'histoire et de philosophie religieuses* (1951), No. 1, p. 41.
[2] *Martini Buceri Opera Latini*, vol. XV, *De Regno Christi*, ed. F. Wendel (Paris, 1955), p. 71.

of the service of God, and with charity towards the neighbour, and to forbid what does not agree with these.'[1]

How far Butzer's book represents the old humanist pedagogic weakness of treating men as though their social, economic, intellectual, and religious lives could be encompassed within the syllabus of a lecture room, is arguable; but this was the age of More's *Utopia*, and of the zealous renewal of study of Plato's *Republic* (a loved work of Butzer's humanist young manhood at Heidelberg). Butzer was uneasily aware of this possible criticism when he wrote at the end of *De Regno Christi* of those 'who consider I have proposed things strange and contrary to the usage of this age, and which one would rather dream of than practise, as if I had built a Republic as Plato did . . .' He insisted, however, that his work should not be judged 'by the judgement of men but by the eternal and immutable Word of God, for these matters are necessary to the eternal salvation of all men'.[2] Whether Hopf is right in asserting without qualification that passages in the *De Regno Christi* were the foundation of the poor law made under Elizabeth I, is doubtful when we bear in mind that in spite of Butzer's protest about all his work being founded on the Word of God, this programme of reform, financial, legal and economic, reflected ideas deriving from the English 'Commonwealth men' and their writings.[3] Or, perhaps, it may be argued that such matters can be regarded—and that Butzer believed them to be so—as legitimate extensions of the fundamental requirements of the Word of God. If other Reformers did not go so far was it not because they hesitated to decide that a particular political programme of reform was necessarily tied to men's eternal salvation? (Calvin, for example, did not build such activities at Geneva upon the same ground as that of men's salvation.)

From this, if nothing else, it is plain that Butzer was concerned with the relations of Church and 'Commonwealth', with Church and society, and his work in England (which reflected the economic problems of the Tudors), as elsewhere, was related to the context in which he was writing. In fact his discussions of the nature of the Church and of Discipline, which was in his eyes fundamental to the well-being of the Church, grew out of the changing environment of Strassburg from 1524 onwards. Here we see that there was one danger which by that year Butzer had not foreseen, and that was the use of his characteristic theme in his treatise of 1523, by Anabaptists who sought a withdrawn society of the pure who fulfilled good works to each other. It was during the years 1524–30 that Anabaptism was most dangerous at Strassburg, and its influence had attracted his fellow-minister Capito. (This was also the period of transition from Lutheran teaching at Strassburg to a South German or Zwinglian type of theology.) From 1526 onwards Butzer led attacks on the Anabaptists, and succeeded, in 1528 and again in 1530, in persuading the Magistrates to issue Edicts against them. In the struggle Butzer saw the need to emphasize the

[1] op. cit., p. 266.
[2] op. cit., pp. 294, 295.
[3] op. cit. cf. Introduction by F. Wendel, p. LII.

visible church against the sectarian principle of the Anabaptists, and to this end he brought together election and works within the church which was *Corpus Christi*, *Sponsa Christi*, and *Regnum Christi*, and particularly he emphasized 'Discipline' as fundamental to the well-being of the Church. Church and discipline, after the first almost naïve assumption on how easy it is to love God and one's neighbour (as shown in *Das ym selbs niemant*), become very soon for Butzer the means which God sets in the world to make this love effective. From this emphasis on Discipline derived the *Disziplinordnung* of 1535 at Strassburg.

Butzer defined the Church in *De vera animarum cura* as 'the Congregation and society of those who in Christ Jesus our Lord are congregated and associated together from the world so that they may be one body . . . from which each and everyone has the office and labour of building up the whole body and all of its members'.[1] In his *Defensio de Christiana Reformatione* of Herman, Archbishop of Cologne, he wrote 'there is the visible church where is the congregation of the faithful, who can be easily discerned . . . who live in the world, though they are not of this world . . . by their fruits . . . by the true confession of Christ, and communication with all members of Christ in the Word, sacraments, and discipline.'[2] Also in this book he explicitly makes 'discipline' a *signum* of the Church. Butzer strove to make visible, incarnate among men, the invisible church of the elect, as the setting from within which Christ through the Holy Spirit works for the advance of His kingdom. In his *Ein summarischer Vergriff der Christlichen lehre* he writes of members of the Church as being built up by Christ; 'He fortifies them, and makes them progress by His constant teaching and His discipline . . . He makes this building up of the new life effective in Him through all His members without exception'.[3] How Butzer conceived the function of the church in the whole of society has already been seen in discussing his *De Regno Christi* above, where he would even go as far as saying that idleness was anti-social and a sin against one's neighbour, supporting himself on the Pauline injunction in Thessalonians 3^{10}.[4] By 'discipline', which should enable the Church to fulfil its duty, Butzer could mean much; the discipline of life and manners, penance, liturgy and ceremonies, fast days, special festivals as 'ways of glorifying God and showing love to one's neighbour'.[5] Discipline 'consists not only in what the pastors and ministers do (who always have the principal duty here) but also everyone in particular has care for his neighbour to confirm him, to advance and exhort him by all possible means to pursue always more and more the way to heavenly life . . . in the authority and name of our Lord Jesus Christ as his disciples'.[6] Discipline, as exercised by the ministers of the Church, braces the Christian and helps him to bear himself as an effective member of the Kingdom of God, and contribute to his own increase in holiness

---

[1] *Scripta Anglicana fere omnia* . . . (Basle, 1577). *De vera animarum cura* . . ., p. 267.
[2] This work was not published until 1613, at Geneva; p. 106.
[3] op. cit., p. 45.
[4] op. cit., p. 88. Butzer cites this text with approval in three places.
[5] *De Regno Christi*, p. 70.
[6] op. cit., pp. 70, 71.

and to that of his fellow citizens. Here it will be seen that discipline involves emphasizing the special ministry within the Church, as distinct from the general ministry of all Church members to each other and to their fellow men, and in particular as part of the Church's διακονία; this is seen in the ministry of 'deacons'. To understand what Butzer means by deacons we must consider his description of the Church's ministers, though here, as on other themes, he does not always write with consistent clarity.

The most convenient sources for Butzer's view of the special ministry in the Church, are his commentary on Ephesians, *De Ordinatione*, *De Vera Animarum Cura*, *Defensio de Christiana Reformatione* and *De Regno Christi*, for here he is clearer than elsewhere in what he wrote about the ministry and especially that of 'deacons'. He more frequently stated that there are two orders or grades of the ministry: 'The ministry of the Church is of a twofold kind: according to the institution of the Holy Spirit, in one is retained the administration of the Word, sacraments, and discipline of Christ, which belongs properly to bishops and presbyters; in the other is the care of the poor, which is committed to those called Deacons.'[1] Though in the same work he wrote later of 'three orders'; the primary order of Bishops (*episcopus*) or Superintendents (*superintendens*) and Presbyters who can be divided into a second and third order, that is, of presbyters proper and those presbyters called deacons.[2] In his work on Ephesians he wrote, however, of the ministry as consisting of evangelists and doctors; pastors, who are bishops and presbyters; and deacons.[3] In his *De Vera Animarum Cura* he wrote of pastors, and doctors, and also deacons as ministers whom the Lord gave to the Church at all times (after the 'extraordinary' ministry of Apostles had ceased); but later in the same work he wrote of *Episcopi* (*inspectores*), *Presbyteri* (*conspectores*) and *Diaconi*.[4] In his *Defensio de Christiana Reformatione* he described the pastoral origins and development of the seven orders of ministry, where he showed deacons to have been assistants to the bishops and presbyters in doctrine, sacraments and discipline. It is highly significant that he concluded that historical discussion with the statement: 'Nulla enim potestas est in Ecclesia Dei nisi ad aedificationem'—the implication of this statement will surely be clear in the context of this essay.

It will be seen that there is lacking here a clearly consistent definition of the nature and functions of the ministry of the Church; however, this is consistent with Butzer's continually guarded way of avoiding too great precision which might weaken the Christian's obedience in the here and now of his life to the Word of God, or his own responsibility in his moral choices. While it is not the clearest of his formal statements, yet since it was addressed to the emperor in 1548 at a time of great urgency which led to conciseness and intensity of statement, *Ein summarischer Vergriff* . . . is a useful point of departure for a closer

---

[1] *Scripta Anglicana fere omnia. De Ordinatione*, p. 238.
[2] op. cit., p. 259.
[3] *Enarratio Epistolae D. Pauli Ephesios*, Basle (1562), p. 117.
[4] *Scripta Anglicana fere omnia. De vera animarum cura*, p. 277.

discussion of what Butzer intended deacons to be and to do. 'We teach that the Holy Spirit has instituted two distinct grades in the ministry of the Church, one which consists of the superior pastors (*Seelesorge*) whom the Holy Spirit describes as overseers (*Auffseher*) and elders (*Elteren*) [the margin has the subtitle here "Episcopos et Presbyteros" [*sic*]] to whom He entrusts the ministry of teaching, of the holy sacraments, and of Christian discipline, that is, the whole cure of souls. The other grade comprises the ministers who assist the others in the ministry of the cure of souls, and tending the flock of Christ and also zealously assisting the poor . . . We teach that these true ministers of Christ, in whatever Church . . . great or small they are, have received from the Lord the same spiritual power and authority, to exercise together ecclesiastical ministry including teaching, the sacraments, and penitential discipline, aid to the poor, in such wise as to feed the flock of Christ according to all its needs, and lead it to eternal life.'[1]

From this brief discussion of the Church and its offices of ministry, it will be seen that Butzer has less to say about the ministry of deacons, in comparison with other ministries, especially the ministering of all Christians to their fellow men, than might be expected; his only statement at length about deacons, and this is almost wholly devoted to their duties, is to be found in the *De Regno Christi*. Nevertheless, some other descriptions of the office of deacon may be useful, since he says little about the definition of a deacon in comparison with what he says about his work in that book.

'Deacons are joined to the ministry of bishops and presbyters to minister to them and especially to care for the poor', he wrote in his commentary on Ephesians 4.[2] In *De Vera Animarum Cura* he wrote that 'the *officium et munus* of Deacons . . . is for the sustaining of the poor . . . Private men, great or small in condition, must contribute to the work of God in the Churches, both from their immovable and movable goods . . . [the Deacons are] diligently to distribute from this to all the poor in the Church, whether local people or strangers'.[3] Butzer, thereafter, having referred with approval to *pulchra iudicia* in the Epistles of St Gregory—*qui pius fuit Romanus pontifex*—on the subject of the work of deacons, added indignantly, 'this office and function are now in the Church, alas, wholly fallen in ruins through pontifical tyranny . . . so that few if any who are Deacons . . . know what their office and function should be . . . they think that their only duty is to sing the Gospel and Epistle at Mass'.[4] In his commentary on Ephesians 4, Butzer showed that διακονία relates specifically to serving others and has nothing to do with 'otiose and vain titles of dignity' whose holders despoil the goods of the Church to ignoble ends.[5]

In the *Defensio de Reformatione Christiana* he claimed that the 'distinction of these ministries in the Churches is not an Apostolic and necessary tradition, but

[1] op. cit., pp. 47, 49.
[2] op. cit., p. 117.
[3] op. cit., p. 277.
[4] op. cit., p. 277.
[5] op. cit., p. 163.

a free matter which any Church can order . . . and no Church is bound to another', and he added that '. . . the ministry of specially approved persons is received with the consent of the faithful'.[1] Butzer, it is plain, accepts as reasonable that in different nations, and under different governments, there will be different ways of arranging for the ministry of the Church, which is not a matter for Christians to quarrel over. The significant thing about a Deacon, therefore, is not so much to define his status and to show his apostolic lineage, but to show what his functions are, and these, with all other gifts (*dona varia, secundum gratiam* . . .) are for *aedificationem communem totius corporis, omniumque membrorum*.[2] Corroboration of this can be seen in Butzer's order for Ordination in his *Pia Deliberatio* for Herman, Archbishop of Cologne, when there is only one ordaining formula for all three offices of ministry, Bishop, Presbyter, Deacon: 'The hand of Almighty God, the Father, Son and Holy Spirit, be upon you and protect and govern you, that you may go and bear fruit by your ministry, and remain in you to life eternal'—'go and bear fruit by your ministry' is the important matter for a Deacon, as for all other Christians.[3]

Chapter XIV of the second book of the *De Regno Christi* is entitled *Lex Sexta de Procurandis Egenis*, that is, the sixth of fourteen laws which 'the Almighty Lord has ordained for His people, for the defence and preservation of the Christian religion'. After the King, Edward VI, has restored the Church's goods, Christ's patrimony, then holy provision and care for the needy poor must be undertaken for 'without it there can be no true communion of saints'.[4] (Did Butzer in his sickness and overwork at Cambridge not realize how utopian this hope was? Could English nobles like the Dudleys be thought of as Magistrates like the Sturms of Strassburg?) For this in all the churches there must be 'Deacons who are men of good report, full of the Holy Spirit and of wisdom', and each church shall have a sufficient number of them to fulfil this duty. The first duty of the deacons is to distinguish between the deserving and undeserving poor, for the former to inquire carefully into their needs; the latter, if they lead disorderly lives at the expense of others, to expel them from the community of the faithful. Care, next, is to be taken for needy widows. The second duty of deacons is to keep a written record of accounts, having sought diligently for the proper collecting of funds from all the parishioners according to their capacity. So that deacons should have the greatest authority among the people, the ancient churches associated them with the holy ministry in the dispensing of doctrine and of the holy sacraments. Next, Butzer repeats the charges against the corruption of this office in papal times in similar words to those quoted above on this point; nevertheless, he has already established at the end of his paragraph on the first part of the office of deacons that 'they must aid and serve the Bishop and the Presbyters in all the discipline of Christ'.[5] Butzer, after giving some historical

[1] op. cit..
[2] *Scripta Anglicana fere omnia. De vera animarum cura*, p. 269, and p. 267.
[3] *Pia Deliberatio*.
[4] op. cit., p. 143.
[5] op. cit., pp. 143, 144, 146 and 145.

account of methods of dealing with the poor with some advice to the king attached, next goes on to reject the customary view that a man has a right to make his almsgiving individually and according to his own views. Butzer is aware, however, that there are some of the poor who will be ashamed to reveal the extent of their need to the deacons, and so discreet neighbours should privately inform them of the fact. On the other hand, he insists that the deacons must be sensitive to the shames of poverty and distribute to the poor with prudence, and not behave like the beadle Bumble in *Oliver Twist*.[1] In all this Butzer is again concerned to show that all Christians are members of one another and there is no place for individualism, either in the great scattering 'largesse' or the small resorting to begging. If dispute should arise in a parish concerning this poor relief then the Deacons should consult with 'the Bishop and assembly of Presbyters', so that 'all things should be done by authority of the Word of God.'[2] Butzer probably thought here of the establishing of many more bishops than those provided for by the ancient dioceses of England, and of assemblies of clergy more frequent and local than Convocations, a foreshadowing of Archbishop Usher's view of a 'moderate episcopacy' and similar themes dear to the Puritans later.

On the title page of *Das ym Selbs niemant* of 1523 there are four citations from Scripture around the printer's woodcut containing the title. Two of these may form a fitting conclusion to this study of Butzer's teaching on διακονία in the Church.

ὁ γὰρ πᾶς νόμος ἐν ἑνὶ λόγῳ πεπλήρωται, ἐν τῷ ἀγαπήσεις τὸν πλησίον σοῦ ὡς σεαυτόν [Galatians 5[14]].

Alles das ir wöllen das eüch die leüt thün sollen das thuend ynen auch ir, das ist das gebatz und die propheten. [Matthew 7[12]].

[1] op. cit., pp. 150, 151.
[2] op. cit., p. 151.

Diakonia in the Thought of Calvin

J. K. S. REID

The Ministry as Diakonia

In the ministry, Calvin sees (*Inst.*, IV.iii.1) the grace, freedom and wisdom of God wonderfully displayed. For the government of His Church is solely administered by His Word. In His freedom, this might quite well have been accomplished by the agency of angels or without any agency at all; in His kindness, He chooses men to be His ambassadors to the world, interpreters of His will, and representatives of His presence (cf. IV.vi.10); and so in wisdom trains us all in humility. Hence 'the principal bond which holds believers together in one body' is the ministry of men (IV.iii.2). Thus God 'consecrates men's lips and tongues to Himself that His voice may be heard in them' (IV.i.5). Accordingly (IV.i.6) the ministry has a dignity which may be neither exaggerated ('it is by no means to be conceded that the Church consists in the assembly of the pastors', IV.ix.7), nor depreciated ('nor could that office (of teacher) be more splendidly distinguished than when He said to them, "He that heareth you, heareth me" (Luke 10[16])', IV.iii.3). While 'more excellent than anything else' (IV.iii.3), yet, whatever its dignity, the ministry serves God, or what is the same thing, is a ministry of the Word.

The path avoiding exaggeration on the one side and depreciation on the other Calvin traces in his treatment of Matthew 20[24-28] et par. (*Commentary on a Harmony of the Evangelists*, ad loc., C.R. 45.556f). This pericope has indeed christological overtones, but for Calvin they are subdued; and it has a general application against the 'concealed flame' of envy in us all. But the lesson of *diakonia* it contains Calvin conceives to be directed almost entirely towards the apostles. 'Primacy has no place in His kingdom . . . Christ appoints pastors of His Church, not to rule but to serve.' Rank is for service; and the ministry is or ought to be the paradigm of service in the Church.

That Christ is the example *par excellence* of service and ministry is recognized by Calvin (see already cited *Comm. on Harm. Ev.*, Matthew 20[24-28]), but not emphasized. That the essence of ministry and all ministry also consists in this, Calvin bases not on an obligatory *imitatio Christi*, but rather upon the undoubted fact that 'the Church has Christ for its sole Head' (IV.vi.9). From this Calvin derives several important conclusions. The immediate use to which he puts it in the passage cited is the exposure of the false claims made by Rome for papacy and hierarchy. But the positive implications range far beyond this. These may be summarily comprehended by saying that the Headship of Christ absorbs into itself all lordship within the Church and thus relativizes all other distinctions, however necessary and right. As Head, Christ exercises a lordship over the Church which does not set Him at such a distance that some kind of subordinate lordship can arise; on the contrary, as Head He is never without the members that constitute His body: 'Rule in the Church belongs to the Head Himself. Where therefore Christ is given His place, there the Church which is His Body may be said to obtain the Kingdom; for Christ wishes nothing in separation from His members' (*Praelectiones in Zechariam* 2^9, C.R. 44.161). Further, all men are put in service: 'He attributes nothing to men but a common ministry, and to every individual his particular share' (IV.vi.10). Where all may thus be subsumed within the category of ministers, within the ministry there is such equality as excludes lordship: 'Monarchy among ministers, or the government of one over the rest, [St Paul] does not only not mention, but indicates that there is no such thing' (loc. cit.). The common character of ministry is represented as collegiate: 'So too Cyprian follows St Paul and defines with brevity and clarity what legitimate government in the Church is. Episcope is one, he says, but part is exercised by individuals corporately (a singulis in solidum). He attributes episcope to Christ alone; but in its administration he assigns a part to individuals, but corporately (in solidum), lest anyone should exalt himself above the others' (*Comm. on Ephesians* 4^{11}, CR. 51.198). In any case, the Ministry itself is no more than part of the Church, and ministers are themselves members of the Church: 'We see how [St Paul] places all men without exception in the body, reserving to Christ alone the honour and name of Head' (IV.vi.9). Further, the Ministry may not be regarded as separate from the Church, nor as monopolizing ministry; and it follows that the relation of laity and clergy has to be defined more carefully in accordance with Scripture. Calvin uses the terms laity and clergy because they are the commonly accepted terms; but he does so reluctantly, because strictly speaking they are imprecise. The real difference between the two is between *public* and *private* ministry in the Church (IV.xii.1; *Serm.* on 1 Timothy 3^{6-7}, C.R. 53.285, 289), between those who *proclaim* the Word and those who *are ruled* by the Word: the ministry to exhort, the people to be exhorted (cf. IV.xii.14, 17; fasting, for example, *enjoined* by the pastors and *imposed* on the people). Not, of course, that the clergy in exercising a public office of this kind are exempted from standing under the Word (see IV.xii.1, where the clergy are subject not only to common discipline but also to a discipline peculiar to themselves).

The simplicity of Calvin's teaching here must not conceal its momentous importance. Not uniquely, but as systematizer and spearhead of Reformed thinking, Calvin is saying nothing more than: *let ministry be ministry*. Thereby instantly the axe is laid at the root of much of the perverse and corrupt practice and thought of the unreformed Church; and on the other hand the truly Gospel elements, of which he never doubts the unreformed Church to be the almost unconscious bearer, are fashioned into a synthesis in which their beauty and power are allowed unimpeded exercise. Rank and dignity, office and function, lay and clerical, equality and diversity—all these elements have their place; but they are now integrated into a whole which really has the appearance of a people of God. The key to this truly biblical synthesis Calvin reiterates ceaselessly in different words and ways. 'When God calls ministers, He sanctions them not to prosecute their own business but that of the Lord who claims their attention; nor to be charged with the rule of the government of the Church, but to be subject to the rule of Christ; in brief, to be ministers, not lords' (*Comm.* on 1 Corinthians 4^1, C.R. 49.362). 'Pastors are not ordained to dominate. Why then? For the service of the faithful . . . servants of Jesus Christ, and of His people and flock' (*Serm.* on 1 Timothy 3^{6-7}, C.R. 53.289). 'The Church cannot be otherwise preserved intact (*incolumem servari*) than by those means which God has been pleased to appoint for its salvation' (IV.iii.2).

We have already seen this expressed: 'Christ appoints pastors of His Church not to rule but to serve' (*Comm. on Harm. Ev.*, Matthew 22^{25}, C.R. 45.557). 'For Christ allowed the pastors nothing more than to be ministers' (ib.; cf. also *Serm.* on 1 Timothy 5^{16-18}, C.R. 53.507, where presiding is to be undertaken not like princes and lords, but *comme un service*). This 'authoritative superintendence over others' is in the Church entirely different from that exercised in the secular spheres. It is true: to serve is also an obligation on 'even kings'. But they can go on governing quite well even when this is forgotten: 'the *manner* in which kings and magistrates serve does not prevent them from governing'. In the case of the ministry it is different: they must 'abstain entirely from the exercise of authority'; for in their case the injunction to minister 'relates to the thing itself, and not only to the disposition'. Ministry has not a *regnum* but a *cura* (*Comm.* on 1 Peter 5^3, C.R. 55.286).

Perhaps a practical remark is here permissible. It is difficult to imagine any single thing that would by itself do more to revive the Church today than a recovered sense of this emphasis so typical of Calvin, that ministry means ministry. The legalism that formalizes ministry into a rank and neglects its essential character of service infects all churches. It is indeed so marked a feature of the Roman Church that, in these days of *aggiornamento*, voices of protest have been raised within it ('see Fr H. Vorgrimler in *Herder Correspondence*, January 1964, on restoring 'the fundamentally service-character of the hierarchy'). But other Churches too are affected. When the ministry is no longer regarded as the prototype of all ministry, when ministry is channelled off into the ministry without remainder, then ministry is emptied of its proper content, and the ministry comes to be regarded primarily as a rank. Nothing does more today to distort the concept of Church or to paralyse its action.

The Ministry of Diakonia

The question as to the number of offices which Calvin recognized as permanently valid has proved troublesome to expositors. The facts in the case are clear enough. In the first edition of the *Institutes* (C.R. 1.186f., 191) he recognizes two only, those of presbyter and deacon. In the final edition (IV.iii.5) the two offices of pastor and teacher are recognized as distinct enough from each other to have respective resemblance to the earlier apostles and to the 'ancient prophets'; and to these two offices two further 'functions' are added (IV.iii.8f), also said to be 'perpetual', the so-called 'governors' and the 'deacons'. Thus four offices are distinguished. But later in the same *Institutes* (IV.iv.1), it is a threefold order that becomes apparent: 'there are three kinds of minister recommended to us in Scripture; so the ancient Church divided all the ministers into three orders'. The order of presbyter is divided into pastors and teachers, now classed together, and those who 'presided over the discipline and corrections'; and there is the third order of deacons. But this coalescence of pastors with teachers is not steadily maintained: in *Comm. on Ephesians* 4^{11}, C.R. 51.197, Calvin declares himself not convinced by those who think pastors and doctors comprise one office: he believes them to differ, but not absolutely. It appears that while both have teaching in common, exposition of Scripture is chiefly (though not exclusively) the duty of doctors, while preaching is chiefly (though again not exclusively) the work of pastors. Theological dons will no doubt take comfort from his judgement that 'et doctor aliquis esse poterit, qui tamen concionando non erit appositus'! If this ambiguity seems surprising, we should reflect that in Calvin's view there is a unity of office even while there is diversity of offices (see J. Bohatec: *Calvins Lehre von Staat und Kirche*, 1937, p. 422), and that consequently the rigidity of the system of orders, as in the unreformed Church, becomes fluid again. In this, we must conclude, he is more in touch with New Testament thought, whether or not we think it right to attempt to reproduce the New Testament situation in later times. For the purpose here it is necessary only to note that in all three distributions of office, whether twofold, threefold or fourfold, the office of deacons is named. The persistence of the office might in any case have been expected in view of Calvin's insistence that ministry in general is service to God and man.

Origin of Diaconate

Calvin has no doubts that Acts 6 refers to the diaconate without equivocation. Here, he says, we have set before us the occasion, the reason and the rite of the creation of deacons (*Comm.* on Acts 6^{1-6}, C.R. 48.117f.). Calvin notes the unpremeditated character of what the primitive Church does here: it is plainly an improvisation to meet a practical exigency. From this circumstance he draws two lessons. The Church of that day might not have seen the advisability of the diaconate had not necessity compelled its creation. And the Church of all times may learn from this that the Church was neither immediately so formed that no correction is needed nor at the beginning so completely built that no perfection can be added. The occasion of the Greeks' dissatisfaction, and consequently of the institution of the diaconate, is the breakdown of a hitherto working arrangement. The apostles as *Dei et pauperum oeconomi* ('stewards of God and the poor') had till now had charge of almsgiving; the complaint of the Greeks showed that this no longer worked satisfactorily. The essence of the *non placet* is carefully defined. It is not that the apostles wish to be relieved of something which it is 'not meet' that they should be doing; it is rather that experience had taught them their inability to carry two burdens, that is both preaching and ministering, and the consequent need of being discharged of one. Again it is not the unimportance of the *cura pauperum* that enables it to be delegated to others; it is rather the demanding importance of the *ministerium sermonis* that leaves them too little time. Calvin takes the opportunity of making a sardonic comparison with Roman Church practice: the other business which leaves *them* no time for care of the poor is their own pursuit of luxury. Care of the poor, Calvin points out, is thus an authentically apostolic obligation for whose discharge purely practical exigencies now demand other arrangements. Hence those who will now discharge it take over not a secular office but a genuinely apostolic function.

That seven are elected Calvin believes to be entirely due to present requirements, and we need look for no more mysterious reason. Assured as he is that it is the historical office of deacons that is being initiated, he has no reason to investigate who exactly they are who first occupy it, and certainly no inclination to adopt the more radical of a wide range of suggestions, that they were simply Hellenists chosen to represent the interests of their group in the council of elders at Jerusalem (so, e.g., R. Bultmann: *A Theology of the New Testament*, 1955, vol. I, p. 56; W. Telfer: *The Office of a Bishop*, p. xiii; J. Knox in *The Ministry in Historical Perspectives*, 1956, ed. H. R. Niebuhr and D. D. Williams, p. 21). The laying-on of hands, by means of which they are installed, Calvin holds to have been by the apostles; but he is at pains to reiterate the view to which he always faithfully adheres, that the rite is one of order and comeliness, a sign of consecration without inherent power resident in itself. The people join in the prayers that are subjoined.

Duty and Function

As already said, Calvin is well aware of the double use to which the word *diakonos* is put. Generally, it signifies 'simply what is meant by minister', and 'all offices of the Church are called Diaconies [*sic*!], that is to say, ministries or services' (*Serm.* on 1 Timothy 3^{6-7}, C.R. 53.289). In its particular use it denotes the diaconate. According to Calvin's developed view, the diaconate is charged specifically with a double duty. There is the *pauperum curam gerere illisque ministrare*, and this is the sole function accorded to them in *Institutes*, edn. 1 (C.R. 1.191). In the 1543 edition (C.R. 1.567), however, in the *Draft Ecclesiastical Ordinances* 1541 (C.R. 10/1.23), and elsewhere, there is added to this the care of the sick. In the final edition of the *Institutes* (IV.iii.9) Calvin states that there were two distinct orders (*gradus distinctos*) of deacon in the primitive Church, and specifies them as those that administer the alms and those who devoted themselves to the care of poor and sick persons. In the *Draft Ecclesiastical Ordinances* the specification is the same ('The fourth order', etc.), though a little more detailed. The first kind of deacon is 'deputed to receive, dispense and hold goods for the poor, not only daily alms, but also possessions, rents, and pensions'—this is the administrative duty. The second kind are those who executively minister to poor and sick: they 'tend and care for the sick and dispense allowances to the poor'. Calvin adduces as ground for this distinction Romans 12[8]: 'He that giveth, let him do it with simplicity; . . . he that sheweth mercy with cheerfulness', a text which he often uses for quite general hortatory purposes, to which indeed it is better suited than to validate an official ecclesiastical structure. It is not unjust to suggest (as J. Bohatec, op. cit., p. 469, *et al.*) that Scripture had less to do with Calvin's diversification of the office into two formal kinds than the practical circumstances with which the Genevan situation confronted him. The 'procurators' and 'hospitallers' may reflect rather the arrangements to which Geneva was already accustomed than an innovation commended by Scripture alone. The way in which Calvin refers to the offices here would agree with the supposition that he was trying to bring under ecclesiastical control arrangements which were already in force.

Spiritual Character of the Diaconate

Calvin shows himself deeply concerned to authenticate the spiritual character of the diaconate. If the offices of procurator and hospitaller had secular precedents and even roots, his sensitiveness at this point would be immediately understandable. It is true that the nature of the duties alone might be held to sanctify the office: 'We know what a holy thing it is to be careful for the poor' (*Comm.* on Acts 6[2], C.R. 48.120). But the anxiety he displays has another significance, too. For one thing all office in the Church is spiritual, in so far as spiritual gift matches and is attached to the diverse ministries discharged in the Church. In this respect the office of deacon is neither other nor less than that of minister or preacher or governor (*Serm.* on 1 Timothy 3[6-7], C.R. 53.290). Again, Calvin is characteristically insistent on the oneness of the people of God. In his treatment of the office of presbyter (especially *Comm.* on 1 Timothy 5[17], C.R. 52.315), he not only repeats his familiar distinction of presbyter and bishop; he adds to this his equally familiar *duo presbyterorum genera*. Both these, each in its own way, serve to emphasize this oneness. By means of the first, one of the breaches that fragment the people of God is closed: the ministry is not divided into two distinct orders. But there remains another breach: the distinction between clergy and laity wrongly conceived and driven so deep that the Church falls apart. Calvin sees that the two kinds of presbyter mend this division. The danger he apprehends and by this means guards against is not that lay presbyters should be put on equality with clerical presbyters: on his view this is sufficiently guarded against by the different functions allotted to each kind. The greater danger is that a clerical element should impose a notion of superordination and subordination that would fragment the people of God. Hence he is not afraid to class the laity as one kind of presbyter that, along with the distinctively clerical presbyter, exercises government in the Church. Calvin holds a similar view, *mutatis mutandis*, with regard to deacons: they are lay no doubt, but they are not for this reason debarred from exercising a spiritual office in the Church. The third consideration arises from the nature of what they are called upon to do. Not only do the deacons stand near the ministers of the Word, but they have the treasures of the Church to dispense (*Serm.* on 1 Timothy 3^{6-7}, C.R. 53.291f). But all alms are sacrifices. Hence those who administer them distribute the sacrifices offered to God and consecrated by Him. It is at this point that the unreformed Church goes so far astray. The only element of the deacon's true office that remains is that he assists. But this assistance is grievously impoverished. For the bishops have made of the deacons nothing but 'domestic servants' (*Serm.* on 1 Timothy 3^{6-7}, C.R. 53.289). The diaconate is no more than a step towards the priesthood. Even worse, their ministering functions have been reduced to 'certain ceremonies about the patten and the chalice' (*Inst.*, IV.v.4; *Comm.* on 1 Timothy 3^{8}, C.R. 52.287), while all the time the revenue of the Church, instead of providing for the poor, is applied to other ends, improper or base. But proper deacons are to be regarded as 'officers of God', and have their place in the *régime spirituel de l'Église*: they have an *office sacré*, and they function *comme les mains de Dieu* (*Serm.* on 1 Timothy 3^{6-7}, C.R. 53.289).

Rank and Other Characteristics

The inclusion of the diaconate within the spiritual government of the Church does not for Calvin mean that it enjoys entire equality with other offices of ministry. Here the concept of rank has to be taken into account. According to Calvin, the real distinction is that of function, and all functions, since 'the natural order is that gifts precede ministry' (*Comm.* on 1 Corinthians 12^{28}, C.R. 49.506), are equally necessary within the ministry of the Church. Yet no office can compete with that of pastor in honour and dignity. Deacons rank after both pastors and governors. Thus (*Comm.* on 1 Timothy 5^{17}, C.R. 52.315) the 'double honour' to be accorded to the elders that rule well, which Chrysostom thought to mean support *and* reverence, Calvin takes as simply a greater measure than is to be accorded to widows, who here are to be reckoned as belonging to the diaconate.

Calvin holds that women have a place among the New Testament deacons. He regards Phoebe (Romans 16^1) as being deacon in the official sense, not merely a servant in general of the Church. The relation of women to the diaconate set forth in 1 Timothy 5^9 is more complex (*Comm.*, ad loc., C.R. 52.310). They are consecrated to the ministry of the Church in a double sense: their poverty is to be relieved, their ministry is to be expended upon the poor: 'there was thus a mutual obligation between them and the Church'. The *Institutes* of 1543 (C.R. 1.451) speaks of 'diaconissae'.

While the distinction between deacons and pastors is clear enough, Calvin characteristically stops short of absolute difference. Each office has indeed its proper function, with its attendant gifts (*Serm.* on 1 Timothy 3⁸⁻¹⁰, C.R. 53.293f.). Deacons have not the *docendi munus* (*Comm.* on 1 Timothy 3⁸, C.R. 52.286). Yet since they sustain a public face in the Church, it is absurd that they should be uninstructed in the faith. They may indeed be gathered together in seminary with presbyters, thus giving unity to the *sancta administratio*.

Ordonnances Ecclésiastiques

The *Draft Ecclesiastical Ordinances* of 1541 (C.R. 10/1.15ff.) supply further details concerning the diaconate, though only some demand attention here. It has been noted that Calvin may here be trying to give ecclesiastical shape to arrangements already working, rather than setting up *de novo* an arrangement for which he found biblical foundation in Romans 12⁷. His injunctions concerning the installation of deacons have a clearly biblical and ecclesiastical stamp. 'The election of both procurators and hospitallers is to take place like that of the elders; and in electing them the rule proposed by St Paul for deacons (1 Timothy 3, Titus 1) is to be followed.' The main charge upon the attention of the procurators is the public hospital, in which are to be lodged separately not only the sick but also those too old to work, widows and orphans, and 'other poor creatures'. But their duties do not end there. There is also a hospital for transient persons; attention is to be given to any recognized as worthy of special charity; and 'care for the poor dispersed throughout the city should be revived, as the procurators may arrange it'. Medical care is to be given by a doctor and a surgeon, and arranged on what we should now call the 'cottage hospital' system. The pastors are enjoined to take active interest in the hospital and to co-operate with the procurators to this end. Mendicancy is to be strongly discouraged, the loiterer to be removed from the church doors and, if insolent, to be handed over to the Lords Syndic; and a total prohibition of begging is to be enforced.

The Seigneury are also involved. It is to them that requests for anything lacking in the hospitals are to be made. There is also a financial obligation. 'If the revenue which their Lordships will assign be insufficient, or should extraordinary necessity arise, the Seigneury will advise about adjustment, according to the need they see.' The financial responsibility thus appears to be twofold. They are to be responsible for the provision of a regular revenue, and this may have to be supplemented in circumstances of unusual need. Calvin does not state the source of this revenue, and we are left to conjecture. If Doumergue (*Jean Calvin, les hommes et les choses de son temps*, vol. V, pp. 225f.) is right, it must be Church endowments, and especially the gifts given for the poor by donors of earlier centuries, which the State had taken possession of and secularized, a process against which Calvin vigorously protested (see the references supplied by Doumergue, ibid.). In any case, the Seigneury rejected the proposal that revenue be assigned by them, and the relevant words are excised from the 1561 edition of the *Ordinances* (C.R. 10/1.102). There remained the 'daily alms' which Calvin never tired of insisting should be rendered gladly, for the Lord loves a cheerful giver.

A further duty fell to the deacons according to the *Draft Ordinances*. They are named among those who administer the chalice: 'none are to give the chalice except the colleagues or deacons with the ministers'. But Calvin does not suggest here that this is an implication of the Acts 6[2] 'serving of tables' from which the apostles resolved to disburden themselves; nor does he there suggest that the duty then allotted to the seven had any eucharistic significance.

The English Reformers and Diaconate

GEOFFREY W. BROMILEY

The general approach of the Reformers to the practice of diaconate does not differ essentially from that of the Middle Ages. Much the same machinery is used and the same actions of giving alms to the poor and visiting the sick and those in prison are to be found. There are, however, three reasons why the issue of diaconate arose with a new urgency and had to be thought out at a new level. The first is economic, the second ecclesiastical, and the third theological.

Economically the age of the Reformation was a period when the slow changes of the later Middle Ages came to a head. The effects of the Crusades and the Black Death, the rise of the mercantile classes and the end of feudalism, the fostering of new industries and the opening up of new trade routes by oceanic exploration—all combined to make the sixteenth century a time of rapid change and accompanying acute distress. This was particularly so on the land, where the old type of economy was yielding before a wave of enclosures, and many of the lesser gentry, as well as displaced and destitute yeomen and peasants, were in no good shape to withstand the incessant onslaught of inflation. The Peasants' War bears ample testimony to the seriousness of the condition in Germany, and the West Country revolt in England in 1549 had an economic as well as a religious basis. Even later, when England became stronger under Elizabeth, the country was still plagued by acute financial and economic problems which created a great deal of poverty and a consequent need for effective measures of relief.[1]

Ecclesiastically, the dissolution of the monasteries caused considerable upheaval in this whole sphere. The monks were extensive landowners, and while it cannot be proved that they were better landowners than others,[2] the change in ownership naturally brought disruption and opened the way for quicker changes. Again, there were still fair numbers of monks and monastic employees in spite of the decline of the preceding century, and the dissolution helped to throw on the labour market recruits who could not easily be absorbed. Finally, the monasteries had carried quite a proportion of poor relief which had now to be taken up by individuals or by the parishes in addition to the existing burden. An intensification of effort was thus imperative.

[1] cf. G. M. Trevelyan, *History of England*, pp. 348, 370.
[2] ibid., p. 311, with bibliography. On this whole question cf. A. G. Dickens, *History of the English Reformation*, pp. 139ff.

Theologically, the Reformation doctrine of justification by faith removed one of the basic props of mediaeval almsgiving, namely, the merit of alms as a good work. Luther's great rediscovery was that justification is by faith without works. The works of Jesus avail for us. They cover all sins and all the penalties of sin. There need be no fear of purgatory nor anxiety to do the works which will bring relief from it. If this is so, a new answer is needed to the question of the meaning and basis of almsgiving. A new form of exhortation has also to be worked out for the stirring of Christians to the practice of liberality. Nor is this an academic matter to be discussed at leisure, for the new presentation is demanded at once against a background of urgent and increasing need.

As regards the general economic problem, the Reformers had not a great deal to offer. They were occupied with their own difficult tasks and in any case they did not regard it as the business of the ministry to advise or to act in secular matters. Luther, with his peasant background, blamed the situation on the development of commerce. Drawing attention to the great amount of waste land, and recalling that man should earn his living by the sweat of his brow (Genesis $3^{17ff.}$), he argued that it is 'more pleasing to God to increase agriculture and decrease commerce'.[1] Calvin, on the other hand, took the initiative of suggesting the setting up of the silk industry at Geneva to absorb surplus labour and to make possible the ending of begging. In England the Injunctions under Edward VI ordered that 'all fathers and mothers . . . bestow their children . . . either to learning or to some honest exercise, occupation, or husbandry . . . lest for lack of some craft, occupation, or other honest means to live by, they be driven to fall to begging, stealing, or some other unthriftiness'.[2] It is interesting that the Lenten fast was also retained in England, not just for spiritual discipline, but in order that 'the nourishment of the land might be increased by saving flesh' and to keep those who 'have good livings, and get great riches thereby, in uttering and selling such meats as the sea and fresh water doth minister to us'.[3] But these are only isolated and sporadic contributions to the general economic problem.

The Reformers certainly had no sympathy with those who tried to solve the problem by revolutionary action. Luther's attitude to the Peasants' War is well known. But Cranmer's Sermon on Rebellion is much to the same effect. He does not deny that the rebels are driven by poverty or that they have real grievances arising from inflation and oppression. Indeed, he condemns very strongly those who 'never cease to purchase and join house to house, and land to land, as though they alone ought to possess and inhabit the earth'. But he argues very strongly that revolution is not the right way to solve economic hardship and injustice. For one thing, it is wrong for Christians to disobey, even because of poverty. Again, 'this sedition doth not remedy, but increase their poverty' by consuming food and hindering the harvest. Thirdly, 'the chief stirrers in these

[1] W.A., VI, pp. 466f.
[2] Cranmer P.S., II, p. 498.
[3] ibid., pp. 507f.

insurrections be ruffians and sturdy idle fellows, which be causes of their own poverty . . . much drinking and little working.' Fourthly, only those who are genuinely poor, not 'poor by their own folly', are deserving of help.[1] In relation to the fourth point, it is worth noting that Luther, too, was against any general scheme of poor relief. 'Do not spoonfeed the masses,' he said. 'If we were to support Mr Everybody, he would turn too wanton and go dancing on the ice.'[2] While there is no doubt much homespun realism in this assessment, the forbidding both of revolt and also of relief creates an almost intolerable situation when, due to more general economic movements, work is simply not to be had even by those who are fit and trained and ready for it.

Behind much of the rebelliousness of the century the Reformers saw not only the desperation provoked by economic change but also the sinister influence of the Anabaptist demand for a community of goods. Against this there is concerted opposition. Luther attacks strongly any organized or compulsory sharing of this kind.[3] Cranmer regards it as plain theft that the rebels should 'take from the rich man what they list without any price', and a reference to Anabaptism may lie behind his statement that there were among the rebels some who 'will needs be called gospellers'.[4] Credal expression was given to opposition to the Anabaptist teaching in the Forty-Two and the later Thirty-Nine Articles (Art. 38). Calvin, too, discussed the community of goods in his Commentary on Acts 2^{44}. He argued that this was a special measure to meet a special occasion, and that it was undertaken on a wholly voluntary basis. It is certainly not to be regarded as a course of action binding on all Christians, as though all title to individual property had to be renounced. Calvin also drew attention to the dangers inherent in this type of action as amply illustrated in monasticism, for, practising poverty in a community of goods, the monks 'call nothing their own, yet stuff their idle bellies with the blood of the poor'. A related issue is that of the equality enjoined by Paul in 2 Corinthians 7^{16}. Calvin does not believe that this can properly be construed as an absolute or organized equality. In his Commentary on Corinthians, ad loc., he states that it is 'not unlawful for the rich to live in any degree of greater elegance than the poor, but no one is to be allowed to starve, and no one to hoard his abundance at the expense of defrauding others'.

How far were the Reformers prepared to go in ensuring the restraint of avarice and the prevention of absolute poverty? A certain cleavage seems to be apparent here. In the larger monarchical states like Saxony and England, where the situation was more complex and authority was more autocratic, Luther and Cranmer adopt a more supine attitude. They condemn rebellion and seek its temporal punishment, but they are ready to leave 'covetous men, which do inclose and possess unjustly the commons',[5] to the everlasting damnation of God, which is no doubt more sure, but which does not greatly help their present

[1] ibid., pp. 193ff.
[2] W.A., XXIV, pp. 676f.
[3] W.A., LII, p. 589.
[4] Cranmer, P.S., II, pp. 195ff.
[5] ibid., p. 196.

victims. Again, they recommend that the able-bodied should work and support themselves, but they are not very active in prompting the government to supply work where there is none to be had. In the less complex and rather more democratic city-state of Geneva, however, Calvin took far more positive steps for the common good, not only by his initiative in relation to the silk industry, but also in his sympathy with legislation to prevent fraudulent commercial practices. He was, in fact, prepared to go further than others in the direction of national as well as individual or ecclesiastical measures for the relief or poverty and the restraint of rapacity. On one point all the Reformers seem to have been in agreement, namely, that there should be a curb on extravagance in dress, jewellery and pleasures, which was both unbecoming in a Christian and harmful rather than helpful to the economy. But their main emphasis here was moral rather than economic.

The answer to poverty was still found in individual benevolence exercised either privately or through the Church. The Reformers themselves all set good personal examples in this regard. Luther, although he claimed that 'God does not want you to give to needy people in such a way that you and yours must also beg and be a burden to other people',[1] was, in fact, generous almost to the point of improvidence, and it was left to his wife to practise what he preached. Calvin in his will provided mainly for his own family, but he did not forget to set aside ten gold pieces for the Boys School and another ten for poor strangers.[2] Cranmer made a serious if not very successful effort to reduce the table expenditure of bishops and other dignitaries so that the money saved might be 'spent in plain meats for the relieving of the poor'.[3] In his last address before execution he could still spare a thought for others, urging the rich among his hearers that 'if ever they had occasion to shew their charity, they have it now, the poor people being so many, and victuals so dear'.[4] Ridley, too, was so concerned about 'a great many of poor men', and especially his 'poor sister and her husband', who had been hard hit by his deprivation, that almost his last act was to send a petition to the queen on their behalf.[5]

Apart from private gifts, the care of the sick and needy was a responsibility of the parish. From an early period it had been the office of the deacon to help in cases of need, and formally this was still true in the Church of England, as may be seen in the bishop's charge at ordination: 'And furthermore, it is his office, where provision is so made, to search for the sick, poor, and impotent people of the Parish to intimate their estates, names, and places where they dwell, unto the Curate. . . .' Under the mediaeval system, of course, the deacon now had another duty, that of assisting in the ministry of the word and sacraments, and it will be noted that the curate was still left with final responsibility in the administering of alms. In other words, the diaconate, as a step to the priesthood,

---

[1] E.A., III, p. 510.
[2] P. Schaff, *History of the Christian Church*, VIII, p. 880.
[3] Cranmer P.S., II, p. 491.
[4] ibid., p. 566.
[5] Ridley P.S., p. 290, cf. the letter on pp. 427ff.

maintained its original duty only in a formal or restricted sense, and the work of diaconate really fell on the incumbent and churchwardens.

Calvin, however, in his reconstruction of the ministry at Geneva, aimed to reform the office of deacon according to the original pattern. On the basis of Romans 12^8 and 1 Timothy 5^{10} he perceived a twofold office, first, that of 'administering the affairs of the poor' and secondly that of 'taking care of the poor themselves'. 'For, although the term has a more intensive meaning, Scripture specially gives the name of deacons to those whom the Church appoints to dispense alms, and take care of the poor, constituting them as it were stewards of the treasury of the poor' (*Institutes* IV, 3, 9). Hence the office of the deacons in the *Ecclesiastical Ordinances* was to have the care of the poor and sick, and of hospitals, and also to prevent mendicancy. Incidentally, imitation of Calvin led to an interesting situation in Elizabethan England, for under the leadership of Cartwright the Puritans argued that a deacon should be debarred from the ministry of word and sacrament. In view of the example set by Stephen and Philip this was regarded by Whitgift as a strange instance of reformation according to the Scriptures.[1]

Funds were raised for poor relief in many different ways. Five main sources of supply can be seen in Reformation England. First, the wealthy were encouraged to make larger bequests, either as gifts or in their wills, for the permanent endowing of a poor fund. Some such endowments came down from the pre-Reformation period, and many parishes have instances of later bequests. Secondly, the ancient custom of giving the collection at Holy Communion to charitable causes was continued. Thus the 1552 Prayer Book orders that this collection should be 'put in the poor men's box'.[2] It was urged that money previously spent on pardons, pilgrimages, etc., should now be devoted to this fund. Ridley, in his diocesan injunctions of 1550, ordained that ministers, in the time of the communion '. . . shall monish the communicants, saying these words, or such-like, "Now is the time if it please you, to remember the poor men's chest with your alms." '[3] Suitable verses of Scripture were also read to encourage liberality. Fourthly, a levy was made on certain clergy whose revenues could stand charitable deductions: 'Because the goods of the church are called the goods of the poor, and at these days nothing is less seen than the poor to be sustained with the same, all parsons, vicars, pensioners, prebendaries, and other beneficed men within this deanery, not being resident upon their benefices, which may dispend yearly £20 or above, either within this deanery or elsewhere, shall distribute hereafter among their parishioners . . . in the presence of the churchwardens . . . the fortieth part of the fruits and revenues of the said benefices, lest they be worthily noted of ingratitude.' When the annual value was over £100, a 'competent exhibition' to one scholar had also to be provided, and thereafter for every additional £100 one additional scholar at Oxford or Cam-

---

[1] Whitgift P.S., III, pp. 58f.
[2] Liturgies of Edward VI, P.S., p. 270.
[3] Ridley P.S., p. 320.

bridge or 'some grammar school'.[1] Fifthly, money from other sources was also made available. Thus 'the money which riseth of fraternities, guilds, and other stocks of the church . . . shall be put into the said chest, and converted to the said use; and also the rents and lands, the profit of cattle, and money given and bequeathed to the finding of torches, lights, tapers, and lamps, shall be converted to the said use.' Fines for the failure to keep registers properly, and, under the Uniformity Act, fines for non-attendance at divine service, were also to go to the same purpose. Should there be a surplus in the poor chest, some of these funds might be used for other purpose, e.g. 'the reparation of highways next adjoining' or 'the reparation of the church'.[2]

Incidentally, the fact that there might be a surplus in some cases is an indication of one of the most serious weaknesses of using the parish as the basic unit of poor relief. In wealthier parishes, where the need is smaller, there is more money available, whereas in poorer parishes the reverse is the case. Again, the situation might fluctuate in a given parish, but, unless a substantial endowment is built up, the time of greatest need will be the time of greatest scarcity. The advantage of more personal responsibility and administration is not to be discounted, but it hardly offsets the need for a broader machinery of distribution for the better sharing of the burden and spreading of the funds available.

Another problem is that some cases of need demanded a type of provision which cannot always be made available on a local scale. Thus, if the field is widened to include education, the founding of a grammar school could not always be met by a private benefaction or local resources. The same was true of hospitals, which would not be needed in every parish and which, even in the cities, could normally be provided only by more munificent bequests. In view of the increased pressure on ordinary resources through economic dislocation and the loss of monastic help, how was this need to be met?

The properties and endowments of the monasteries and chantries seemed to supply the answer, since these represented the charitable giving of the past and there could be nothing wrong in turning them to a more genuinely biblical purpose. But in the larger states the ruling classes who carried through the dissolution had very different ideas. Instead of regarding dissolution as a redeployment of the Church's resources, they regarded it as a disendowment. Indeed, they treated it as a disendowment, not in the national interest, but in their own interests. In the England of Edward's reign this led to a sharp collision between the Reformers and the ruling nobility. To the Reformers the released properties belonged to the Church and ought to be devoted to the extension of the ministry, the establishment of schools and hospitals, and the furtherance of other charitable causes. The nobility, however, had legal control, and refused to listen either to advice or to warning.

The Reformers did enjoy some small success, largely through enlisting the support of the young king himself. At the suggestion of Ridley, Edward founded

[1] Cranmer P.S., II, p. 500.
[2] ibid., pp. 500, 503.

sixteen grammar schools and seems to have planned a further twelve colleges. Again, shortly before his death, he was so moved by a sermon of Ridley on the duty of helping 'the poor and unlearned' that he sent for the bishop and asked what could be done. Out of this request came Christ's Hospital to provide education for the poor, St Bartholomew's for the treatment of wounded soldiers, the sick and diseased, and Bridewell for the correction of the idle and unthrifty poor.[1] On the other hand, Cranmer and Ridley 'were both in high displeasure . . . for repugning as they might against the late spoil of the church goods, taken away only by the commandment of the higher powers, without any law or order of justice, and without any request of consent of them to whom they did belong'.[2] Latimer, Lever, Bradford, and Knox all spoke out so sharply in the same conflict that 'these men, of all other, these magistrates then could never abide'.[3] But the battle was a thankless one, and the financial and economic difficulties of the reigns of Mary and Elizabeth made it quite impossible that there should be any reconsideration of the matter later.[4]

The reorientation of Church expenditure was an important part of the diaconate as all the Reformers conceived of it. Luther put the matter bluntly when he stated that 'it is better to give your neighbour a penny than to build St Peter a church of gold'.[5] Calvin, too, argues that the Church has been guilty of gross misdirection of money, not only in respect of monasteries, masses, pilgrimages, and the like, but also in respect of extravagant vestments and furnishings. Discussing the incident of the anointing in his Commentary on John 12, he denies that this is a precedent for 'costly extravagance in worship'. It is a special instance, for the incarnate Lord is present in person. Now that He is no longer on earth, attention is to be given to the poor who are still with us. As Calvin puts it, 'alms, by which the wants of the poor are relieved, are sacrifices acceptable, and of sweet savour to God . . . Any other kind of expense in the worship of God is improperly bestowed.' The mediaeval Church might argue, of course, that Christ Himself is still present by transubstantiation, but denial of the real presence in this sense was an integral part of the Reformation, not only in Switzerland, but also in Edwardian England. Hence the redistribution of ecclesiastical wealth was a natural step for the Reformers to take, and if they had had full freedom to carry out their plans any losses suffered by the dissolution of the monasteries would have been more than redressed by the new educational, medical and general philanthropic programme which would have been made possible.

The Reformers could appeal to their theological reconstruction in favour of the diversion of money from extravagance in Church life and practice to poor

---

[1] Ridley P.S., xiii, n. 1. For additional information cf. Dickens, op. cit., who argues that much more was done than often supposed (pp. 210ff.).
[2] Ridley P.S., p. 59.
[3] loc. cit.
[4] In contrast, Zwingli enjoyed such success in redeploying ecclesiastical revenues in Zürich that the poor fund was more than trebled in a brief span, cf. J. Rilliet, *Zwingli* (1964), pp. 90ff.
[5] W.A., X, 3, p. 282.

relief, but in terms of practical motivation the theological reconstruction seemed to work against them. The mediaeval understanding was simple and effective from the popular standpoint. Only a few might be inspired to follow the so-called evangelical counsels and give alms of all that they possessed, but the spiritual advantages secured by ordinary almsgiving were a sufficient driving force to ensure regular gifts to all branches of the Church's activity. Perhaps self-interest played a big role here, but self-interest is a powerful motive. Reformation theology, however, destroyed this motive, for almsgiving can neither help to justify before God nor secure the reduction of purgatorial penalties. Why, then, should Christians provide the money needed for the diaconal programme?

The first answer comes in the form of scriptural injunction. Reformation theology teaches the supreme authority of Scripture as the norm of faith and conduct. But Holy Scripture is full of commands and exhortations to give to the poor. Some of these are collected in the Prayer Book for use at the appropriate point. Nor are they to be read merely as human commands, for, quite apart from the inspiration of Scripture as God's Word, Christ Himself makes the duty of almsgiving quite plain. As Calvin says in his Commentary on Matthew 5^{42}: 'Christ demands from his own people disinterested beneficence.' The disciple, as disciple, is pledged to liberality towards the poor. This is part of the very essence of his discipleship.

Appeal to authority, however, carries the risk of emphasizing almsgiving merely as a duty, and this can easily lead back to the view that justification is by fulfilment of duty rather than by faith in Christ's perfect fulfilment. How is this emphasis on duty to be reconciled with the essential emphasis on faith? The answer is to be found in the more general discussion on the relation between faith and works. This is a basic theme in the Homilies on Salvation, Faith and Good Works which are usually attributed to Cranmer, and the points made by Cranmer will throw a good deal of light on this question of the motivation of almsgiving.

It is faith alone which avails for justification before God. But justifying faith is no mere belief. It is a dynamic and active faith which finds spontaneous expression in fulfilment of the Law, in works of love. Hence a good work like almsgiving might well serve as a test of the genuineness of faith. If the command to give alms is not fulfilled, there is little point in appealing to faith, for the faith to which appeal is made is shown to be empty protestation. True faith is not 'idle, unfruitful, and dead, but worketh by charity' and 'may be called a quick or lively faith'.[1] In this sense it may be said that 'the trial of all these things is a very godly and christian life'.[2]

This aspect of the matter carries the demand for solemn searching of heart and life on the part of all who make a profession of Christian faith. If a lack of love for others is revealed, e.g., by a lack of liberality, this is not a simple failure which can easily be remedied by amendment. It may be the sign of a deeper lack.

[1] Cranmer P.S., II, p. 135.
[2] ibid., p. 139.

There is no real obedience, because there is no real faith. This, in turn, is a fearful possibility, for if there is no real faith there is no real salvation. In other words, the element of anxious concern is not entirely banished. Indeed, it arises with even greater seriousness, for what is at issue now is not the degree of purgatorial penalty but eternal life or eternal perdition. This is why the Injunctions can give the impressive warning that to relieve the poor is 'required earnestly upon pain of everlasting damnation'.[1] Cranmer uses the strongest possible terms in this connexion: 'They that be christened, and have knowledge of God and of Christ's merits, and yet of set purpose to live idly, without good works, thinking the name of a naked faith to be sufficient for them . . . upon such presumptuous persons and wilful sinners must needs remain the great vengeance of God, and eternal punishment in hell, prepared for the devil and wicked livers.'[2]

Yet, while it is true that almsgiving is a test of faith it is no less true that faith is a test of almsgiving. Great pains are taken by all the Reformers to make it plain that what matters is not the deed only, but the living source of the deed, the inward motivation. In this regard four main points are made, first, that true almsgiving will proceed from faith, secondly, that it will be motivated by genuine love, thirdly that it will be done as to Christ, and fourthly that it is a worship of God.

True almsgiving will proceed from faith. Cranmer here quotes Chrysostom to the effect that 'as men . . . first have life, and after be nourished; so must our faith in Christ go before, and after be nourished with good works. And life may be without nourishment, but nourishment cannot be without life . . . He that doth good deeds, yet without faith, he hath not life.'[3] Commenting on the statement of Augustine that 'there is one work, in the which be all good works, that is, faith which worketh by charity', Cranmer himself adds that if a man has faith he has 'the ground of all good works', but if he does not, he has only 'the names and shadows' of virtues. Works not done 'in faith for the honour and love of God, they be but dead, vain, fruitless works'.[4] Thus, to stimulate genuine liberality, it is not enough to call for a solemn searching of the life as a test of the genuineness of faith. The one thing necessary above all others is to issue the call for faith itself, to preach the Gospel in the power of the Spirit in order that faith may be evoked. Then, 'as soon as a man hath faith, anon he shall flourish in good works'.[5]

True almsgiving is motivated by genuine love, for faith itself is the response of love. This truth brings into sharp focus the inadequacy of self-interest as a motive. This motive may produce cash, but it is of little spiritual profit. Luther stated this very plainly once when he gave a gift to a beggar and his companion, Jonas, said that God would reward him. Luther replied: 'One should give will-

[1] ibid., p. 503.
[2] ibid., p. 140.
[3] ibid., p. 143.
[4] ibid., p. 142.
[5] ibid., p. 143.

ingly, moved by a love that is very ready to give.'[1] Luther also put it very succinctly when he said that 'he who has given someone his heart will also give him his purse'.[2] This is also the point at issue in respect of the secrecy of almsgiving: 'Benefactions . . . should be given quietly and without seeking one's own benefit.'[3] Calvin had the same truth in mind when he said that what Christ commands is 'disinterested beneficence' (on Matthew 5^{42}). Charity imposes duties, but 'these are not fulfilled by a mere discharge of them . . . unless it is done from a pure feeling of love'.[4] Cranmer links this whole matter with his primary concern for faith as the motivating spring. He quotes Augustine to the effect that 'the intent maketh the good works; but faith must guide and order the intent of man', 'and the faith which does this is a true faith that worketh by love'.[5] In other words, the true motivation of love is inseparably connected with the faith which is 'a sure trust and confidence in God's merciful promises . . . whereof doth follow a loving heart to obey his commandments'.[6]

True almsgiving is done as to Christ. This truth, clearly taught in the Parable of the Sheep and the Goats and equally clearly implied in the inclusion of the second commandment within the first (cf. Matthew $22^{37ff.}$; 1 John 3^{17}), is emphasized by Luther when he speaks of giving 'for the sake of God'.[7] It is also given as one of the main reasons for almsgiving in the Injunctions under Edward VI. Christians should be liberal because whatever is given for the comfort of the poor 'is given to Christ Himself'.[8] This brings us back, of course, to the basic theme that love for God is inseparable from trust in Him for salvation. The love for Christ which impels a man to serve Him in the form of the needy neighbour is the love which arises only as response to the great love wherewith He loved us. Hence the surest way to stir up the desire to give to others as to Christ is to present the Gospel and to call for faith as committal to Him who came in the form of the servant for us.

Finally, true almsgiving is worship of God. This aspect is well brought out by Calvin in his contrast between extravagant expenditure in worship and the alms which are 'sacrifices acceptable, and of sweet savour to God' (Commentary on John 12). It is worthy noting that Calvin with his fine Biblical sense is not afraid to speak of sacrifices in this connexion. He obviously does not mean offerings brought with the intention of placating God or making satisfaction, e.g., for the temporal penalties of sin. He has in view the sacrifices which are acceptable because they are the self-offering to God which is the response to God's self-offering for us. This is the heart of Christian worship, so that in a deeper sense the Injunctions under Edward VI can say that 'to relieve the poor is . . . a true

---

[1] W.A., *Tischreden*, IV, No. 4109.
[2] W.A., XLIV, p. 539.
[3] W.A., *Tischreden*, IV, No. 4162.
[4] *Institutes* III, 7, 7.
[5] Cranmer P.S., p. 142.
[6] ibid., p. 133.
[7] Cf. W. A., *Tischreden*, II, No. 1426.
[8] Cranmer P.S., II, p. 503.

worshipping of God'.[1] The call to worship, which is fundamental to Christianity itself, is also a call to the giving of alms.

From a practical point of view the diaconal programme of the Reformation was not eminently or uniformly successful. In the main this was due to circumstances over which the Reformers had no great control. The economic situation was particularly unfavourable. The failure to secure the redirection of former ecclesiastical resources was a serious blow. The sharp break from former practices created difficulties, and there was a serious dearth of trained ministers to give the people the necessary evangelical and theological instruction. In England the topsy-turvy nature of the Reformation added to the confusion. With available resources the Reformers did reasonably well in a very difficult situation. Perhaps they could have taken the opportunity to press for a bolder reorganization of the diaconate. Perhaps they could have thought more broadly in terms of diocesan or even national schemes. Perhaps they might have done more to encourage the voluntary sharing of possessions instead of attacking the Anabaptists and the monks on this matter. But to say what should have been done is often easier than to do it in the circumstances of the time.

From what one might call the prophetic standpoint the Reformers displayed on the whole a certain timidity which was no doubt part of their life in a more autocratic polity, but which was not altogether in keeping with their desire for Biblical reformation. One can sympathize with their conviction that official support may bring about demoralization. One may approve their avoidance of clericalism, i.e. the interference of ecclesiastics in details of government. One may recognize that even at considerable personal cost they did condemn the avarice of the rich as well as the restiveness of the poor. Yet the fact remains that even the able-bodied and willing may be victims of economic circumstances, that it is the duty of any right-minded government to take all possible steps for the relief of such victims and the redress of the circumstances, and that it is the office of ministers of the Gospel to remind rulers of this responsibility, if not as a duty of charity, certainly as a duty of justice. Something of what was needed may be seen in isolated cases, but it was hardly adequate to the need of the hour. What was finally required was a broader conception of diaconate to include the concern of Christians for their fellow men, not merely in terms of what can be done for the needy in and through the Church, important though this is, but also in terms of the testimony to be borne to those in civil authority in the interests of a just and responsible social and economic order.

From a theological point of view the Reformers showed a fine grasp of the true and necessary basis of diaconate, and this is their main contribution. If there is one weakness, it is perhaps that they do not go far enough in making the diaconate of Christ Himself the starting-point, centre and goal of all else. Yet they do this implicitly, for, sweeping aside the distortions of mediaeval teaching and practice, they try to fashion their understanding in Biblical terms, and in so doing they are necessarily brought back, not merely to faith, but to the

[1] ibid., p. 503.

object of faith, i.e. to the loving action of God Himself in Jesus Christ. In effect, this divine diaconate is the basis of all else. Even if in a given situation there is a measure of practical and prophetic failure, it provides the controlling principle in terms of which alone the diaconate of the Church can and should be exercised.

This has two implications of the greatest importance. It is a reminder that diaconate, for all its practicality, is first and finally a theological question, not in the sense of a theoretical question, but in the strict and proper sense of the term 'theological'. New insights and better techniques may emerge, but these can never lead to true Christian diaconate if the theological question is not answered, or if the right answer is not given to it. The so-called Social Gospel must still be the Gospel if it is not to degenerate into mere sentimentalism on the one side or mere sociology on the other. It must still be the Gospel of the grace of God in Jesus Christ. It must rest on the theological foundation which underlay the whole thought and action of the Reformers.

Secondly, the warning is given that the diaconate and its fulfilment stand in the closest possible relation to evangelism, i.e. to the ministry, which is itself diaconate, of the Gospel, the basis of diaconate. A plea for giving or a call for social action can have only a superficial response if not preceded, accompanied, and motivated by a proclamation of the self-giving of God and a summons to the response of self-giving to God. The Reformation itself, especially in the larger and more difficult states, did not succeed as well as one might have hoped at this level of living and effective evangelism, and it may be that in the last analysis the weakness of its practical diaconate is not unrelated to this failure. What is certain is that there can be no Christian diaconate in the genuine and abiding sense except in the context of the living and effective proclamation of the Gospel. The diaconate is one and indivisible. It cannot be sundered within itself any more than it can be severed from the divine diaconate in Jesus Christ from which it derives and of which it is itself a part.

The Puritans

GEORGE YULE

Because Jesus Christ is for the world, the Church which is the Body of Christ must also be for the world. Frequently, however, it has set itself up apart from, and even against the world. Even at the Reformation, as Barth has pointed out, the Reformed definitions of the Church as the Elect, the Congregation of the Faithful, never gave any indication of the Church being for the world as the servant people of the Servant Lord.[1] Absorbed with its fight against Rome, attempting to set its house in order, it made an emphasis that was understandable but disastrously wrong, for part of its fight against Rome, and part of its setting of its own house in order by its Christological correction, should have been this insight of the Church as being for the world. At times this insight did break through. Luther's rediscovery of *sola gratia* is the very basis of it, and one can see in the writings and activities of Butzer, and the way in which Calvin began to rethink the function of the Diaconate, a real advance. But too often there was a stress on the Church's purity and self-discipline which had more than a touch of Pelagianism about it, and an absorption with questions of Church order, plus an uncritical acceptance of many of the unjust and insensitive social attitudes of the time, which, combined with the ordinary human ability to rationalize one's self-interest, deflected the Church from a thorough-going reorientation of its thought in regard to the fellow man.

In this essay I wish to examine the attitude to this problem of those members of the Church in England in the sixteenth and seventeenth centuries who were commonly called Puritans. Their influence on the later history of the Anglo-Saxon churches has been far reaching, and it has been suggested in the famous thesis of Weber and Tawney that their emphases played a not inconsiderable part in the development of *laissez-faire* capitalism—with its disregard of the fellow man.

Puritans are a difficult group to delineate. They were essentially members of the Church of England, though in the seventeenth century they were often looked on as also including the radical separatist groups, and after 1662 the term is normally used for the Independents and so-called Presbyterians who were ejected from the Church of England for failure to conform to the fairly rigid tests the State imposed. The best definition for Puritans of the sixteenth century

---

[1] *Church Dogmatics*, IV, iii, pp. 764ff.

is the phrase they used to describe their own outlook, when they said that their document *A Parte of a Register* was written by those who 'desire the Reformation of our Church in Discipline and ceremonies according to the pure word of God and the law of our land'.[1] This definition shows their emphasis on the purity of the Church, based on strict Biblical precedent. There was no hint of separation of Church and State; they fully accepted the idea of the Christian Commonwealth and indeed looked to the godly prince to bring about reform. What aspects of the life of the Church needed further reform, and to what extent this reform should go, of course varied. Consequently it was impossible to say clearly who was or who was not a Puritan, and Bishops Grindal, Hutton, and Jewel would come under this definition almost as well as Hooper, Travers, and Cartwright. Nevertheless the general attitude was clear enough, and came out in particular issues.

How did the Puritans regard the services of the Church to those in need? Did they see the further 'Reformation of our Church . . . according to the pure word of God' as including the Church's outreach to the needs of mankind? Occasionally they did, but on the whole other preoccupations, Church government, vestments, and the Church's relationship to the State, along with peculiar emphases in theology, prevented this becoming a dominant interest—although it was an interest. And indeed it needed to be, for the question of poverty particularly was acute in sixteenth- and early seventeenth-century England.

Poverty and insecurity had been the common lot of most of the peasantry in the subsistence economy of the Middle Ages. But shortage of labour following the Black Death had enabled the peasant and artisan to improve their positions considerably in the fifteenth century, and in England villeinage was almost abolished and many feudal services replaced by a fixed and often nominal payment. However, with the increasing population from mid-fifteenth century, combined with inflation in the sixteenth, new and acute problems arose. To offset the inflation and to increase their standards of living in an increasingly opulent and extravagant age, the landowning classes raised rents, often enclosed lands, and attempted, at times, to take over the common fields. This process, known as the enclosure movement, seriously affected many of the peasantry, and a number were forced to leave their holdings. In some counties up to one-sixth of the villages became depopulated.[2] This, occurring with an increase in population, created an acute problem of poverty in Tudor England, particularly in the towns to which the landless labourers migrated. The monasteries, previously looked upon as a source of poor relief (though, in fact, only 3 per cent of their vast income had gone to this purpose), were dissolved by Henry VIII and the crisis was further accentuated. The maldistribution of wealth can be seen for example, from the tax returns for the subsidy levied by Henry VIII in 1524; a third of the population owned no property beyond the clothes they stood up in and a few sticks of furniture, while on the other hand, taking Exeter and

[1] *A Parte of a Register*, Preface.
[2] M. Beresford, *The Lost Villages of England*, pp. 166–76.

Coventry as examples, 2 per cent of the taxable population owned no less than 45 per cent of the wealth.[1]

The Reformation came on the scene of and in part accentuated this economic revolution. The dissolution of the monasteries led to unparalleled speculation in land and consequently aggravated the problems, as speculators frequently increased rents and enclosed lands to the detriment of the peasantry.[2]

Under Edward VI the English Church, helped by such leading Continental refugees as Martin Butzer, Peter Martyr, and John à Lasco, moved doctrinally into a reformed position. These Reformers had looked for social regeneration as the fruit of regeneration in the Church.

Like as we suffered ourselves to be ignorant of the true worshipping of God, even so God kept from us the right knowledge how to reform those inconveniences which we did see before our eyes to tend unto the utter desolation of the Realm.[3]

Martin Butzer's *De Regno Christi* was a manual of instruction for the godly prince to establish the kingdom of Christ, for 'neither the Church of Christ nor a Christian Commonwealth ought to tolerate such as prefer private gain to public weal, or seek it to the hurt of their neighbours'.[4] At the suggestion of Ridley, Edward VI founded sixteen grammar schools and established Christ's Hospital, St Bartholomew's, and the Bridewell for the relief of the poor. 'Sir, I have promised my brethren, the citizens,' wrote Bishop Ridley, 'to move you because I do take you for one that feareth God and would that Christ should lie no more abroad in the streets.'[5]

But as Tawney has put it:

The Christian prince strove, but not, poor child, as those that prevail. The classes whose backing was needed to make the Reformation a political success had sold their support on terms which made it inevitable that it should be a social disaster. The upstart aristocracy of the future had their teeth in the carcase, and having tasted blood were not to be whipped off by a sermon.[6]

The leading Protestant divines, the Commonwealth men, Latimer, Becon, Lever, and Ponet, had led the attack on the rack-renting landlords and usurers. For them, as Ridley said, 'Christ had lain too long abroad . . . in the streets of London, both hungry, naked and cold'.[7] But the positive attitude of the Edwardian Reformers was not continued after Protestantism was re-established under Elizabeth. There was nothing like the 'Commonwealth group.' This was partly because the ranks became divided. The Queen insisted on a Reformation settlement that was more conservative than that for which any of the Reformed party

---

[1] W. G. Hoskins. 'Provincial Towns in the Sixteenth Century', *Trans. Royal Hist. Soc.* (1956), pp. 17-19.
[2] R. H. Tawney, *Religion and the Rise of Capitalism* (1936 ed.), pp. 137-47.
[3] Quoted in Tawney, op. cit., ch. 3, n. 10.
[4] Quoted in Tawney, op. cit., p. 142.
[5] *The Works of Bishop Ridley* (Parker Society), p. 535.
[6] Tawney, op. cit., pp. 142-3.
[7] *Works*, op. cit., p. 535.

hoped. Consequently the radicals found it difficult to remain in a church that exhibited, in their eyes, so many of the 'dregs of Popery'.[1] This is where one can begin to talk about a Puritan group—though the word is not used till much later. Their whole emphasis was on the purity of the Church. The Reformation in England under Elizabeth, they said, had gone halfly forward and more than halfly backward.[2]

At first their attention was on vestments, 'those relics of the Amorites'.[3] Was not the wearing of popish garments to seek their patterns 'out of the cisterns and puddles of our enemies' instead of from the fountain of Scripture? And 'as touching the Lord's Supper who can refrain tears to declare how miserably it is transformed into the old stage-like frisking and horrible idol-gadding'.[4] When the Puritans were defeated on this issue by the bishops acting on the queen's instructions, they then turned their attention to the government of the Church, and the question of discipline, which absorbed their attention until this move collapsed under government and episcopal pressure in the early fifteen-nineties.[5] It was at this time that a Presbyterian form of Church government was looked on as a *de fide* matter prescribed in detail in Holy Scripture. In this pattern of Church government deacons had a place—not the type of deacon prescribed in the Prayer Book, the subpriest, a type 'which never came from heaven',[6] but the type described in the Scripture where 'it is evident that the office of deacon consisteth only in the oversight of the poor'.[7] Deacons whose 'special fitness is in merciful compassion of those in necessity and an upright and just conscience in (their) dealing' were to look after alms given to the poor. Each parish was to have its pastor, doctor or teacher, elders, and deacons elected to help the pastor as the only Church ministers left us by Christ.[8]

In this whole discussion the emphasis was on the abolition of episcopacy and the institution of a lay eldership, and one feels that deacons were included along with elders simply because they happened to be mentioned in the New Testament. Their office was never discussed in detail; indeed, the tendency was to say that the Church of England already had them, but under a different name; as Travers said, 'Little change is needed to turn collectors, churchwardens and sidesmen into elders and deacons, for the deacon's office is but to distribute the church's alms.'[9]

Occasionally more thought was put into the matter. In the fifteen-eighties the leading Presbyterian Puritans organized a number of secret meetings on the style of presbyteries which met regularly, kept records, and sent representatives to

[1] *Second Parte of a Register*, i: 136-8.
[2] ibid., ii: 60.
[3] *Zürich Letters* (Parker Society), ii.151.
[4] Quoted in *Puritan Manifestoes* (ed. W. H. Frere and C. E. Douglas), p. 50.
[5] See Patrick Collinson, 'John Field and Elizabethan Puritanism' in *Essays for Sir J. E. Neale* (ed. S. T. Bindoff, J. Hurstfield, C. H. Williams).
[6] *Seconde Parte of a Register*, 1:130.
[7] ibid., 1:127.
[8] ibid., 1:165-6.
[9] ibid., i:170.

secret general assemblies. They hoped to have a Presbyterian organization to take over the government of the Church in England should Parliament abolish Episcopacy. The records of the Dedham Classis in Essex have been preserved and the question of the care of the poor of the parish came up. It was suggested that collections be taken up for the poor at communion, that 'so many as be of ability invite to their houses one couple of such of their poor neighbours as have submitted themselves to the good orders of the Church and walk christianly and honestly in their callings',[1] and that every quarter the ministers 'with two or three of the ancients of the town with one of the Constables, do visit the poor and chiefly the suspected places, that understanding the miserable estate of those in wante and the naughty disposition of disordered persons they may provide for them accordingly'[2] Cartwright, arguing with Whitgift, said that the evils of the time were due to lack to enforceable discipline by an eldership, and that despite the excellent laws, there were still so many rogues and vagabonds to the manifest breach of God's law and the hazard of the Commonwealth because the office of deacon was abolished. However, he gave no hint as to how the deacons should operate, as if the restoration of the form would work the miracle—'The Lord would give no blessing to those good laws because his order was neglected.[3]

During the discussions of the Westminster Assembly of Divines when the Church of England adopted a Presbyterian polity due to Parliament's temporary need of the Scots Army in the Civil War, the Diaconate was never fully debated. Months were spent discussing the eldership and the powers of presbyteries, but deacons were dealt with in one day,[4] and in the actual *Directory of Government* all that was said was that they were not to preach nor administer the sacraments, 'but to take special care in distributing to the necessities of the poor' and, finally their office was perpetual.[5]

The purity of the Church was uppermost in their minds, and they never thought through the implications of the office of deacon. The State was taking more and more responsibility for the poor, and nobody appears to have worked out how the system of deacons was to function alongside the system of poor relief of the secular authorities. It was a complex situation for, as Tawney remarks, if the Church of the Middle Ages was a kind of State, the State of the Tudors had some of the characteristics of a Church.

With the defeat of the attempt to change the government of the Church of England to a Presbyterian form, English Puritanism itself changed. There had been premonitions before, as will be seen, but after 1590 Puritanism took on many of those moralistic attitudes which were not markedly present before, but with which the word Puritan is normally associated.

[1] R. G. Usher, *The Presbyterian Movement, 1582–1589*, p. 100, and Collinson, op. cit.
[2] Usher, ibid.
[3] J. Strype, *Whitgift* (Parker Society), i:132.
[4] *Journal of the Assembly of Divines* in Lightfoot, *Works*, xiii:83.
[5] *Form of Church Government sub Deacons.*

The Puritans' problem was how to show their loyalty to the pure word of God when the law of the land prevented their attempts to purify the discipline and ceremonies of the Church. Official discipline by eldership was prohibited. A rigid discipline could only be imposed by exhortation. Now began the great age of Puritan introspective writings, of sermons, of catechisms, most of which had a very individualistic and moralistic ring about them. Cartwright, the great Elizabethan Puritan, had denied any ethical distinctiveness.[1] 'Puritans, unspotted brethren and such like . . . names we abhor and detest and openly profess that in ourselves we find nothing but sin and uncleanness.'[2] But the seventeenth-century Puritans often saw themselves as the holders of a stricter moral attitude than their fellows. Mrs Hutchinson writes:

Whoever was zealous for God's glory or worship, could not endure blasphemous oaths, ribald conversation, profane scoffs, sabbath breaking, derision of the word of God and the like—whoever could endure a modest habit or conversation or anything good—all these were Puritans.[3]

William Perkins was perhaps the most influential Puritan at the end of Elizabeth's reign, and it is instructive to examine his attitude to those in need. It has been argued that Perkins was responsible for a new attitude towards poverty because he concluded that the very poor must be wicked, since 'rogues, beggars and vagabonds . . . commonly are of no civil society or corporation': 'they join not themselves to any settled congregation for the obtaining of God's kingdom': they 'are (for the most part) a cursed generation'.[4] But as the author of this view, Mr Christopher Hill, freely admits,[5] there are countless places in Perkins's works which attack covetousness, usury, unjust dealing, and these could hardly be acceptable to the grasping bourgeois members of the congregation which, we are told, heard Perkins preach with avidity. Hill gets over this difficulty by saying that they just did not listen to those bits. Self-deception does indeed go to great lengths, but this particular version of it is incapable of proof or disproof, and Perkins's undoubtedly very great influence must surely have exercised itself in a more plausible, if more subtle way.

Those, for example, who hoarded grain to sell at a higher price in times of scarcity must have been singularly deaf if they fancied Perkins was bolstering up common trade practices.

Truly I perceive you are a hard-hearted man, void of any compassion to the poor; you have been one of those who have brought our country into such misery. And to you the prophet Amos speaketh after this manner, 'Hear this, O ye that swallow up the poor . . . "Ye are cursed idolators because ye set your

---

[1] A. F. S. Pearson, *Thomas Cartwright and Elizabethan Puritanism*, p. 89.
[2] *Second Parte of a Register*, i:85–86.
[3] Lucy Hutchinson, *Biography of Colonel Hutchinson* (Everyman edn.), p. 64.
[4] Quoted in J. E. C. Hill, 'William Perkins and the Poor' in *Puritanism and Revolution*, pp. 227–9.
[5] ibid., p. 230. I am deeply indebted to Mr Hill's essay; by his great knowledge of the period he has opened up many problems, and has made us ask new questions on this topic.

hearts upon your riches."[1] If ye loved God "ye would also love your poor brother in whom God's image appeareth. Those who refuse to lend freely to the poor . . . are the bane and plague of the commonwealth: these are they that make beggars and vagabonds." '[2]

As for the enclosing landlords:

they are unmerciful men: surely they eat the bread of oppression and the very stones in the walls and the beams of their fair buildings cry unto God for vengeance against them.[3]

The attitude of his disciple William Ames, who eventually was forced into exile in Holland, where he became professor of theology at Franeker and exercised a wide influence, was similar.

To be willing to buy cheap and sell dear is (as St Augustine observes) common, but yet a common sin.[4]

Such usury which is commonly practised by Usurers and Bankers is deservedly condemned of all, because it is a catching art and no regard of charity or equity being had, lays in wait for other men's goods.[5]

All men should practice liberality and although they should aid the good rather than the bad, 'yet we must not therefore be curiously inquisitive into the hidden faults of the poor, for charity doth not easily think evil'.[6] Poverty is a foul scandal in a city and community where everyone is not provided with necessary food.[7] He ends his *Cases of Conscience* with an attack on covetousness and a plea for contentment.

This type of ethical exhortation was common with most of the leading Puritan divines. Preston, the most influential Jacobean Puritan, wrote:

If a man be rich, it is a thousand to one but that he trusteth in his riches. A man's calling is not to gather riches . . . but the end of our calling is to serve God and man.[8]

Others, such as John Downham, also emphasized Christian charity in alms and works of mercy,[9] and the tradition continued, and indeed reached its culmination, with Baxter, who set out in his *Christian Directory*, in greatest detail, the right Christian behaviour in different relationships and situations—in the way both masters and servants should be treated, in buying and selling, in letting and hiring.

Baxter was a conservative, who tended to accept the social relationships of

[1] William Perkins, *Works*, iii:465.
[2] ibid., i: 774.
[3] ibid., iii:465.
[4] William Ames, *Cases of Conscience* (1639), p. 236.
[5] ibid., 240.
[6] ibid., 255.
[7] ibid., 267.
[8] John Preston, *A Remedy Against Covetousness*, 1633, pp. 40-41.
[9] John Downham, *A Guide to Godliness* (1622), pp. 137, 157.

his time, but within that framework he set scrupulous standards. The rich must not give mere token gifts to the poor; God 'will not be put off with your tithes or scraps'. 'All usury against justice or charity is wicked.' 'Lending is a duty when we have it and our brother's necessity requires it.' Oppression of the poor is a heinous crime, and unmerciful landlords are the common and sore oppressors of the countrymen.[1]

It is hard to see in all this an active encouragement of the *laissez-faire* business immorality associated with eighteenth- and nineteenth-century capitalism. Indeed, recent research has shown that the efforts of the Puritan preachers were not without effect. Professor Jordan has analysed the amounts left to religious and charitable enterprises from 1480–1600, and although his comparative statistical method, which ignores the rise in population and the rise in prices, is certainly in error, so that one cannot say this was a more generous age than its predecessor, nevertheless vast sums were given, particularly by the merchant classes—the heart of Puritanism—to relief of the poor, help of prisoners, and education, as well as to the setting up of Puritan lectureships and the financing of ministers, whereas the mediaeval system of alms, administered by the monks, was casual and ineffective in its incidence, and nearly a quarter of alms given went towards chantries and their prayers for the dead. After the Reformation there appears to have been an onslaught on poverty and ignorance. Thirty-five thousand donors, two-thirds of whom came from London and Bristol, gave £3 million (in our money well over £100 million), over 60 per cent of which went to relief of the poor in endowments, almshouses, hospitals, and schemes of rehabilitation, with about 25 per cent to education.[2]

This was a real achievement. But there was another side to the question, which can be seen in some of the statements made by Perkins, Ames, Dod, and Cleaver, to name but a few, about the vagabonds and beggars. Ames wrote that as idleness was the mother and nurse of many vices,

the lusty beggards and vagabonds are not to be suffered. Firstly, because they openly oppose themselves to the Divine Ordinance. Secondly, they are a burden to others without necessity. Thirdly because they defraud those who are poor indeed of some part of the alms they would receive if they had not been prevented by such. Fourthly, they do not carry themselves as members of any church or commonwealth. Fifthly, they directly set themselves to many kinds of wickedness.[3]

Although one can have some sympathy with those who must try to deal with a vast social problem of unemployment and begging that had got out of hand and menaced the stability of society, yet these writers showed less social sensitivity than say More, Latimer or Starkey, who were also faced with these

[1] Richard Baxter, *Chapters from a Christian Directory*, ed. Jeanette Tawney, pp. 127, 129, 138ff.
[2] W. K. Jordan, *Philanthropy in England 1480–1660, The Charities of London 1480–1660—The Aspirations and Achievements of an Urban Society* and *The Forming of the Charitable Institutions of the West of England 1480–1660*.
[3] *Cases of Conscience*, p. 249.

problems. Why did they fail to see in the beggars and vagabonds the 'image of God'?

Here is another aspect. After his clear exposition of the dangers of riches and covetousness, Preston added:

> On the other hand, if a man by diligence in his calling have riches follow him, he may take them as a blessing of God bestowed on him as a reward of his calling ... The more diligent a man is in his calling, the more God doth bless him and increase his riches.[1]

Man must not set his heart on riches, and be tempted to use unlawful means to get them. But 'the method God useth to enrich men is this. He first bids us seek the kingdom of heaven and the righteousness thereof, and then all these things shall be administered unto us as wages.'[2] He answers the question of care for one's estates by saying that it is lawful to do so, 'observing the right rules in doing it'. He must stick to his own calling, leave time for his private service of God, and his aim must be on God's glory and the public good, not on riches.[3]

Lacking in this is the consequence of the Incarnation—the servant—Lord's love for all mankind in all its need—and hence the Church as the Servant People.

It is instructive to see how these writers posed their problems. The most notable of them, William Perkins, named his large book on Christian ethics *Cases of Conscience* and, in a very scholastic fashion, determined in detail what was or was not permitted to the individual Christian in each situation. The third section is headed 'Concerning man as he stands in relation to man', but although there is much real and helpful insight, and at times a deep compassion for the fellow man, the general orientation is in a different direction—how can the individual Christian be kept pure and holy. The Church was seen primarily as the Holy Community, and therefore the function of Christian ethics was to keep each member in a state of holiness. This was to be achieved by the minute individual examination of conscience, first in relation to what was demanded by God in His worship, and then what God demanded in relation to our neighbour, but the effect was a twofold distortion. *Sola gratia* was stressed as the basis of justification, but it would almost appear that one can earn one's sanctification without it, and secondly, the neighbour became almost a means for one's individual exercise in godliness rather than primarily a person for whom Christ died.

William Ames's book with the same title, *Cases of Conscience*, showed the same preoccupation, although it, too, mingled real insights—'in pity and its works we do especially put on the image and likeness of God'.[4]

It is significant that Ames bemoaned that the papists had far more books of

[1] *A Remedy against Covetousness* (1633), p. 42.
[2] ibid., p. 43.
[3] ibid., pp. 44ff.
[4] *Cases of Conscience*, p. 258.

this type than the Reformers, and that the children of Israel should 'need to go down to the Philistines, that is, our students to Popish authors', 'to sharpen Share, Mattock, Axe or Weeding Hook'. He reluctantly acknowledged his own debt to them,[1] and his emphases and the layout of his work show that it was greater than he realized. He began with a minute examination of the states of the conscience, later quoting in detail the refinements of William of Paris on temptation, and in Book Three analysing Christian virtues and vices. Throughout his centre of interest is the individual and his holiness.

This tendency is seen most clearly perhaps in John Preston's *A Remedy against Covetousness*, where one would think, surely, the Church's concern for the fellow man would be most obvious. But it was a highly individualistic work, almost devoid of Christological control. Wealth will be no use to you in the day of death, goods are in themselves vanity. Riches must not be sought by unlawful means, by gaming, usury, and the like, and if a man is wealthy it is a thousand to one but that he trusteth in his riches. All very true, but not dominated by *sola gratia*. And so consequently he could go on to assure his hearers that the righteous are rewarded with riches as wages.[2]

What was the cause of this attitude? One cannot read the Puritan literature of this period without becoming very conscious of the immediacy of the Word of God in the Bible for them. God spoke to them directly out of the very words of the Bible, and although no theory of verbal inspiration was worked out, their belief was not dissimilar. We cannot understand the Puritans without seeing this. 'We must be subject to God,' said Preston, 'not only in the main commandments but to every part of it.'[3]

It is this conjunction of Biblical literalism with the primary idea of the Church as the Holy Community that caused these Puritan writers to bring forward their schemes of ethics in this manner. Their whole emphasis was on discipline, on purity of life and worship according to what they found in the written word of the Bible. A word from Leviticus or Deuteronomy, unless it could be glossed over, was interpreted in the same way as a word from the Gospels.

This was a source of strength; the denunciations of Amos against the sins of neglecting the poor, the exhortations of Paul to love and care, the word of our Lord for the poor and outcast, were all faithfully discussed. But then also were the more prudent passages from Proverbs and the less incisive ones from Titus. And so, for example, Ames in his discussion of usury[4] wrote that Scripture did not take away all usury altogether, because the Jews were permitted to take usury of every stranger that was not poor. By the same method he showed that what was prohibited was 'that which is exacted from the poor', 'that which bites and gnaws; that is, when a debt is exacted with rigour and the damage of the

---

[1] ibid., Preface, pp. 2, 3.
[2] *A Remedy against Covetousness*, p. 42.
[3] J. Preston, *The Church's Carriage* (1638), p. 105.
[4] Ames, *Cases of Conscience*, pp. 240ff.

neighbour, that which is repugnant to charity'. The Bible was looked at very much as a book of precedents.

They could make a wooden interpretation of it that was harsh to those considered the 'idle poor'. The Apostle said that he that will not labour must not eat, therefore those able to work were not to be relieved, wrote Perkins.[1] Yet, because there was to be no beggar in Israel, Ames could write, 'It is a foul scandal in a city or community where everyone is not provided with necessary food',[2] and this attitude led many Puritans to give to almshouses and poor relief, and a man like Samuel Hartlib, the friend of Milton, to realize the inadequacies of the current systems of relief.[3]

This type of moral self-absorption, which could lead Perkins to talk of liberality as a *remedy* for covetousness[4] was largely due to the hold that the doctrine of predestination had gained over them. Calvin had warned against exploring the labyrinth of this doctrine, and looking to oneself and one's works as evidence of one's election was to look to a very unsteady prop.[5]

However, following Beza, many English theologians from Perkins onwards not only took the doctrine out of the context of Christology where Calvin had finally placed it, but tried to explore the labyrinth in detail and tended to see good works as a sign of election. The intolerable strain this put on people made them absorbed with the question of their own election. These cases of conscience over minutiae of personal conduct become understandable, and added to their idea of the Church as the Holy Community rather than as the Servant People, and their use of the Bible as a book of precedents rather than as the witness to the Incarnation, the wonder is perhaps that so much real compassion did come through.

In short, what we have is the beginnings of Covenant Theology which after Perkins in England superseded Calvin's more Christological emphasis. The grace of God in Jesus Christ is displaced from the centre. God's covenant of free grace is made into a contract. As in the Middle Ages, where the Sacrament of Penance is made a condition for receiving mercy, so in this new Protestantism repentance becomes a kind of condition and faith is turned into a work, while good works become the sign of one having closed with God in this contract. Such a theology naturally tends towards an individualistic moralism and pietism. The centre of gravity has shifted from Christ to man's response, and it is not surprising that there is a failure to see the Church as the servant people of the Servant Lord.

The part that rationalization and class interest played in all this is a complex question. What people assume that these leading Puritan writers and preachers said about covetousness and hard-heartedness is not always what they actually said—about how these 'deprive us of all pity and compassion against those that

[1] *Works*, II:145.
[2] *Cases of Conscience*, p. 261.
[3] Samuel Hartlib, *The Parliament's Reformation* (1646).
[4] *Works*, II:148.
[5] Calvin, Institutes III. xiv. 19. See W. Niesel, *The Theology of Calvin*, pp. 168ff.

are in want', and niggardliness 'keepeth men not only from the communicating of their goods to others, but also from enjoying them for their own benefit, committing therein a double theft', and how one must conduct business in the spirit of one running a public service.[1] Was there, then, anything in Puritan social teachings as distinct from other contemporary Christian emphases to attract the merchant classes because of their laxity? The explanation for the common failure of Puritans to do much about the crushing poverty in the eighteenth and nineteenth centuries, and for the close link-up between nonconformity and the middle classes is more likely to be found in the form of covenant theology and Biblicism which lent itself to an inward-looking and individualist view of Christian holiness, especially when after 1662 all nonconformists were debarred from the universities and therefore from the professions, and so perforce engaged very largely in commercial enterprises.

Many Puritans did not show much imagination about how to deal with poverty, because they themselves did not experience it personally. By contrast, the Puritan Sects of the Civil War period were more perceptive—far more of them came from the 'lower' orders of society, and were particularly strong in Cromwell's rank and file of soldiery, and in the poorer urban classes, especially in London.

Even more than other Puritans, these sects stressed the necessity of the Holy Community, and in the interests of purity broke away altogether from the established Church, to set up their voluntary covenanted communities where they could practise the full purity of worship and discipline as they saw it. They completely severed the connexion between Church and State in the interests of reformation, and sharply divided the sphere of grace from the sphere of nature. Then, however, unlike many other Separatists, they argued that as they had Christian liberty and Christian equality in the sphere of grace, by analogy there should be civil liberty and civil equality in the sphere of nature, and many of these groups showed rare social concern.[2]

A heterogeneous group of Puritans—Baptists, incipient Quakers, Brownists, and the like, came together in the Leveller Movement, which advocated many far-reaching reforms, to reform the law by reduction to 'the nearest agreement with Christianity'; to abolish tithes 'and other enforced maintenances for there be no ground for either under the Gospel'; to release imprisoned debtors, abolish 'the oppressive monopoly of Merchant Adventurers and others'; for Parliament to provide some powerful means to 'reclaim' (the word is significant) 'men, women and children from begging and wickedness, that this nation may be no longer a shame to Christianity therein'.[3] These demands culminated in radical political programmes—to abolish the veto of king and Lords, and a remarkable widening of the franchise to include even the poorest, so that they might have some say in the formulation of the laws. As Rainsborough, their spokesman at

[1] John Downham, *A Guide to Godliness*, p. 157.
[2] A. S. P. Woodhouse, *Puritanism and Liberty*, Introduction, pp. 60, 68, 69.
[3] Quoted in Woodhouse, ibid., pp. 320–2.

the debate in Cromwell's Army Council at Putney in 1647, said:

For really I think that the poorest he that is in England hath a life to live as the greatest he, and therefore truly sir, I think it is clear that every man that is to live under a government ought by his own consent to put himself under that government. I do not find anything in the law of God that a lord shall choose twenty burgesses and a gentleman but two or a poor man shall chose none.[1]

The same radical demands for the abolition of tithes, release of imprisoned debtors and reform of the laws were made by the non-democratic Fifth Monarchists, a Millenarian group prominent after the suppression of the Levellers.[2]

All the radical groups coming partly from the more orthodox Puritans had an intense concern for social righteousness. A Baptist preaching before Cromwell at his Headquarters in 1647, Thomas Collier, said on the text 'Behold, I create a new heavens and a new earth'—

It shall be a new earth in relation to the manner of the persons ruling, it is a new earth in which shall dwell righteousness, 2 Pet. 3.13, this is the great work that God hath to effect in the latter days of the Gospel, to reduce magisterial power to its primitive institution . . . This is the great work right honorable, that God calls for at your hand, whom he hath raised up for that end . . . to loose the bands of wickedness, to undo the heavy burdens, to let the oppressed go free, to break every yoke . . .

and he concluded with a detailed list of wrongs to be righted. All of this, he said, came from Scripture, 'although I trust I shall deliver nothing unto you but experimental truth'.[3] And this can also be understood in a way Collier did not quite intend, for he and his associates had a closer experience of poverty which enabled them to express in much more precise and relevant terms the social concern felt also by Perkins, Downham, and the others. Despite the fact that they held the same views of Biblical literalism, and had as great an emphasis on the Church in terms of a holy community, their closer association with the outcast and the oppressed enabled them to express their faith by care of those outcast and oppressed more easily, whereas Puritans in higher social classes tended with their refined individualistic moralism to weaken in humanity.

Consequently, because of their other preoccupations and because of a failure to see the Church as servant people of the Servant Lord, the Puritan groups in Britain did not develop the idea of the diaconate, but applied it in a rather wooden way. Care of the poor was limited largely to works of mercy by the individual, and indeed, except for the Sect-type Puritans, few creative suggestions were put forward to alleviate poverty.

[1] ibid., pp. 53, 56.
[2] S. R. Gardiner, *History of the Commonwealth and Protectorate*, ii: 269ff.
[3] Woodhouse, op. cit., p. 390.

Diakonia in Modern Times
Eighteenth–Twentieth Centuries

FREDERICK HERZOG

The Isenheim Altar, until the late eighteenth century the centre of the Antonite convent chapel at Isenheim in the Alsace,[1] in a unique way exemplifies the nature of Christian care for the sick and the poor. The Antonites, recognized as a brotherhood by Pope Urban II in 1095, were devoted to the care for the sick, especially the victims of the plague and syphilis epidemics. While receiving at Isenheim whatever medical attention was available at the time, the sick were also brought to the chapel to sit or lie in front of the altar (probably completed in 1516) and to look at the paintings: 'Participation in the liturgy could render the sufferer oblivious to the most terrible afflictions and enable a salutary germ of hope to spring up within him, stirring the other healing processes to life. Face to face with Christ crucified, hanging in dreadful isolation on the cross of shame, the ailing could forget their own sufferings, even the direst and most excruciating agony of mind and body.'[2]

At Isenheim care for the sick lay in the message of the paintings as well as in the hands of the religious. The Biblical word that fits this type of care best is *diakonia*.[3] The term describes as an act that shares in Christ's diakonia, in his servanthood most fully embodied on the Cross.

Luke relates that Jesus thought of himself as *diakonos* (Luke 22[27]).[4] The believer who seeks to follow Him cannot but share in His care for the marginal figures of life. Its distinct characteristic is the fusion of care for the body with care for the soul.[5]

---

[1] When at the time of the French Revolution the Isenheim convent was dissolved and most of its furnishings were destroyed or disappeared the altar was saved. Today it stands in the Unterlinden Museum at Colmar. See Robert Gall, *Schlüssel zum Isenheimer Altar* (Colmar, 1960), p. 11.

[2] Pierre Schmitt, *The Isenheim Altar* (Berne, 1960), p. 6; cf. Walter Nigg, *Maler des Ewigen* (Zürich and Stuttgart, 1961), pp. 45–54.

[3] In the Greek *diakonia* covers waiting at the table, serving food, etc. ThWNT, II, pp. 81ff. Under the impact of the Gospel such acts of menial service became expressions of the love of neighbour. RGG³, vol. I, p. 620.

[4] The life and work of Jesus is the archetype of *diakonia*. The love of the Christian is grounded in his servant attitude. RGG³, vol. II, p. 162. cf. Heinz-Dietrich Wendland, 'Christos Diakonos-Christos Doulos' in *Christos Diakonos* (Zürich, 1962), p. 14: 'The Son of man . . . serves in suffering. He is the Servant of God who fulfils diakonia through his death.' (*Christos Diakonos* referred to as '*CD*' hereinafter.)

[5] Erich Beyreuther, *Geschichte der Diakonie und Inneren Mission in der Neuzeit* (Berlin, 1962),

Lex Christi Lex Orandi et Credendi

The Isenheim Altar testified to Christ's servanthood in a sanctuary. The witness of the paintings as well as the work of the religious was tied to *leitourgia*, the worship of the community. Jesus Christ Himself rendered obedient service in terms of *leitourgia* before God. His work of mercy grew out of His worship of God. It was God's very being that informed His acts of mercy. Worship of God lies at the heart of *diakonia* and not moralistic perfectionism. Christ's *diakonia* qualifies Christian worship in a specific way. Learning to fulfil the *lex Christi*, 'Bear one another's burdens and so fulfil the *law of Christ*' (Galatians 6²), is the heartbeat of Christian worship as well as of faith. The *lex orandi* is not of itself the *lex credendi*. Both are subject to the law of Christ.[1]

For the neighbour *diakonia* embodies a love that in *leitourgia* is received as God's love. Sharing completely in the mysterious love of God, it does not calculate whether the neighbour merits love. The basic question of *diakonia* is not whether the neighbour needs my love, but whether I am capable of sharing God's love.

With the discovery of the priesthood of all believers in the reformation of the sixteenth century new vistas for understanding the Christian life opened up. In the gradual discovery of the diaconate of all believers the reformation continued.[2] While the seventeenth century was still very much concerned with consolidating the reform of the Church in systems of orthodoxy, the eighteenth century began to interpret the reformation in new experiments of Christian living. Since then *diakonia* as a core concept of the Christian faith slowly moved across the consciousness-threshold of the Church.

Diakonia in Education

'I teach them what I know. I make them rehearse their geography, their history of nature. And while I show them how to knit I tell them Bible stories.[3] In these words Louise Scheppler (1763–1837) summarized her effort in the *poêles à tricoter*, the 'knitting-stoves' of the Ban-de-la-Roche. She was a maid in a manse, but also a born teacher. Gathering children around living-room

---

p. 12 (referred to as 'GD' hereinafter). cf. Arthur Rich, 'Diakonie und Sozialstaat' in *CD*, p. 36; W. Schneemelcher, 'Der diakonische Dienst in der alten Kirche' in Herbert Krimm (ed.), *Das diakonische Amt der Kirche* (Stuttgart, 1953), pp. 60f. (the book edited by Krimm referred to as '*DAK*' hereinafter). A beautiful expression of the *wholeness* of *diakonia* is related by J. C. van Dongen, 'Die Diakonie in der reformierten Kirche der Niederlande' in Herbert Krimm (ed.), *Das Diakonische Amt der Kirche im ökumenischen Bereich* (Stuttgart, 1960), p. 108. Ottho Gerhard Heldring, the pioneer of home missions in Holland, had a well dug for the poor population of a village when he read the story of the Samaritan woman (John 4): Christ can also quench another thirst! (The book edited by Krimm will be referred to as '*DiÖB*' hereinafter.)

[1] For a more detailed examination of the relationship of worship and *diakonia* see my article, 'The Montreal "Crisis" of Faith and Order', *Theology and Life*, vol. 6, No. 4, 1963, pp. 314ff.

[2] Johann Hinrich Wichern's 'Gutachten, die Diakonie und den Diakonat betreffend' in *Gesammelte Schriften* (Hamburg, 1902), vol. III, pp. 821–99, of 1856, is a milestone in this development. See also J. C. van Dongen, op. cit., p. 118.

[3] Octavie de Berckheim, *Souvenirs d'Alsace* (Neuchatel and Paris, 1889), p. 121.

stoves, she was one of the first kindergarten teachers.[1] Behind her work stands the struggle of Jean-Frédéric Oberlin (1740–1826) to educate the people of his parish, that is, to lead them out of ignorance and poverty into a better day.[2] In 1767, when Oberlin arrived in the Vosges mountain village of Waldersbach, some forty miles south-west of Strassburg, most of his parishoners barely eked out a living. They spoke patois, a dialect neither French nor German, which isolated them even more in their mountain valleys.[3] Oberlin realized that they could not be effectively helped by alms from the outside. They had to be able to stand on their own feet. Thus he began a great educational effort,[4] teaching them how to improve their soil,[5] how to raise better vegetables and build roads and bridges.[6] Central to his effort was the creation of schools. The so-called *poêles à tricoter* were the most elementary level. The education effort, however, was only part of the overall pastoral care of Oberlin. It was in terms of his comprehensive *diakonia* that he became influential in the Church.[7]

Oberlin began his work in an age that was awakening to the need for education. In the sixteenth and seventeenth centuries in Europe hordes of beggars were roaming the countryside. The main Christian reaction had been almsgiving. In 1701 appeared a tract which is characteristic of the new approach of the eighteenth century: August Hermann Francke's *Segensvolle Fusstapfen des noch lebenden und waltenden, liebreichen und getreuen Gottes*.[8] Francke (1663–1727) here describes the beginning of his educational effort with orphans and the children of the poor which grew into the so-called Franckesche Anstalten, leading from elementary school to college. A publishing house and a pharmacy were soon added. Both enterprises prospered and contributed major funds to the educational projects. At the time of Francke's death altogether 2,500 students

[1] Erich Psczolla, *Louise Scheppler: Mitarbeiterin Oberlins* (Witten, 1963), p. 44, claims that Louise Scheppler rejected the idea that she founded a kindergarten. See also René Voeltzel, *Louise Scheppler et les 'Petites Ecoles' du Ban-de-la-Roche* (Taizé, 1963), p. 20; for post-Oberlin developments Martha Buch, 'Oberlin und Fröbel', *Jahrbuch der Elsass-Lothringischen wissenschaftlichen Gesellschaft*, vol. VI, 1933, pp. 121–43.

[2] Henri Ochsenbein, 'Die diakönische Tätigkeit der protestantischen Kirche in Frankreich' in *DiÖB*, p. 72, calls Oberlin an 'exemplary deacon'. Alfons Rosenberg, *Der Christ und die Erde: Oberlin und der Aufbruch zur Gemeinschaft der Liebe* (Olten and Freiburg, 1953), p. 283, speaks of Oberlin as 'a deacon of Christ'.

[3] It was by no means a completely impoverished language. See Jeremie Jacques Oberlin, *Essai sur le patois lorrain des environs du comté du Ban de la Roche* (Strasbourg, 1775), pp. 120ff.

[4] Jean Paul Benoit, *J. F. Oberlin: pasteur d'hommes* (Strasbourg, 1955), p. 168, speaks of Oberlin as 'pédagogue avant tout'. In Camille Leenhardt, *La vie de J. F. Oberlin* (Paris and Nancy, 1911), pp. 33ff., the educational effort of Oberlin is considered first.

[5] Karl Eduard Boch, *Das Steintal im Elsass: Eine geschichtliche Studie über die ehemalige Herrschaft Stein und deren Herren, sowie über die Entwicklung des gesamten Wirtschafts- und Geisteslebens im Steintal* (Strasbourg, 1914), p. 234.

[6] Oberlin centred his *diakonia* in the improvement of his parish and rejected the suggestion that he build a diakonic institution. See Ernst Schering, *J. F. Oberlin: Sternetunde der Sozialpädagogik* (Bielefeld, 1959), pp. 40, 46, 50.

[7] See Johann Hinrich Wichern, *Die innere Mission der deutschen evangelischen Kirche* (Hamburg, 1849), pp. 143, 216.

[8] Translated into English by Anton Wilhelm Böhme under the title *Pietas Hallensis; or, an abstract of the marvellous footsteps of divine providence* (2nd ed., 1707). See Erich Beyreuther, *August Hermann Francke* (Marburg, 1961), p. 199.

and personnel were associated with his schools. The responsibility for educating the poor had dawned on him as they came to the door of his manse to beg. 'For some time I had bread distributed to them in front of the door. But soon I thought that this was a welcome opportunity to help the poor people in their souls through the Word of God.'[1] Francke catechized them for about fifteen minutes. Seeing the need to instruct the children more extensively, he opened a school.

Francke already realized that poverty could not be overcome by almsgiving. It was also not a matter of merely getting the poor off the street.[2] That had been attempted before in many quarters.[3] The time had come to try something new.[4] Man had to be equipped with knowledge. Understanding himself and his environment better, he could throw off the shackles of poverty. Elementary education as introduced by Francke quickly spread throughout Germany; princes and governments assumed responsibility.[5] With one difference: education as public education was no longer tied to conversion![6]

The Emerging 'Public Welfare' Concern

Pietism, of which Francke was an outstanding representative, had an individualistic bent. Ironically, although aware of the failure of mere almsgiving, it generally continued it in a somewhat sublimated form. Instead of individuals, now a few institutions were supported by a number of like-minded Christians. Pietism was unable to awaken the Church as a whole to the needs of society, not to speak of providing leadership.[7] Soon the enlightenment took its place as a formative influence.

As 'the exodus of reason from its self-inflicted captivity' (Kant) the enlightenment continued to stress education as the best means to improve the human condition. But those who believed in the enlightenment no longer based their ideals on the Christian faith. Man had become his own measure. Charity work now found two different expressions, one rooted in man's own capacities and

---

[1] *Wahre und umständliche Nachricht von dem Waisen-hause, und übrigen Anstalten zu Glaucha vor Halle* (3rd ed., 1709), p. 2.

[2] As to what had been done before Francke, see, for example, Willi Grün, *Speners soziale Leistungen und Gedanken. Ein Beitrag zur Geschichte des Armenwesens und des kirchlichen Pietismus in Frankfurt a.M. und in Brandenburg-Preussen* (Würzburg, 1934).

[3] Francke had been especially impressed by what had been done in Dutch institutions. See Gerhard Uhlhorn, *Die christliche Liebestätigkeit* (Moers, 1959), pp. 608ff. (reprint of second edition; referred to as *Uhlhorn* hereinafter).

[4] With special reference to the tons of gold expended on the poorhouses in Holland Francke states that the Halle *Anstalten* are a much greater and more important work. See August Hermann Francke, *Der Grosse Aufsatz* (Otto Podczeck (ed.), Berlin, 1962), p. 41. Francke's self-confidence seems to be rooted in his conviction that *diakonia* in education can accomplish what mere almsgiving never could.

[5] H. Heppe, *Geschichte des deutschen Volksschulwesens* (Gotha, 1858), vol. I, p. 53.

[6] cf. Herbert Krimm, 'Diakonie' in *Evangelisches Soziallexikon* (Stuttgart, 1954), p. 224: In Pietism 'education and conversion were inseparable'.

[7] One must keep in mind, however, the long-range effect of Pietism: 'Historical research sees in Puritanism the beginning of capitalism, in German Pietism the beginning of socialism.' Erich Beyreuther, *GD*, p. 41.

the other in Christianity.¹ The feeling of a specific community responsibility for the sick, the poor, etc., emerged.² The Church could still contribute benevolence funds. But leadership was not expected of it.

Even though communities began to take matters into their own hands, the earth did not become a paradise. Political and economic conditions kept the majority of the people poor. Wars and famines followed each other. In the famine of 1772–3 there were 150,000 dead in Kursachsen alone. Man had not learned as yet effectively to control his societal well-being. In the last part of the eighteenth century begging was again on the increase. In Cologne one counted 10,000 beggars among a population of 40,000. The intelligentsia found plenty of opportunities for discussing proper measures to improve the conditions of the poor. Programmes and ideals, however, were not enough to wipe poverty off the face of the earth.³

Prefigurations of Later Developments

The care of the sick remained negligible in large parts of Europe in the eighteenth century. Even in a city like Hamburg, a community that prided itself in an awakened social consicence, two hospital patients still had to share the same bed. Untrained attendants reluctantly performed the necessary chores. This does not mean that a better approach had not been as yet discovered. But men were still unable to cope with the vast needs of their day on a broad scale.

Already in the seventeenth century France's Vincent de Paul (1581–1660) in his *filles de la charité* had taken a big step towards a more thorough care for the sick. In the Middle Ages, although occasionally women had worked in this field, the male orders had been predominant. The Antonites are an example. Vincent de Paul gave the woman an independent place. No cloistered nuns, the *filles de la charité* were free to respond to need wherever it was found.⁴ As early as 1652 three members went to Poland. But it was not before the beginning of the nineteenth century that they extended their work to Germany.⁵ Two or three decades later the Protestant deaconess appeared on the scene.

Another example of the slow process in which the Church became conscious of *diakonia* is the diaconic congregation. Jean-Frédéric Oberlin in the Ban-de-la-Roche came as close as any single individual in the eighteenth century to realizing local *diakonia*. Rejecting the suggestion of building an institution, a poorhouse or an orphanage, he spent his energies on the socio-economic improvement of his parishioners as well as on their spiritual and intellectual growth. All efforts, such as the schools, the agricultural societies, and a type of

---

[1] *Uhlhorn*, p. 674.
[2] Gerhard Noske, 'Geschichtliche Voraussetzungen der heutigen Diakonie' in *Heutige Diakonie der evangelischen Kirche* (Berlin, 1956), p. 10.
[3] *Uhlhorn*, pp. 676ff.
[4] For specific characteristics see Léonce Celier, *Les Filles de la Charité* (1929), pp. 115ff.
[5] *1660–1960 Monsieur Vincent vit encore. Sa survie par ses Filles de la Charité au long des siècles* (Paris, 1960), p. 27.

bank where his parishioners could loan money, contributed to the growth of a diaconic congregation.[1] Only in the twentieth century, however, was the significance of the diaconic congregation more widely appreciated.

From Diakonia in Education to Diakonia in Social Service

An increase in knowledge meant an increase in man's capacity to master his environment. Education led to industrialization. One can often observe how the one directly works into the hands of the other. Upon Oberlin's initiative a Swiss entreprenneur, Jean-Luc Le Grand (1755–1825), built a factory in the Ban-de-la-Roche. Occasionally even the idea of founding a 'Christian industry' was promoted. Two men, Philipp Matthäus Hahn (1739–90) and Gustav Albert Werner (1809–87), built factories in Germany on the principle of Christian co-operation between employer and employee. But their efforts stood outside the main current of the times. Both Church and State in the eighteenth century had been unable to solve the problem of poverty. Inexorably the poor of the eighteenth became the proletariat of the nineteenth century. The victims of the anonymous forces creating the modern masses presented a new challenge for *diakonia*.

Industrialization on a large scale with its ensuing social blight hit England first. Robert Owen (1771–1858), co-owner of a cotton mill and thoroughly acquainted with the social conditions of the people, already in the early nineteenth century outlined a broad programme of social reform.[2] His influence on the 1819 labour legislation, the First Factory Act, was considerable.[3]

Besides the new problems created by industrialization society still faced the old ones carried along from the past. Already before the turn of the century the English philanthropist John Howard (1726–90) had visited European prisons and hospitals and exposed the abysmally poor conditions in widely read reports.[4] It was especially in the area of concern for prisons that Elizabeth Fry (1780–

---

[1] Oberlin was influenced by the Moravians, who began to establish themselves in the Alsace as early as 1735. (For Moravian beginnings in the Alsace see G. Koch, 'Le rayonnement de la piété morave en Alsace' in *Le messager evangelique*, No. 9, March 1, 1964, p. 5). By way of the Moravians, Oberlin was linked to the educational effort of the Halle *Anstalten*, whose product Zinzendorf was. In Zinzendorf *diakonia* in education expanded into ecumenical *diakonia*. Important attempts at ecumenical *diakonia* are already found in August Hermann Francke. See Erich Beyreuther, 'Ökumenische Diakonie im deutschen Protestantismus bis zum Beginn des 19. Jahrhunderts' in Christian Berg (ed.), *Ökumenische Diakonie* (Berlin, 1959), pp. 43ff. If space would permit it would be important to describe Zinzendorf's significance for *diakonia* more fully. We call attention to Heinz Renkewitz, 'Der Diakonische Gedanke im Zeitalter des Pietismus' in *DAK*, especially the section, 'Die diakonisch handelnde Gemeinde: Zinzendorf und die Brüdergemeine', pp. 282ff.

[2] Robert Owen, *A New View of Society and Other Writings* (London and Toronto, 1927), p. XII.

[3] When in 1818 Owen made a trip to France and other European countries he also paid a visit to Oberlin. See Helene Simon, *Robert Owen: Sein Leben und seine Bedeutung für die Gegenwart* (Jena, 1905), p. 144.

[4] Translations soon began to appear: John Howard, *État des prisons, des hôpitaux et des maisons de force* (Paris, 1788); John Howard, *Nachrichten von den vorzüglichsten Kranken und Pesthäusern in Europa* (Leipzig, 1791).

1845) made her impact. Wichern called her 'a queen in the realm of mercy'.[1] While for some time in England great personalities continued to tackle the problems in a more individualistic manner,[2] the Germans began to launch concerted *diakonia* efforts—stimulated by the English pioneers.[3]

The New Deacon

August Hermann Francke could still afford to wait for the poor to knock at his door. Johann Hinrich Wichern (1808–81), some hundred years later, in the slums of Hamburg, sought out the outcast child. In 1833 he founded in Hamburg the 'Rauhe Haus', a home for vagrant boys in connexion with a Sunday School enterprise brought into being under English influence.[4] Most of these boys had been running around in rags tied together with strings. Wichern even found children of a drunk who were drunk, too. Those he gathered he united in family-type groups of twelve to fourteen under the care of a 'Bruder', an older brother, and educated them, combining theoretical with practical concerns, shoemaking, tailoring, baking, etc.

With Wichern's 'Bruder' a new type of deacon originated. In 1839 Wichern founded a 'Bruderhaus', an educational institution for deacons who would go into slums, jails, and other places where most pastors would not go and perhaps could not go without neglecting what they considered their foremost duties.[5] The general outlook of the Church had not been geared to the social needs of the people. Even towards the end of the nineteenth century a professor for practical theology at the University of Berlin still advised his students not to make any calls. Too close a contact with the people would make the mantle of the prophet fall off their shoulders.[6]

In order to be fair one must recall the circumstances under which many pastors in Europe were working. At a time when Cincinnati, Ohio, was as large as Hamburg it counted 144 churches and chapels, while Hamburg had about a dozen.[7] At the same time the largest congregation in Berlin consisted of 89,000 'souls' shepherded by five pastors. Wichern's deacons were supposed to bring change.

The New Deaconess

The very year Wichern founded the 'Rauhe Haus' in Hamburg, in 1833, the

[1] Johann Hinrich Wichern, *Die Behandlung der Verbrecher in den Gefängnissen und der entlassenen Sträflinge* (Hamburg, 1853), p. 12.

[2] For a review of English *diakonia* discussions see Paul Philippi, *Christozentrische Diakonie* (Stuttgart, 1963), pp. 22ff. As key work is cited J. S. Howson, *Deaconesses; or the official helps of women in parochial work and in charitable institutions* (London, 1862).

[3] Johann Hinrich Wichern, *Die innere Mission der deutschen evangelischen Kirche*, p. 25.

[4] *Uhlhorn*, p. 721. As regards English influence see also pp. 731ff., 739ff., 755. Contacts between English and German Protestantism go back much farther. See Erich Beyreuther, *August Hermann Francke und die Anfänge der ökumenischen Bewegung* (Leipzig, 1957), p. 122.

[5] As regards Wichern's hesitation to call the 'brothers' deacons see Ernst Schering, *Erneuerung der Diakonie in einer veränderten Welt* (Bielefeld, 1958), pp. 66f. (referred to as '*ED*' hereinafter).

[6] Günther Dehn, 'Adolf Stöcker', *Zwischen den Zeiten*, No. 8, 1924, p. 26.

[7] J. Wichern, *Das Rauhe Haus und die Arbeitsfelder des Rauhen Hauses* (Hamburg, 1833), p. 90.

first dismissed female prisoner entered the asylum of Theodor Fliedner (1800–64) at Kaiserswerth am Rhein. Fliedner was pastor of a small struggling 200-member congregation.[1] In 1835 he organized a knitting school in order to give the unwanted woman, just dismissed from prison, something to do. In 1836 a kindergarten followed. The same year the school for female nurses was founded.

While Wichern's enterprise had brought forth the new deacon, Fliedner's produced the new deaconess.[2] In Fliedner's day the abominable conditions of the German hospitals had hardly improved over the eighteenth century. Usually two patients still had to share the same bed. If one patient died after 10 p.m., the other had to lie next to him until morning.[3] Understandably one preferred to be sick at home. Only the poor and lonely, those for whom no one could care at home, and occasionally journeymen were forced to choose these places of misery. Now Fliedner's deaconesses took over.[4] A new type of care for the sick began in Protestantism.[5]

There is no need to recount the well-known story of the deaconesses. Suffice it to say that their work of love benefited also specific types of sick, such as the epileptics. In the care for the epileptics Friedrich von Bodelschwingh's (1831–1910) Bethel (near Bielefeld in Westphalia) began to play an outstanding role.[6] Von Bodelschwingh himself injected into the *diakonia* that characterized the nineteenth century a special quality. Not confining himself to the service for the sick, he became involved in politics in order to realize his social reform programmes. Making use of the existing political structures he had himself elected a representative of the Prussian 'Landtag'.[7]

[1] Fliedner collected money for his charge in Holland and England. See Theodor Fliedner, *Collektenreise nach Holland und England, nebst einer ausführlichen Darstellung des Kirchen-, Schul-, Armen- und Gefängniswesens beider Länder* (Essen, 1831), vol. I, pp. 14ff.

[2] It was not completely without precedent for Fliedner. On his trip to Holland he had discovered deaconesses among the Mennonites, women who in the Mennonite congregations were responsible for the care of the poor. Fliedner refers to their work as an institution of primitive Christianity which ought to be imitated. Theodor Fliedner, ibid., pp. 150ff. Another influence on Fliedner was an essay by the Protestant minister of Bislich bei Wesel, Friedrich Klönne, who discusses the possibility of reviving the work of the primitive Christian deaconess (published in Leipzig in 1820).

[3] *Uhlhorn*, p. 743.

[4] Biselotte Katscher, *Geschichte der Krankenpflage* (Berlin, n.d.), pp. 53–73. It is noteworthy that Florence Nightingale received training in Kaiserswerth. A little of what Fliedner had received in England he could now return.

[5] For a survey of Roman Catholic care for the poor, the sick, etc., in modern times see Joseph A. Fischer, 'Die katholische Caritas in der Neuzeit' in *DAK*, pp. 388–432. Fliedner's relationship to Roman Catholic models is briefly examined in Theodor Schäfer, *Die Geschichte der weiblichen Diakonie* (Stuttgart, 1887), pp. 299f., and *Uhlhorn*, p. 731. Uhlhorn denies that Fliedner imitated the Roman Catholic orders of nursing. But for the general development of the deaconess idea he feels that both the apostolic deaconess as well as the Roman Catholic orders of nursing were influential. W. Löhe wrote in 1860: 'We must confess that the deaconess of the 19th century is not the . . . local church deaconess, but a Protestant copy of the Roman Catholic sister of mercy.' Quoted in Friedrich Thiele, *Diakonissenhäuser im Umbruch der Zeit* (Stuttgart, 1963), p. 75.

[6] In 1872 Bodelschwingh took over the leadership of two institutions, a home for epileptics and a home for deaconesses, which grew into the Bethel *Anstalten*. Martin Gerhard, *Friedrich von Bodelschwingh* (Bethel, 1952), p. 13.

[7] ibid., pp. 552ff.

The Limits of Diakonia in Social Service

Wichern expected the Church to be concerned with the 'whole' man, to save the people bodily as well as spiritually. He formulated the task as *innere Mission*, at type of 'home mission' directed toward the Church itself, an external and internal renewal of the German people who nominally at least were Christians.[1] He recognized the guilt of the bourgeoisie for the social dilemma and understood the proletarian plight, 'but the new type of the proletarian as *socio-political element* who has nothing in common with the "naturally" poor of all times did not enter his field of decision'.[2] It was detrimental to his intention that he aligned himself with the State when in 1857 he became 'Oberkirchenrat', an appointee of the Prussian church government.

Since the *innere Mission* stopped where for the rising proletariat the demands only began, the movement lost contact with the working class.[3] Too much alignment with the State meant too little critical distance to those responsible for the social dilemma. Since practice did not conform to theory in Wichern,[4] his revolutionary discovery that individual charity (*Liebestätigkeit*) had to be broadened to a *diakonia* wrestling with the social structure had no effect on society. Wichern was afraid of revolutionary change and practically also took the attitude that 'all revolutions are against the kingdom of God'.[5] The fact that he had been a student of Schleiermacher might explain part of his inability to attain a more radical understanding of the relationship of Christianity and culture.[6]

The limits of *diakonia* in social service of nineteenth-century Protestant Germany were especially revealed by two men, Adolf Stoecker (1835–1909) and Friedrich Naumann (1860–1919). Stoecker, since 1874 'Hofprediger' in Berlin (the 'personal preacher' of the Kaiser), realized that Wichern's *innere Mission* offered no solution to the tough social problems.[7] He began to approach it in political terms and founded the Christian-Social Worker's Party. It failed miserably, however. To add insult to injury, the Kaiser dismissed the political preacher. Later in a famous telegram he declared: 'Stoecker is finished. Christian-Social is nonsense.'[8]

---

[1] It would be wrong to claim that Wichern created the *innere Mission*. Uhlhorn sees Wichern's significance in the fact that Wichern crystallized the already existing concerns: 'He did not call the *innere Mission* into life. It was there before.' *Uhlhorn*, p. 728. Wichern himself saw it that way: 'The totality of these hidden, gradually appearing Christian efforts to save—this is for us the *innere Mission*.' Johann Hinrich Wichern, *Die innere Mission der deutschen evangelischen Kirche* (Hamburg, 1849), p. 3. Or more specifically: the *innere Mission* is "the total work of that love . . . which wants to renew . . . the masses of Christendom internally as well as externally." p. 4. For a critical evaluation of the concept *innere Mission* see *Uhlhorn*, p. 726.

[2] Karl Kupisch, *Kirche und soziale Frage im 19. Jahrhundert* (Zürich, 1963), p. 17.

[3] ibid., pp. 18ff.

[4] cf. the examination of Wichern's theory in Heinz-Dietrich Wendland, *Der Begriff Christlich-sozial* (Köln and Opladen, 1962), pp. 15ff.

[5] A famous word of Gottfried Menken, quoted in Emmanuel Hirsch, *Geschichte der neuern evangelischen Theologie* (Gütersloh, 1954), vol. V, p. 96.

[6] *Uhlhorn*, p. 721.

[7] Karl Kupisch, *Zwischen Idealismus und Massendemokratie: Eine Geschichte der evangelischen Kirche in Deutschland von 1815–1945* (Berlin, 1955), p. 103.

[8] ibid., p. 109.

The fact that Naumann founded a party without the word 'Christian'[1] in its name did not keep it from failing likewise. Naumann realized that Christian-social politics was impossible. Jesus offered no basis for socio-political theory.

Both Stoecker and Naumann keenly saw the shortcomings of *diakonia* limited to social service. In a world of power struggle the Christian, if he wanted to get involved in the world, would also have to get involved in the power struggle. *Diakonia* in politics, 'political *diakonia*',[2] beyond *diakonia* in mere social service was inescapable. But since a political party did not seem a workable expression of *diakonia* in politics,[3] what would be a more effective form? Was it not basically a matter of finding a form that would genuinely express the specific quality of *diakonia*? Stoecker and Naumann knew of no answer.

The Emerging Welfare State

While in Europe the 'professional' deacon and deaconess proved only partial answers to pressing social needs, they did give the European discussion on *diakonia* in the last hundred years its peculiar slant.[4] Some areas of the world did not develop a marked need for professionalized *diakonia*. The United States are the most striking example. The four deaconesses Fliedner personally brought to the Lutherans of Pittsburgh in 1849 were unable to enamour American women with the idea.[5] It was not before 1884, when seven deaconesses from Iserlohn (Westphalia) arrived in Philadelphia, that the deaconess became a more attractive professional option among the American Lutherans. Later the Evangelical Synod, the Episcopalians, and the Methodists also introduced deaconesses. But the overall situation did not call for professional *diakonia*. Fliedner's complaint, more than a decade and a half after he had imported the first deaconesses, that no American woman had joined their ranks needs no reading between the lines to sense the American climate in matters of *diakonia*: 'O ye North American maidens and widows with your many Dorcas societies for clothing the poor, etc., why do you neglect the care of the sick? In ten thousands of his brothers and sisters the Saviour calls you not only with the words, "I was naked", but also with, "I was sick, did you visit me?"'[6]

It has been observed that the term *diakonia* is only today becoming more

---

[1] Günther Dehn, op. cit., p. 43: 'Naumann was able to do the liberating deed of giving up the predicate "Christian" as description of his endeavors.'

[2] Helmuth Schreiner speaks of the 'political *diakonia*' of Stoecker, 'Wichern, Löhe und Stoecker', in *DAK*, p. 348.

[3] For the problems connected with the use of the phrase 'political *diakonia*'—a phrase we have generally tried to avoid—see reference of footnote 12, p. 148.

[4] The work of the deacons and deaconesses was by no means accepted universally. For an early critique see Agénor de Gasparin, *Des corporations monastique au sein du protestantism* (Paris, 1855), Vol. II, pp. 136ff. The author objects to the inroads of the monastic spirit in Protestantism. The problems and reservations have not become less within the last hundred years. See, for example, Heinrich Leich, *Sterbende Hutterhaus-Diakonie?* (Bielefeld, 1956) and Friedrich Thiele, *Diakonissenhäuser im Umbruch der Zeit* (Stuttgart, 1963).

[5] Theodor Fliedner, *Nachricht über das Diakonissen-Werk in der christlichen Kirche, alter und neuer Zeit* (Kaiserswerth, 1856), p. 21.

[6] ibid.

current in America, signalizing a more Church-oriented interpretation of the social responsibility of the Christian.[1] Although *diakonia* did not become as professionalized in America as in Europe, the churches engaged in work that brought similar results. When in 1955 the National Council of Churches made a first national survey of the *diakonia* efforts in the churches co-operating in the Council it counted 2,783 health and welfare institutions. Of the number 18 per cent were homes for old people, 14 per cent neighbourhood centres, and 10 per cent establishments for children.[2] It is important to note in this context that of the total number of hospitals in the United States only one-sixteenth are Protestant whereas one-eighth are Roman Catholic.

For the development of *diakonia* in the United States the sharp separation of Church and State has been beneficial. It kept Church members from acting in terms of benevolence only. It was their obligation as citizens to be politically responsible for the marginal figures of life.[3] In the face of an increasingly brutal industralization the obligation was too often forgotten. But the Social Gospel, most illuminatingly embodied in the figure of Walter Rauschenbusch (1861–1918), was characterized by its effective nurture of the social responsibility of the Christian as a citizen in an industrial society at least in some denominations.

One can easily understand why the United States as a whole did not know of a marked development from *diakonia* in education via *diakonia* in social service to a more political *diakonia*. A growing frontier nation at one and the same time faced a plurality of needs. Many of the American pioneer colleges were immediate expressions of *diakonia* in education. Simultaneously the new communities had to be structured socially and politically. One must also keep in mind that in the vast unpopulated spaces of the New World there were always new opportunities, so that the social needs were seldom as pressing as in Europe. Wherever such needs did make themselves felt the multiplicity of the denominations worked against a common Christian approach. When in the thirties the Great Depression radically confronted the American for the first time with the modern social and political dilemmas he built the welfare state, guided by the democratic vision. The economic homogenization of the West since World War II is perhaps the main reason for the emergence of the welfare state as ideal, if not as reality, in most parts of our hemisphere.

Because of the different socio-economic development Christian thought in the United States did not regard *diakonia* as a master-image. What Christians did not feel called upon to do externally in terms of Social Action they sought to manage internally under the guidance of the stewardship idea.[4] In view of the

---

[1] E. Theodore Bachmann, 'Diakonie in den Vereinigten Staaten' in *DiÖB*, p. 171.
[2] ibid., p. 210. For a bibliography on *diakonia* in the United States see pp. 218f.
[3] Johann Hinrich Wichern, *Die Behandlung der Verbrecher und der entlassenen Sträflinge*, p. 10: American developments already early in the nineteenth century could serve as models for amelioration of conditions in Europe. Work in Boston influenced the founding of the rheinisch-westfälische Gefängnisgesellschaft.
[4] See Martin O. Dietrich, 'Stewardship' in *DAK*, pp. 433–42. Little has as yet been done in serious theological comparison of *stewardship* and *diakonia*. The equation stewardship = *diakonia*

secularization of many of the activities of the Church the desire recently has been expressed to reintroduce the challenge of genuine *diakonia*.[1]

Diakonia in Politics

The complex power structures developed by the State to provide for education[2] and social security[3] need constant surveillance and correction lest they become ends in themselves. In what form can *diakonia* share in this task? A recent test for finding an answer has been the struggle for Civil Rights in the United States.

One is tempted to list non-violence, the technique of the sit-ins, as the most modern expression of *diakonia* in the political realm. But it is not a direct expression of reconciling love.[4] Going beyond direct nonviolent action,[5] *diakonia* in politics can attempt, however, to transform the societal structure. What is possible was shown by Dr Eugene C. Blake when on 24 July 1963 he appeared with Rabbi Irving Blank and Father John Cronin before the Committee on the Judiciary of the House of Representatives. Introducing his testimony, he said: 'Mr Chairman and members of the Committee, my name is Dr Eugene C. Blake. Accompanying me are Rabbi Irving Blank and Father John Cronin. It is an unprecedented and indeed historic event that I speak for the social action and racial action departments of the National Council of Churches, the National Catholic Welfare Conference and the Synagogue Council of America.'[6] After

---

is not as simple as some recent literature on the subject would have us believe. There are good reasons for seeing the term stewardship without a halo. cf. Gibson Winter, *The New Creation as Metropolis* (New York, 1963), p. 97: 'Terms such as "vocation" or "stewardship" avoid . . . basic questions. In fact, stewardship is little more than a fundraising "gimmick" in most churches.' One should read Dietrich's article in the light of Winter's critical remarks. Hans Christoph von Hase, 'Die Wiederentdeckung der dienenden Gemeinde' in *Diakonie der Gemeinde* (Stuttgart, 1961), p. 41, seems to sense the problem when he stresses that the diakonic aspect of stewardship as yet has been too little tested (referred to as '*DG, Vol. I*' hereinafter).

[1] E. Theodore Bachmann, op. cit., p. 211.

[2] Sheldon L. Rahn, 'Neue Formen des Dienstes' in *Diakonie als ökumenische Aufgabe II* (Berlin, 1963), p. 45: 'The time is past in which it was necessary for the church to be a pioneer, to organize most of the social, health and educational services . . .' (the symposium referred to as '*Diakonie II*' hereinafter).

[3] Uhlhorn could already claim that the views about the task of the State had completely changed since the middle of the nineteenth century: 'Until then one acted according to the principle *il mondo va da se* (the world runs by itself), now one cannot assign enough tasks to the state. . . . The care for the lower classes is part of it.' *Uhlhorn*, p. 759. While in retrospect it appears that the State at the time did not assume enough responsibility or was not responsible in the right way, the change in attitude since the beginning of the eighteenth century is obvious.

[4] cf. William Robert Miller, *Nonviolence: A Christian Interpretation* (New York, 1964), p. 177: 'Nonviolence . . . is not love; nor is it a method for resolving conflict. It is a way of waging social conflict that is compatible with love. It does a minimum of damage and holds the door open to creative, constructive possibilities. But it has no intrinsic power to heal and to build anew. For this we must look beyond nonviolence to active, agapaic love and reconciliation.'

[5] If one wishes to speak of the nonviolence of Jesus one first must qualify. There are different motives of nonviolence. Each motive determines a specific technique. cf. André Troomé, *Jésus-Christ et la révolution non violente* (Geneve, 1961), pp. 192, 197.

[6] 'Testimony on Civil Rights Legislation Presented to Committee on Judiciary, House of Representatives', *Religion and Labor*, vol. VII, Nos. 2-4, October-December 1963, p. 1.

enumerating the various denominations and religious organizations represented by the three bodies, Dr Blake outlined the theological and social factors calling for speedy enactment of just legislation.

Not all such action will immediately reach the public limelight, and yet will be *diakonia* in the political realm. An example is Fritz von Bodelschwingh's (Friedrich von Bodelschwingh's son) successful intervention for epileptics who had been condemned to euthanasia by measures of the Third Reich. Von Bodelschwingh was able to reach Hitler's personal physician, Dr Brandt. No one else in Germany got through to the one truly responsible 'and encountered him directly in a battle with his soul. Even in his final words at the Nürnberg trials before his execution Dr Brandt, Hitler's personal physician, remembered: only one man had tried to stop him, Pastor von Bodelschwingh.'[1] Von Bodelschwingh succeeded. Thirty thousand were saved from mercy killing. The whole programme was called off.

Whether *diakonia* in the political realm immediately reaches the public limelight or not, it always leads to a clear confrontation of State and Church. When during World War II the Netherlands were occupied by Germany the deacons of the Dutch Reformed Church assumed the care for the politically persecuted, supplying food and providing secret refuge. Realizing what was happening, the Germans decreed that the elective office of the deacon should be eliminated. The Reformed Synod on 17 July 1941 resolved: 'Whoever touches the diaconate interferes with what Christ has ordained as the task of the Church. He touches the cult of the Church.'[2] Whoever lays hands on *diakonia* lays hands on worship! The Germans backed down. In taking *diakonia* seriously in a concrete political situation the Church begins to grasp her very being.

The Theological Rediscovery of Diakonia

In commenting on the resolution of the Dutch Reformed Synod of 17 July 1941, Herbert Krimm observes that perhaps not all Reformed theologians in the Netherlands had been conscious before of the close relationship between *diakonia* and *leitourgia*.[3] It is fair to say that few theologians also outside of Holland were aware of the issue. A remarkable change has taken place within the last two decades.

One concrete example:[4] on 6 November 1961, at the celebration of the seventy-fifth anniversary of the Swiss institution for epileptics in Zürich, three theologians of note lectured in the presence of 150 ministers and fellow theologians on the nature and task of *diakonia* 'in the very hall in which otherwise the

[1] Erich Beyreuther, *GD*, pp. 203f.
[2] Herbert Krimm, 'Diakonie als Gestaltwerdung der Kirche' in *CD*, p. 62. cf. J. C. van Dongen, op. cit., pp. 112f.
[3] Herbert Krimm, ibid.
[4] Another important example is the *Diakoniewissenschaftliche Institut* at the University of Heidelberg. See Paul Philippi, 'Diakonie als Wissenschaft?' in Gerhard Noske (ed.), *Heutige Diakonie der evangelischen Kirche* (Berlin, 1956), pp. 63–68; Herbert Krimm, 'Akademischer Nachwuchs für die Diakonie' in *Jahrbuch der Inneren Mission und des Hilfswerks der Evangelischne Kirche in Deutschland* (Stuttgart, 1964), pp. 29–39.

male epileptics eat their meals and on Sundays the entire congregation of the institution gathers for worship. Especially for those among the listeners who were representatives of the *diakonia* work of the Church it was like early dew in a dry summer. For here it happened that three distinguished representatives of theological scholarship allotted to *diakonia* an essential place within the Church.'[1]

Theology is beginning to learn that the basic structure of the Church is diaconic. Proclamation, pastoral care, Christian education, Church government and administration, stewardship and charity work have diaconic character.[2] The language used in the ecumenical church to express this understanding may differ, the principal witness is the same.[3] This is due to at least two factors: the growing similarity of economic and cultural structures in every continent[4] and the breadth of the ecumenical conversation.[5]

Recent thinking on *diakonia* centres its understanding of the diaconic character of the Church on Jesus as *the* deacon. Thus a 'christocentric *diakonia*' is being developed.[6] In terms of the Protestant principle one author has expressed it in the words: *sola gratia, sola fide, solus Christus, sola Christi diakonia*.[7] The *sola Christi diakonia* implies that man's needs are ultimately met only by God's own intercession for man in Christ. Since the full manifestation of God's intercession still lies in the future, *diakonia* is directed toward the coming of God's kingdom. In *leitourgia* the Christian time and again is confronted with the eschatological dimension of his existence. Separated from *leitourgia*, *diakonia* would be the same as secular welfare work.[8]

Problems of definition are inevitable of which a few seem especially pressing: the relationship between the diaconic task of the Church as a whole and the specific diaconic office,[9] the difference between political *diakonia* and a more comprehensive societal *diakonia*,[10] the unity between political or societal *diakonia* and other aspects of *diakonia*,[11] the limitations of using such qualifications as political or societal,[12] the difference between *diakonia* and mission[13] and the

---

[1] Walter Grimmer, 'Vorwort' in *CD*, p. 7.
[2] Heinz-Dietrich Wendland, *Botschaft an die soziale Welt* (Hamburg, 1959), p. 254.
[3] Gibson Winter, *The New Creation as Metropolis*, p. 150: 'The notion of the servant Church owes much to . . . World Council discussions.'
[4] cf. *Uhlhorn*, pp. 767, 799f.
[5] For *diakonia* this was crystallized at New Delhi. See W. A. Visser 't Hooft, *The New Delhi Report* (London, 1962), p. 111.
[6] Paul Philippi, *Christozentrische Diakonie*, pp. 227ff.
[7] Ernst Schering, *ED*, p. 34.
[8] Heinz-Dietrich Wendland, 'Die dienende Kirche und das Diakonenamt' in *DAK*, pp. 443ff.
[9] Hans Christoph von Hase, *DG, Vol. I*, pp. 26ff.
[10] Heinz-Dietrich Wendland, *Botschaft an die soziale Welt*, pp. 263ff.
[11] Wolfgang Schweitzer, 'Fürsorgerische und gesellschaftliche Diakonie' in *Deutsches Pfarrerblatt*, 62. Jahrg., 1962, pp. 125–7; and the reply by Herbert Krimm, 'Christos Diaconos', ibid., pp. 533–5.
[12] Theodor Schober, 'Der missionarische und diakonische Ansatz im Leben der Christusgemeinde' in *Jahrbuch der Inneren Mission und des Hilfswerks der Evangelischen Kirche in Deutschland* (Stuttgart, 1964), pp. 20ff.
[13] ibid., pp. 11ff.

place of *diakonia* in the context of theology as a whole.[1]

But the problems of definition are only secondary as compared with the significance of the great socio-economic change in many parts of the world. What does it mean to live diaconically in the modern welfare state?[2] Must *diakonia* conform to the social change? Or should it seek to transform the structure of society according to the Gospel image of man and human community?[3] New forms are sought that could transform the world.[4] In many areas of the West only preliminary spadework has been done for the creation of new forms.[5] Occasionally the desire is expressed to find new tasks for old forms, as may be the case with the Hospitallers, the Order of St John, which goes as far back as the year 1099, the time of the Crusades.[6] More frequent is the demand for new forms of old tasks, as with the deaconesses.[7] The principal intention is to supplement the 'saving' Rescue Mission *diakonia* of the past with a 'formative' Industrial Mission *diakonia* for the new society.[8]

The frequent intermingling of *diakonia* and public welfare in the history of the Church[9] and the replacement of large areas of *diakonia* work by public welfare[10] forces theology to ask whether there is anything distinctive about *diakonia* that the State cannot offer.[11] Here theological reflection on *diakonia* joins the basic theological quest of our day. The recent stress on Jesus as *the* deacon points to the core of the contemporary theological concern: what is the distinctive characteristic of Jesus? The quest for new forms of *diakonia* is essentially the search for a form of life that can express the unique quality of Jesus' life—a form that man cannot produce by his own power.

The attempt of finding answers takes on ecumenical dimensions. Orthodox ecclesiology has an important contribution to make to the asking of the right questions.[12] The unusual interest in *diakonia* in Roman Catholicism of late promises to make a conversation on *diakonia* the cutting edge of the Roman Catholic-Protestant dialogue.[13]

---

[1] Eugen Gerstenmeier, ' "Wichern Zwei." Zum Verhältnis von Diakonie und Sozialpolitik' in *DAK*, pp. 529ff.

[2] Ernst Schering, *ED*, p. 22.

[3] Leslie E. Cooke, 'Die Verantwortung der Kirchen in der Sozialarbeit' in *Diakonie II*, p. 12.

[4] Sheldon L. Rahn, 'Neue Formen des Dienstes' in *Diakonie II*, pp. 44–59.

[5] Hans Christoph von Hase, 'Die christliche Gemeinde und die gesetzliche Neuregelung der Jugend- und Sozialhilfe' in *Jahrbuch der Inneren Mission und des Hilfswerks der Evangelischen Kirche in Deutschland* (Stuttgart, 1963), p. 26.

[6] In the same yearbook, ibid., pp. 91–102, the essay on 'Evangelische Ritterschaft in unserer Zeit'. See especially p. 95: 'Bridgebuilding toward Diakonia.'

[7] Friedrich Thiele, *Diakonissenhäuser im Umbruch der Zeit*, pp. 26ff.

[8] cf. Eugen Gerstenmaier, op. cit., pp. 501f.

[9] Schneemelcher, op. cit., p. 64.

[10] Uhlhorn, p. 667. It was noticeable since the days of Pietism.

[11] The question is already part of the ecumenical conversation. See Eugene C. Blake, 'What Makes Christian Service Distinctive?' in *Consultation Digest* (World Council of Churches, 1962), pp. 53–59.

[12] See Iwan Pereswetow, 'Zur Geschichte der karitativen Tätigkeit in der orthodoxen Ostkirche mit besonderer Berücksichtigung der russischen Kirche' in *DAK*, pp. 231ff.

[13] From the growing literature we cite Karl Rahner and Herbert Vorgrimler (eds.), *Diaconia in Christo* (Freiburg, 1962).

Local Diakonia

In the ecumenical movement[1] the trend toward local ecumenicity is paralleled by the emphasis on local *diakonia*.[2] It is very much part of the ecumenical concern for 'all in each place'.[3] It involves the fusion of the call to unity[4] with the call to service.[5] The new interest in local *diakonia* does not mean to suggest that diaconic congregations do not exist.[6] But in terms of a comprehensive ecumenical concern new reflection is called for. What is the structure of the diaconic congregation? Does it need a professionally trained deacon? What is the place of the deaconess?[7] Oberlin already hoped that laywomen could work as deaconesses in the local congregation, much as laymen were acting as deacons.[8] The 'professional' deacon and deaconess and the 'lay' deacon and deaconess need not exclude each other as long as both are able to embody the unique dimension of the Christian life.

Drawing its strength from *leitourgia*,[9] *diakonia* must be related to the primordial structure of human existence. Too often the 'rich' and 'healthy' Christian has condescended in 'diaconic paternalism' to the less fortunate—to improve his condition, to make him feel good or to convert him. As a result the real point of *diakonia* has been missed. Primarily the poor and the sick does not need me, but I need him. Is it not in the poor and sick that I meet Christ and in this encounter learn to love with the love of God? Is it not in the lowliness of the outcast that I am confronted with God's very being?

Christ? The love of God? God's very being? In the poor and the sick? In the outcast? *Diakonia* makes us ponder in action the mystery of the relationship between suffering and God. Words can only witness to the mystery, the way the words of John the Baptist witness on the Isenheim Altar—written near his large pointing finger: *illum oportet crescere, me autem minui.*

---

[1] Since ecumenical *diakonia* is such a vast field, a special chapter is devoted to it in this volume. It seems pertinent to note at this point that space does not permit us to call attention to a great number of diakonia efforts in the ecumenical church of today which demand equal consideration. The name of Albert Schweitzer symbolizes all these efforts.

[2] Hans Christoph von Hase, 'Die Wiederentdeckung der dienenden Gemeinde' in *DG*, Vol. I, pp. 15-43.

[3] Sheldon L. Rahn, op. cit., p. 45.   [4] W. A. Visser 't Hooft, op. cit., p. 116.

[5] ibid., p. 111; P. C. Rodger and L. Vischer (eds.), *The Fourth World Conference on Faith and Order* (London, 1964), pp. 87ff.

[6] See Arvo J. Laarjarinne and Theodor Schober, *Die diakonische Gemeinde am Beispiel Finnlands* (Neuendettelsau, 1963); J. C. van Dongen, op. cit., p. 115.

[7] Hans Christoph von Hase, 'Der Aufbau der dienenden Gemeinde' in *Diakonie der Gemeinde* (Berlin and Stuttgart, 1964), Vol. II, p. 28.

[8] An outline of Oberlin's views were printed under the title, 'Oberlin et les Diaconesses' in *La Diaconesse*, vol. 34, No. 4, Oct.-Dec. 1935, pp. 2ff.; German translation by Paul Werner, 'J. F. Oberlins "Diakonissen" bereits gegen Ende des 18. Jahrhunderts' in *Die Diakonisse*, 9.Jg., Heft 2, Feb. 1934, pp. 54ff. See also 'Gedanken von Joh. Friedrich Oberlin über ein Wiederaufleben des apostolischen Diakonissenamtes in der Gemeinde', *Der Armen- und Krankenfreund*, 83.Jg., Heft 1/2, Jan.-Feb. 1931, p. 5. For a critical evaluation of the place of the deaconess in the primitive church see Johannes Leipoldt, *Die Frau in der antiken Welt und im Urchristentum* (Leipzig, 1955), p. 210; for the deacon see Ernst Barnikol, *Das Diakonenamt als das älteste Leib- und Seelsorge vereinende Amt der Gemeinde* (Halle, 1941), p. 14.

[9] Theodor Schober, *Gottesdienst und Diakonie* (Stuttgart, 1965), pp. 9ff.

Christological Understanding

W. A. WHITEHOUSE

I

To work in the personal service of another human being is, once more, the least coveted role in human society. Young persons may have to do this as part of their apprenticeship. Shop assistants and bus conductors must do it, but can protect themselves to some extent from the thought of indignity by 'serving the management' rather than the customers. Personal secretaries can bask in the dignity of their boss and enjoy the game of managing him—and can leave him for another if they are defeated or bored. Domestic servants, and more especially those who must serve their employers or their employers' 'guests' at table, are no longer in a worse position to look after themselves than are others engaged in direct personal service; but this occupation, lightly undertaken to earn money in a vacation, has revealed to many students the perils and indignities of being in personal service to their fellow men and women. They have tasted, in a greatly alleviated form and by uncommitted sampling, something which was a painful commonplace in Hellenistic society. It was scandalous for Jesus to interpret His own role, and to present the terms of discipleship, by using this model. But He did so, with the personal service of the table-waiter firmly in view.

Then, as now, the general idea of occupying oneself and expressing oneself in 'service' was not unacceptable. To serve a respected householder or farmer, to serve the community in the apparatus of government, to serve God from some niche in the religious establishment, these were possible ways of enriching one's life and of giving to it value and meaning. (To serve a commercial enterprise is a quite recent addition to the list of worthy causes.) To serve one's mere fellow man who happens to be in need was not, and is not, comparably worth while. If done at all, it is done occasionally, as an act of condescension or as an act of religious obligation. Judaism conjoined love of neighbour with love of God. Indeed, any religion which expresses among other things a community's will to survive is likely to prescribe some form of neighbourly service to the needy. What is scandalous about the teaching and example of Jesus is the suggestion, embodied in His choice of model, that those who follow Him must spend themselves in direct personal service to any who call upon them, without calculation and without any safeguards of dignity. Their true dignity will emerge precisely in so doing, but it will not commend itself as such to those wise in the ways of this world. Nietzsche saw the point with rare clarity after it had been masked for centuries by the dignities of 'Christendom'. The disciples of Jesus will, it is true, be serving Him, serving, too, the 'cause' which He embodies, and (so He assures them) serving God, by putting their resources at hazard in this way. But faith and obedience may have to do without the comfort of being able to regard Him, or His 'cause', or the God whose name He invokes, as obviously adequate grounds from which to derive authentication for such a programme of living.

The scandal is aggravated when one reflects on that aspect of the public ministry of Jesus which particularly struck the theologians of 'the Social Gospel' in the nineteenth century: His deliberate turning to the poor and the incompetent rather than to the able and influential. To help such lame dogs over their various stiles is a humane procedure, and indeed may be an important safeguard for the community against social collapse. But to make this the corner-stone in a policy for world-regeneration is utterly 'unrealistic'. Those who call for personal service most loudly and most frequently will always be 'the poor'. One need not hold them in contempt (though the 'realistic' tendency is always in this direction), but to suggest that personal service to their manifold needs is the lever which alone will avail to transform and regenerate the world is folly. It is perhaps excusable and comprehensible and in some mysterious way right, in a Jewish religious leader, who identifies 'the poor' with 'the pious and therefore the oppressed'; but the actual conduct of Jesus can be neither justified nor explained in terms of that handy assumption. The 'poor' to whom He turned were persons whom it is unrewarding to serve (even, one might add, on that assumption); and to give Himself to them in the humble role of *diakonos* was to lay Himself open to degradation and wasteful self-destruction. In doing precisely this, the Son of Man gave up his own life. But He did so with confidence that this would provide 'for many' the means of procuring their emancipation (Mark 10[45]).

Among 'the many', first and most evidently, are those who hear the news about Jesus Christ, leap to lose their chains, and therefore receive it as 'the word of the truth' (Colossians 1[5]). In His case, they are persuaded, such spending of life in diaconal service has been authenticated, first in His own resurrection from the dead and now in His coming to them as their living Lord through the Holy Spirit to give them the freedom of faith. His lifetime of diaconal service was rooted in God. They do not, however, proceed by one short direct step to obey the injunction 'Go and do thou likewise' (Luke 10[37]). This would be to step aside from one religion of righteousness by works to another one—to 'an impractical and inept idealism' which is even less appropriate to the condition of men and their world than whatever religion it is which they are ready to abandon. They do indeed turn to God from idols, to serve a living and true God (1 Thessalonians 1[9])—a possibility to be joyfully welcomed in principle. But they serve Him first by the gratitude of faith; by acknowledging the grace with which He has emancipated them from the dominion of darkness and transferred them to the kingdom of His beloved Son 'in whom we have redemption, the forgiveness of sins' (Colossians 1$^{13-14}$).

Their gratitude is for services which they can neither repay nor emulate. In the servant-manhood of Jesus they recognize the Christ of God, the authority of God's anointed Servant; they see deeper, and identify this authority as the authority of God Himself in person, the Lord of all who has come to men as a neighbour in this world to serve them in their deepest need. His service to them has turned them into accepted fellow servants with Jesus, in a service to the world which God Himself is giving in His Christ. Yet they dare not say: 'I will therefore give myself as a Christ to my neighbour', until they have first suffered the judgement and transformation of human self-awareness out of which there emerges the qualifying clause: 'just as Christ offered himself to me'. Vivid in their minds is the picture of Christ giving Himself to His disciples in the diaconal service of washing their feet. At the heart of that episode is the word to Peter, who had found in Jesus a cause to serve and a master to emulate: 'If I do not wash you, you can have no part in me' (John 13^8). Those who are to serve must first let themselves be served. Only as beneficiaries of His unique personal service to them can they follow Jesus in freedom and light, being effectively emancipated from the darkness of this world's preoccupations. Among such preoccupations there is a certain interest in serving adequate causes or serving an adequate Lord, and the gratitude of faith includes testimony to the fact of having found such a Lord and such a cause. But the judgement and transformation in human awareness which Christian faith entails bring emancipation even from this subtle interest. In this life, believers are content to follow Jesus on the road of diaconal service whose end is the Cross. Those who make Christ's life their own believe that 'when Christ, who is our life, shall be manifested', they with Him shall also be manifested in glory (Colossians 3^4); and such hope provides in them a steady source of discipline and determination without which it is hardly possible to continue steadfast on so inglorious a road. But those who are to tread it must do so as men *prepared* always to find that it is intrinsically inglorious—though dignities, graces, and gratifications *may* be added, and to reject them when offered, to tread the road grimly wearing a hair-shirt for its own sake, is as bad in its own way as to depend on service being ennobling. Those who are prepared for the road have their feet washed by Him into whose death they are baptized; and this ever-renewed foot-washing means ever-renewed emancipation from ungenerous and self-regarding preoccupations including those of a religious kind.

Discipleship therefore means actually following Jesus in the paths of mundane personal service to those who call out from conditions of need however crude. The parable of judgement (Matthew 25$^{31-46}$) speaks to men in this world whose fellow men are physically short of food and drink, actually lonely and unwelcome in society, short of clothes, in poor health, locked up in prison. Discipleship is judged by the actuality of mundane service which makes its own quite concrete and practical difference to their condition. The service must be offered in its own right and for its own sake, but it is, in fact, set by God in a dimension deeper than humanitarianism or social therapy. Those conditions of deprivation, incompetence and bondage, are symbolically (and perhaps symptomatically) significant for the entire being and experience of every man in so far as he has not yet responded to the ministry of Jesus, Servant and Lord. He is ready to make our mundane service part of His own unique service; and what we have to offer may be viewed without presumption as a potential witness to, and vehicle for, the personal service which He alone can give. It bears witness, or may do so, in that it comes through servant-disciples who owe their freedom to services rendered; but more directly may it do so through its own intrinsic, but borrowed, grace.

'As our heavenly Father has in Christ freely come to our aid, so we ought freely to help our neighbour through our body and its works, and each should become as it were a Christ to the other that we may be Christs to one another and Christ may be the same in all; that is, that we may be truly Christians.' Luther's words express the hope of bringing the help of the Gospel, in, with, and under the practicalities of neighbourly help. It is not, in the last resort, for us to calculate for this; though what we can do 'through our body and its works' is never dissociated from what we simultaneously provide 'through our soul and its words', and we must reckon with the possibility that this will be used as God's vehicle for His own word. It is not, however, for the servant-disciple to assess what service is likely to be 'spiritually profitable', nor how to make it so. Like a waiter, he is at the beck and call of everyone in that part of the room where he happens to be. Their calls for mundane service must be answered with mundane efficiency 'through the body and its works'.

II

So far, with assistance from Luther's *Treatise on Christian Liberty*, we have considered how the Christian is conformed to his Lord as 'a perfectly dutiful servant of all, subject to all'. The prospect is scandalous to anyone who wishes to conduct his life as an essay in self-fulfilment. Such a person (and he is alive in all of us) may, when he becomes a Christian, conspire with his obituarist to produce a career which both can regard as 'self-fulfilment in a lifetime of service'. By so doing he will have distorted in practice what he ought to have been giving. The neighbourly personal service open to an individual under the Cross is piecemeal. It lacks the self-justifying cohesion to which so satisfying an epitaph seeks to draw attention. An obituarist is professionally obliged to disregard the fact that a really Christian life is a life broken and thrown away. This is not to deny that God may grace such a life with fullness and dignity in His own way, and that hints of this may be vouchsafed even in this world's experience. It serves merely to stress the truth that a Christian 'lives not in himself but in Christ and his neighbour . . . in Christ through faith, in his neighbour through love'.

But Christ whose accepted fellow servants Christians are is more than an exemplary individual. In Him, so faith acknowledges, the Son of God assumed the role of King and Priest whose office it is to make all creatures relate with God and with one another in mutual grace and self-giving. Taking the form of a servant, born as man, humbled in obedience even unto death on a cross, He is now exalted, to be owned as Lord by every creature, to the glory of God the Father (Philippians 2^{7-11}). His service to 'the many', which at present only believers accept and acknowledge, incorporates their emancipated lives into 'a royal priesthood, a priestly kingdom'. Of this, the Church is the visible embodiment. To live in Christ by faith is to take one's place in the community of His Church. The discipleship of each individual, called to live in his neighbour by love, is caught up into a corporate service which has direction, scope, and shape of its own. It is in this fellowship of service that believers receive their high privilege, granted by grace and secured only through the Holy Spirit, that God's own service to His world in the person of Jesus Christ should be mediated through their persons and their actual worldly service.

Before saying any more about this, a word of warning must be interposed. It is improper to treat participation in the Church's corporate service as one element, perhaps optional, in the whole service to which individuals are called. A calculated risk has been taken in this essay by adopting an order of discussion which might suggest such a view. It is more nearly true to regard the individual's personal service to his fellows as the developed expression of his Church membership—but not if this leads him to distort his service to men in life's common ways by twisting it into some kind of service to the Church and making it ecclesiastically meritorious. The discipleship of each individual is caught up into the corporate service of the Church and is constantly renewed, as we shall see, at that centre; but each service, corporate and individual, has its own distinct and proper shape. There is some truth in the impropriety of viewing participation in the Church's special and limited service as one element in the individual's total service. Luther took risks here when he fought to make plain the freedom with which a Christian man gives himself in service. It is, I believe, still necessary to do so.

The *direction* of all Christian service is sufficiently indicated by the phrase: 'a diaconal service of reconciliation' (2 Corinthians 5^{18}, to be understood in the light of all that precedes that verse from 3^4 onwards, and with attention to chapters 8 and 9, where there is lavish and varied use of 'diaconal' terminology).

The *scope* of reconciliation is the whole creation, viewed from Christ as its centre and now brought by His service under His dominion. To live in Christ by faith is therefore to have one's own small being rooted in that principle which gives cohesion to all things; in Him all the fullness of God has chosen to dwell, that through Him God may reconcile to Himself all that is (Colossians $1^{17, 19-20}$).

The first question is about the scope of the Church's own distinctive service. Its members have usually been unwilling to demarcate at all rigidly the frontiers of this new visible community; yet for some purposes it is proper to define them, and this rather precarious human decision can be safeguarded against the twin perils of arrogance and indifference if it is accompanied by recognition that the sphere of the visible Church and the sphere of Christ's Lordship do not in all respects coincide. The expression of Christian faith and life in diaconal service has for its scope a sphere of operation which transcends the apparent frontiers of the visible Church, but is nevertheless encompassed by Christ. He has defined this sphere, and He has done it not by first identifying Himself with the Church but first by identifying manhood with Himself. No human experience is alien to Him, and inasmuch as you do or do not render diaconal service to any human neighbour in need, you do it or don't do it to Him. (Matthew 25[44f.].).

It is rightly said that there is a mystery here, a mystery of the presence, in the person of each actual needy neighbour, of the Lord 'to whom to refuse anything is a monstrous sacrilege' (Calvin's comment on Matthew 25[40]); and that Jesus wants His disciples to know about this mystery, so that their actual service may be cleansed from all taint of patronage and all will to impose. It is rash, however, to try to develop an understanding of this mystery—in terms, perhaps, of some 'identity-mysticism'—lest the service should come to seem rewarding in a religious sense to him who gives it, when nothing more can be at stake than its being actually helpful to him who receives it. Yet Calvin's moralizing, however valid, may not be quite sufficient to bring out in the right way this mystery and its power to safeguard the quality of 'obedient' service. Eschatological parables, as Hoskyns said, serve to strip us naked of transient preoccupations and little moral busynesses, so that ultimate facts and duties stand out in luminous simplicity. In this parable we hear how our lives are set in a fellowship of diaconal service where Jesus, the Christ of God, makes the call of the needy His own call and makes the answering word or gesture or helping hand His own as well. In Him it is all being justified, reconciled to God and sanctified, so that in the end it may be glorified.

The Church does not monopolize this fellowship of service; it knows about it and must bear explicit witness to it. It must do so by being itself a fellowship of service, in a way and a shape which are the more eloquent for being special and limited. This, however, raises a complicated question about scope which must be noticed before leaving that topic for the third one, which is shape. New Testament evidence about the Church's effort to express itself as a fellowship of service frequently suggests that such an effort, made as it is by believers, must be made in terms of the needs of believers. This is intelligible in the circumstances and it poses no great problem in a community which all the time is addressing itself with success to the task of drawing others in. With Christians for whom the whole of their society was 'Christendom', no problem is raised at all. For us, however, the Church is a community whose domestic life can all too easily be shut off from the main stream of society, so that a self-contained expression of diaconal service within the fellowship of the Church has no witnessing power and is spoiled in its very character by a taint akin to incest.

In the course of transition from 'Christendom' to present post-Christendom conditions, the Church has retained an interest in special activities and institutions through which, from the early days of 'Christendom', it tried to extend diaconal service into the whole fabric of society. It now has to reckon with a general verdict that these are rightly conducted under an aegis other than its own. It may, indeed, concur with that verdict. The Church's special interest in these activities and institutions is not so central as it once was to its own, or anyone else's, concern. They are residual lines of penetration for the Church with its distinctive witness, but they cannot be regarded in this light without embarrassment.

This is germane to the question about *shape* for the Church's life as a fellowship of service. There is something to be said for working towards an answer beginning from need and not from willingness to serve, and beginning from need outside the Church's domestic life. Since face-to-face personal service to persons is a vulnerable and wearing occupation, the Church ought not to relax its corporate concern that teachers, doctors, nurses, welfare officers, prison visitors, be raised up from its own membership, to help in manning the relevant services and maintaining their quality. But a distinction between these vocations to service and those open to an accountant, an assistant in a public library, a saleswoman, or a garage mechanic, is not easily drawn under modern social conditions —and neither should we expect it to be, when the 'waiter' model for diaconal service is kept in mind. The residual lines of penetration do not stand out with their former distinction. Alongside all such lines of direct personal service to persons, furthermore, there are the great service-complexes of the national establishment and of industry and of semi-public and private administrations— new material for theological evaluation only in the sense that this has traditionally been confined to 'the State' in its varied manifestations, but now requires revaluation in a wider context and with more attention to the 'personal' nature of service in these complexes. There is a give-and-take of service between the Church and all parts of this worldly network. The problems involved are treated elsewhere in this symposium. They are mentioned here simply as a reminder of the rather puzzling conditions under which the Church must try today to shape its own life as a fellowship of service, and, in its *special and limited way*, be eloquent of the truth which it knows about through the Gospel of Jesus Christ. Traditions inherited from the apostolic age and from the epoch of Christendom are neither sacrosanct nor sufficient in new circumstances, though to consult such traditions, as preceding essays have helped us to do, is rewarding.

It is as a fellowship of believers that the Church must still shape its own life. In the conduct of its own peculiar affairs it can learn a great deal about human needs and can do experiments in the art of meeting them as a fellowship of believers. But as such it lives all the time in an open commitment to serving unbelievers, serving *with* unbelievers, and being served *by* unbelievers. No aspect of its domestic structure is insulated from the effects of such a commitment, least of all its structure for diaconal service.

When we move right into the Church's domestic life it is plain first of all that its members are united in a fellowship of service to God offered through Jesus

Christ. This is personal service offered to a neighbour, for in Christ God has given Himself to His people as their God and as such He has become their neighbour. But He is not a neighbour who needs either man's work or His own gifts returned. He asks for faith. Faith expresses itself in worship; and worship is the surrender of human interests, in adoration, to a Lord whose influence upon the being and well-being of the worshippers they wholly accept and wholly trust. Because God blesses human beings in all acts of worship where self-preoccupation is lost in praise of His goodness, their 'service to Him' is transmuted into a new experience of 'being served'. In this experience they are turned afresh towards neighbours on the other side, so to speak; towards their fellow men whose cause God has made His own in Jesus Christ.

Our human neighbour does need our resources; and if they are laid open to *him* in an offer of personal service, no one can say what he will do with them— and with the person in whom they inhere. In this direction there is no question of faith in one's neighbour, no worship of humanity, no unconditional devotion even to its more worthy preoccupations. In direct association with the Church, as contributor to its special and limited service, the Christian participates in a service to men which has been distinguished since very early days (Acts 6[2]) as 'preaching the word of God' and 'serving tables'. In both respects the Church demonstrates by Christian discipleship how men can help one another, having first been helped by Christ. To divorce the two distinguishable aspects is always wrong. But it is right to observe that it is through the second motif, 'serving tables', that the Church's special witness to diaconal service has been explicitly developed.

Christians who seek precise bearings from the New Testament for the shape and structure of obedience must take what comfort they can from experts in this field. It is evident that in New Testament times the Church paid explicit attention to the actualities of personal diaconal service, and shaped its life accordingly. How it did so is not very clear. Some of its members, presumably those who most obviously filled a role of personal assistants to their fellow men, attracted to themselves the title *diakonos* (Philippians 1[1]; 1 Timothy 3[8–13]); and *diakonia* is evidently the name (not, of course, in all cases) for one special activity among others, presumably of a 'table-serving' kind. It is difficult to see what more should be made of the evidence than what stands in *A Platform of Church Discipline Gathered out of the Word of God*, presented to the Synod at Cambridge, New England, in 1649. 'The office and work of the Deacons is to receive the offerings of the church, gifts given to the church, and to keep the treasury of the church: and therewith to serve the *Tables* which the church is to provide for: the *Lord's Table*, the table of the *ministers*, and of such as are in *necessitie*, to whom they are to distribute in simplicity' (c. VII, par. 3). It is also difficult to hold back an opinion that something has gone wrong when such deacons are regarded as inferior personal assistants to the 'priestly and ruling' ministers, with servant-status less essential to the fundamental structure of the Church than that of the clergy proper.

To be unconcerned about structure, to confine concern in the case of deacons to their clerical status, to assume that the economic realities of the Church's life (treasury-keeping) may casually be conformed to the world's current practices— all these attitudes may cloak a fundamental lack of concern for the *actuality* of diaconal service within and beyond the Church's domestic life. If so, they betray the Gospel and depart from original apostolic tradition. Less heinously, they could be merely symptoms of a high-minded attitude to sordid practicalities— which has its endearing side, though it is sinful and imperceptive. To suppose that the Church is engaged in a 'spiritual service', which in principle is not impaired if its resources for practical mundane support are abused or squandered or left unused, is to work with false distinctions and ill-conceived priorities. It is tempting to say that, in this matter at least, the Church may find some significance in the lack of adequate help from tradition, and should let the contemporary situation structure its theology and its practice. After all, the whole point is to *serve*; and usually this means to be imposed upon, without imposing. But tradition, critically consulted, may help to renew and inform a concern for structure within the Church; and though, in diaconal service, it must be prepared for being imposed upon by men in their actual needs in the world as it is, its action must everywhere bear the stamp of standards imposed from a kingdom not of this world.

III

Luther's *Treatise on Christian Liberty* was a christological demonstration that God's truth about His world and about human living shines out in Jesus Christ, but had been obscured and opposed in mediaeval ecclesiasticism. Luther helped it to shine out again as light; light in which men may find and develop genuinely human lives. To do this work of theological clarification is to give personal service to persons—and to invite obloquy by doing so, whether it be done with Luther's epoch-making incisiveness or with Barth's daunting thoroughness. Barth has provided the same positive help, but with thorough-going attention to the ways in which this truth is obscured and opposed in modern humanitarianism. In his *Church Dogmatics*, Volume IV, Parts 1, 2 and 3, he demonstrates how men live as beneficiaries of the Lord who became Servant, the Servant who became Lord; and how, by our engagement in diaconal service, His justification of us and His sanctification of us are concretely shown forth in prophetic declaration. Faith working through love expresses the hope in which man as such is called to live. This hope is true to a world where man is to live as the accepted partner of God, purged from the pride and healed from the sloth which corrupt his authentic humanity; and in this hope, truth prevails over falsehood. The truth shines out as a light in which all may live, and to the hidden realities of righteousness by faith and sanctification in love there is added the visible testimony of wisdom—knowledgeable practice. Authentic humanity comes to us from its source in Christ Jesus, whom God made our wisdom, our righteousness and sanctification, our emancipation (1 Corinthians 1^{30}); and in us, as in Him, the substance of knowledgeable practice is diaconal service.

'The true community of Jesus Christ is the society in which it is given to men to see and understand the world as it is, to accept solidarity with it, and to be pledged and committed to it' (*Church Dogmatics*, IV, 3, p. 780). Experience of this will vary with time and with place. Those who at present speak about it from a place in radically secularized societies tend to stress (cf. Hromadka) the unhelpfulness of 'high-sounding doctrines, lofty ideals or moral demands and aims' and ask for greater readiness 'to follow Christ's example of serving at the lowest levels of humanity'. Readiness so to do should not, perhaps, entail complete neglect of service on other levels, including those where doctrines, ideals, demands, and aims are very much to the point; though it is right to observe that men sick from the effects of an ideological diet are not helped by having a rival ideological diet served up to their tables, particularly one which they have already rejected as debilitating. In every cultural situation at present wise diaconal service must have a more helpful content than that.

Barth's balanced and penetrating account of the world as it is, and of humanity pledged with Christ to solidarity with it and to service, rests on preparatory work done in Volume III, Part 2, the theological account of man as the creature of God. Those who are ready to be helped by Barth, but are not prepared to let him do their thinking for them, must make an effort to relate what he has to suggest (in Volume IV) about the actualities of life in service to his earlier analysis of manhood as being-in-encounter. To understand how man *is with* his neighbour and in limited ways *can be for* his neighbour, is to know the conditions of service. It is also to appreciate how, in diaconal service, the Church and the Christian should be *at their most human*.

Secular humanitarianism, like mediaeval ecclesiasticism, bears its own witness to God's truth, even while suppressing it by pride and wickedness. And secular humanitarianism may help the Christian community to learn (if it will learn from no other source) that it must come out from behind the protective masks of religiosity and self-interested ecclesiasticism and act with the unadorned integrity of generous men. The eleven-page discussion of possible confusions between 'humanity' and 'Christian love' (III, 2, pp. 274–85) gives salutary help in this matter. Christian diaconal service, though proceeding from love and renewed by love, is *essential humanity*; it stands or falls by that criterion, a fact easily obscured when it is conceived explicitly as the outworking of Christian love.

God's truth shines out and prevails in the wisdom of diaconal service; and, in a special and limited way, this fact can be focused in Church Order, which itself should at all points be eloquent of the Gospel. Church Order expresses the full life of the Body of Christ, and the expression of this particular aspect has to be related to the total structure by which that is done—a total structure which may be shaped by a central Papacy, an Episcopal Bench, a hierarchy of Church Courts, or a network of localized Church Meetings and Synods. My own experience falls within the last of these areas, and, unlike most professional theologians, it includes service as a deacon (and vivid youthful impressions of the diaconal practice observed in the village church where I grew up) in a pattern of Church Order derived by way of seventeenth-century Congregationalism from Calvin at Geneva. The practice involves the 'social diaconate' of an elected group of men and women, whose humanity is certainly unadorned, but displays in rough and ready ways varying from person to person some integrity which warrants election. These men and women prepare the Table for the Lord's Supper, carry the food on it to the congregation, receive the collection, and entrust to one of their number the charge of giving quiet help from that money to anyone known to be in particular distress. In the village church where I grew up breaches in human relationships within the congregation were healed more often by the deacons than by the minister, and it was they who cared most effectively for the lapsing and the lapsed. It was they who saw to it, often in the absence of a minister, that congregational activities were maintained and financed. They knew better than any minister how to deal with local mischief-making, a matter of some importance when the congregation, along with two others of different Church Order, was a focus of village interest. They also knew how to deal with patronizing or imposing interventions from higher ecclesiastical sources, intent, in most instances, on marshalling financial and economic resources in their own way, which often seemed to be neither Christian nor consistent with human dignity.

From this special and limited domestic Church experience, deacons were equipped to go out, as many did, to public positions of social responsibility and to care in a humanly acceptable way for persons and their affairs outside the Church. Such special diaconal service was also a help to all Church members who went out in their company.

The Diaconate in the Anglican Communion

THE ARCHBISHOP OF CANTERBURY

It is stated in the Preface to The Form and Manner of Making, Ordaining and Consecrating of Bishops, Priests and Deacons according to the Order of the Church of England that 'from the Apostles' time there have been these Orders of Ministers in Christ's Church: Bishops, Priests and Deacons'. The diaconate is thus continued and esteemed as one of the three Orders of Ministers in the Church of God. Furthermore a man is made a deacon in the Church of England only by episcopal ordination 'To the intent that these Orders may be continued and reverently used and esteemed in the Church of England; no man shall be accounted or taken to be a lawful Bishop, Priest or Deacon in the Church of England, or suffered to execute any of the said functions except he be called, tried, examined, and admitted thereunto, according to the Form hereafter following, or hath had formerly Episcopal Consecration or Ordination.'

The Church of England cherishes the scriptural evidence for the place of the diaconate in the Church. Both the Collect and one of the lections in the service for the Ordering of Deacons refer to St Stephen and his colleagues in Acts 6 as being the first deacons. Modern Anglican exegesis might put less weight upon that passage, where the term 'deacon' does not occur, and more weight upon the evidence of the New Testament as seen in such passages as Philippians 1^3; 1 Timothy 3^{8-13}; Acts 20^{17}.

From the definition of the diaconate as one of the three orders and from the solemn language of the rite of the making of a deacon it is clear that the order is regarded by the Church of England as having religious and theological importance. The candidate is asked if he trusts that he is 'inwardly moved by the Holy Ghost' to take upon him this office and ministry, and the office is bestowed by the formula 'Take thou Authority to execute the office of a Deacon in the Church of God committed unto thee'. Furthermore the rubric prescribes that at the beginning of the service there shall be a sermon 'declaring the Duty and office of such as come to be admitted Deacons; how necessary that Order is in the Church of Christ, and also, how the people ought to esteem them in their duties'.

At the same time the Ordinal presupposes that a man is likely to be a deacon, not necessarily for longer than one year, before he is ordained to be a priest. The

Collect at the conclusion of the service asks that those ordained deacon 'may be found worthy to be called unto the higher Ministries in the Church'. A rubric lays down that after the service 'it shall be declared unto the Deacon, that he must continue in that office the space of a whole year (except for reasonable causes it shall otherwise seem good unto the Bishop) to the intent he may be perfect and well expert in the things appertaining to the Ecclesiastical Administration'. If he be found faithful and diligent 'he may be admitted by his Diocesan to the order of priesthood'. This sequence is not prescribed, but the implication is that one who did not follow it would be unusual and exceptional.

The duties of the deacon are indicated in the questions and the exhortation read to him by the bishop in the service. He will read the Scriptures in the Church, assist the priest in divine service and specially in administering the Holy Communion, instruct the young and in the absence of the priest baptize infants and preach (if he be so permitted by the bishop). He will also assist in the planning and distribution of poor relief in the parish.

Such are the facts which indicate the several features of the Anglican conception of the deacon as set out in the formularies. If on the one hand the diaconate is normally the first step in the course of those who are soon to be priests, it is at the same time an office with distinctive role and functions. The necessity of a man remaining a deacon *for a whole year* is to be seen in contrast on the one hand with the perpetual diaconate in some parts of Christendom, but on the other hand with any idea that the diaconate is but a preliminary rite towards a priesthood which might be immediately conferred.

In the history of the Anglican churches the diaconate has in the main borne the character which the formularies describe, of an office entered for a short time by those who subsequently become priests. The functions have continued except that there are forms of society, such as the modern English welfare state, wherein the administration of poor relief by the Church may figure very little; and preaching is commonly entrusted to the deacon as well as to the priest. The deacon is thus in some respects an apprentice, learning under the priest the practical rudiments of pastoral work before becoming a priest himself. Emphasis is commonly placed upon the *training* of a deacon. He is in the parish not only to assist but to learn, and the bishop will require evidence of his promise as a learner of pastoral craft and evidence of his continuing theological study before he agrees to lay hands upon a man for the conferring of priesthood. The diaconate is thus a road of preparation for the priesthood which enhances the solemnity or the latter order.

On the other hand, there has been frequently within the history of the Anglican Churches, and perhaps chiefly in modern times, a feeling that the normal Anglican practice devalues the significance of the order of deacon in the Church of God. Hence attempts are made to revive a perpetual diaconate. The rubrics of the Prayer Book do not exclude this, for there is no obligation for a deacon to become a priest. In a good many places within the Anglican Communion perpetual deacons are now to be found: men without the theological attainments or the distinctive calling for the priesthood, who are yet set apart as deacons for an office of teaching, pastoral assistance, and administration.

The development of a perpetual diaconate, lawful under the Anglican rubrics but contrary to what they suggest as the norm, of course raises problems. If the perpetual deacon is employed in a whole-time paid service, the desire for the priesthood may in course of time be felt. If, on the other hand, he is a man whose diaconate is discharged in the midst of some other professional calling, it may be asked whether the ordination to the diaconate may not unnecessarily obscure the role of the *layman* as rightly assisting in the Church's pastoral work and administration. It is hard at present to predict what or how widespread may be the outcome of experiments towards a perpetual diaconate in the Anglican churches.

I would here mention that the order of deaconess, revived in the Church of England a century ago, enlists the service of women in many parts of the Anglican Communion. It is understood that the order of deaconess is, as in the early Church, an order for women other than the three orders to which men are admitted. It is beyond the prescribed scope of this essay to describe the many roles of the service of women, for instance as teachers in schools and colleges, as pastoral workers in hospitals and universities, and as members of the active and contemplative religious orders.

As to the order of deacon in the Anglican churches, whether it remains in accordance with the pattern set in the Ordinal or whether it develops along the lines of the recovery of an office of perpetual deacon, the theological significance of the order should not be overlooked.

The Reformers rejected any idea that the office of a minister could supplement or interfere with the uniqueness of the offices of Jesus Christ. But the offices of Jesus Christ may be *reflected* in the lives of His ministers, and the titles of the orders in the Church have overtones recalling the offices of Christ. *Christ is Bishop*, the ruler and shepherd of the people, and His ruling and shepherding is inseparable from His feeding them with the truth of which He is teacher. *Christ is Priest*, the offerer and the intercessor, whose manward role as teacher and absolver of the people is inseparable from His Godward role on their behalf. *Christ is Servant*, and if His supreme act of service was to give His life a ransom for many (Mark 10^{45}) the spirit of service marked His every action towards the apostles and mankind (Luke 13^{27}).

These offices of Christ are reflected in the orders of minister in the Church. The bishops rule and shepherd, teach and feed, effacing themselves as they work in the name of the great Shepherd of the sheep. The priests preach and teach, absolve and care for the people in a life always Godward in offering, adoration, and self-consecration through Jesus the great High Priest. The deacons assist. Their role is limited, there are functions which they may not perform; but their office as assistants is made glorious by the motif of Jesus who was amongst the apostles as their servant.

It is in their distinctive roles, each with its powers and each with its marked limits, that the orders in the Church serve God's glory, in the spirit of Jesus, the

Bishop, the Priest, the Servant. Now, where men permanently fulfil the office of deacon this theological principle is apparent enough. No less apparent is the theological principle where men fulfil a brief diaconate before becoming priests. Bishop Lightfoot of Durham used to say that the priest is still a deacon, and the bishop is still both deacon and priest. Anglican thought would probably agree that in a real sense that is so. The man consecrated to be bishop will carry into that office, with its distinctive authority and functions, the priestliness of the order to which he already belonged. So, too, will the deacon when he is ordained priest carry forward the role of servant into the office wherein new authority and new functions are given to him. What can more root ecclesiastical office in the principles of Christ than an order, obligatory as the first step for all who will become priests or bishops, whose functions are limited on every side and whose essence is to be the servant of the other ministers and of the people?

The Diaconate in the Roman Catholic Church

H. FRANCIS DAVIS

Within the limits of the Catholic Church, the principle, and to some extent the practice, of a permanent diaconate has always been admitted in the Catholic churches with an Eastern rite. This is not usually sufficiently borne in mind, either by Catholics or by non-Catholics. It is, however, recognized and safeguarded by the Decree on the Eastern Catholic Churches, Rome, March 1964, in the following words: 'For the purpose of restoring the ancient discipline of the sacrament of Orders to the Eastern churches, this holy Council desires that the institution of the permanent diaconate should be restored where it has fallen into disuse.'[1]

There is not as yet a Code of Eastern Canon Law, but it is probable that the functions of deacons in the Eastern rites will be similar to those recognized in the Eastern Orthodox Churches.

In both East and West the diaconate has remained in principle an order of service, as its name and origins indicate. Naturally there has been some variation in the type of service suited to the needs of each particular age and place. The service rendered by deacons to the Church has been principally an assisting of bishops and priests in liturgy, works of charity and catechizing. But in the Western rites of the Catholic Church, which at the moment is numerically far the greatest part of that Church, the diaconate in modern times, up to Vatican Council II, has been (*a*) restricted to liturgical service, and (*b*) a temporary order for those intending to continue into the priesthood. The temporary nature of the diaconate has not meant, of course, that the liturgical functions of the deacon are omitted, but that they must normally be carried out by priests, acting in virtue of the order of deacon which they had received before their priestly orders.

The deacon's liturgical service, like diaconal service at all times, has excluded presidency and leadership. The deacon has never been understood to possess the power of consecrating the Eucharist or absolving from sin or anointing the sick. In a similar way, any pastoral work done by the deacon has always been understood as being done under the leadership of bishop or priest. Since bishop and

---

[1] 'Ut antiqua sacramenti Ordinis disciplina in Ecclesiis Orientalibus iterum vigeat, exoptat haec Synodus, ut institutum diaconatus permanentis, ubi in desuetudinem venerit, instauretur' (Decretum de Ecclesiis Orientalibus Catholicis, 17).

priest are defined ultimately by their relation to the Eucharist, the deacon's service, whatever its nature, has been understood as ultimately a Eucharistic one. If in the future the office confided to the deacon is extended, it will be extended only to those functions which a sound theology sees as an extension of the Eucharist. Clearly, religious instruction is intimately related to the latter, as is also the extension of *agape* to the care of the sick and needy. It would seem that matters of economic administration are no more directly related to the diaconate than to the priesthood or episcopate. Such matters have to be attended to, whether by priest, deacon or lay assistants. But they are not as such the exercise of sacred orders.

In mediaeval and modern Western practice, up to a year ago, the service asked of a deacon had been exclusively liturgical. By virtue of his ordination, the deacon becomes the assistant of the bishop or priest at solemn mass. By delegation, he is deputed to help in the administration of other sacraments. The Roman Pontifical calls him 'comminister et cooperator corporis et sanguinis Domini'. It is his privilege to sing the Gospel at a solemn mass. In the *Ordo Missae* of 1965 the reading of the Gospel at a non-sung mass is the exclusive right of a deacon or priest. He is allowed to carry the Blessed Sacrament from one altar to another, even though there is a priest present who could do this. He may also expose the Blessed Sacrament, and replace it in the tabernacle after exposition; but he himself is not permitted to give benediction with the sacrament on such occasions. He has the right to bless the paschal candle, even in the presence of the bishop. He may preach also, provided the local ordinary (the bishop, vicar-general or vicar-capitular) gives him mission and permission.

When delegated, for a just cause, and with permission of the ordinary (cf. above) or even his parish priest, he may (i) lawfully administer solemn baptism to infants or adults; (ii) distribute Holy Communion, with the customary blessing afterwards (with or without the sacrament); (iii) give himself Holy Communion even merely for the sake of his own private devotion; (iv) preside over funerals, whether of adults or of small children. As will be seen later, an important addition to these liturgical functions has been recognized by Vatican II, the Constitution on the Church.

The distinctive liturgical vestments of the deacon are the dalmatic (or conobium), at one time reserved to the Pope and certain privileged bishops, and the transverse stole over the left shoulder. His special place during the Mass is on the step immediately below the predella or footpace. It is also his privilege to sing or read the Gospel from the ambone or special elevated place set apart for this purpose. St Thomas still regarded it as the deacon's office to preach the Gospel by way of catechizing, 'per modum catechizantis' (*Summa Theol.*, pars III, LXVII, art. 1, ad lim.).

In recent years there have been certain foreshadowings of a restoration of the diaconate, even before the Constitution on the Church of November 1964. On 1 February 1957 a series of directives were issued for the ceremonies of Holy Week. These directives allowed, for the sake of a more solemn observance of the special Holy Week ceremonies in small churches, the use of a deacon assisting the celebrant, even when no other sacred ministers were available. On 1 January 1961 bishops in mission countries were empowered 'to grant that solemn Mass and other solemn liturgical functions may be celebrated with the assistance of a deacon only, if other sacred ministers are lacking'. In the recent *Ordo Missae*, Vatican, 1965, rules are finally laid down for a Mass with a deacon (i.e. without other sacred ministers) as a general permissible alternative where the full ceremonies are not possible. In other ways, there has been a tendency to interpret the rules about the delegation of deacons for distributing communion, preaching, etc., rather less restrictively than previously; and in many places this has become fairly common, where deacons are available. But, at least until the end of 1964, deacons who were not also priests were usually in short supply for obvious reasons.

Before speaking of the new movement for a restoration of a permanent diaconate in the West, at least where the need for it was felt, it would be well to say something of Catholic theology on the diaconate. Since the Middle Ages there has been a slight shift of emphasis here. In the thirteenth century the main interest was on the relationship of the diaconate to the priesthood on the one hand and to the subdiaconate and minor orders on the other. The emphasis in modern times is more on whether the diaconate is part of the sacrament of Orders, and whether it was specifically or merely virtually instituted by Christ. The question came up in St Thomas's *Summa Theologica* under the aspect of the unity of Orders. It was felt that, among the sacraments, Orders gave rise to a special problem. For, while baptism or confirmation were conferred once for all, Orders was conferred in different stages. Were the earlier stages really part of the sacrament? If so, were there seven, or possibly eight, sacraments of Orders, or were the earlier ones not part of the sacrament at all, or what? For St Thomas, there was a special problem regarding the episcopate. Was it a distinct order from the priesthood? Since this does not touch the diaconate, it does not concern us here. The second problem does concern us. Are the diaconate and lower orders sacraments, or part of the one sacrament of the priesthood? St Thomas's answer was that the priesthood is of such a nature that its powers can be divided, and the ministerial aspect of them, i.e. the diaconal aspect, can be given without the special sacrificial aspect. Many theologians today would accept this explanation as valid for the diaconate. But they would not usually go so far as St Thomas, who extended it to the subdiaconate and minor orders. Only in the priesthood and the episcopate is given the sacrificial fullness of the priestly ministry. The diaconate would be, not a different sacrament, but the same sacrament given in its aspect as an office and power of service.

From the time of the Council of Trent onwards interest shifts for apologetic reasons to the divine institution of the diaconate and its sacramental nature. Arguments in favour of these affirmations begin to be sought more from Scripture, Liturgy and Tradition, rather than exclusively from 'theological reasons'. In favour of its divine institution was its early existence, which is attested in the

New Testament and in the earliest traditional documents. Against its direct and specific divine institution was the lack of any saying of our Lord with regard to it. The Council of Trent is usually cited in favour of its divine institution, where it condemns those who say there is not in the Church a divinely constituted hierarchy consisting of bishops, priests, and ministers (Sess. XXIII, canon 6). It seems that the word 'ministros' must at least include deacons. Trent says further that sacred ordination is a true and proper sacrament instituted by Christ, and it elsewhere says that there are other orders, major and minor, apart from the priesthood. But it does not explicitly say that all the orders are instituted specifically by Christ, nor that all are sacraments or parts of the sacrament. (cf. Trent, Sess. XXIII, canons 2 and 3.)

Many theologians today attempt to solve the problem by applying to its solution a modern theory that Christ left to the Church considerable power with regard to the sacraments. He did not, according to this view, give the Church power to institute new sacraments. But He did give it a certain latitude in the choice of the exact rite of conferring it, and, in the case of Orders, He left it to the Church whether to give the power of Orders wholly or in part, according to circumstances and needs. This view is more or less supported by Yves Congar and Karl Rahner.

As far as the diaconate is concerned, this view is supported by recent studies on the liturgy of Orders. Diaconate has in common with the episcopate and the priesthood the ceremony of the laying on of hands. This ceremony is absent from the rite of conferring the subdiaconate and the minor orders. The argument has been immensely strengthened since 1931 by the studies of Cardinal Van Rossum regarding the so-called 'mater and form' of Orders. The terms 'matter and form' are, of course, mediaeval technical terms to signify that part of the rite which constitutes the very essence of the ordination. The rest of the rite is, in this terminology, regarded as mere ceremony; so that, if it were omitted, the Order would still have been conferred, provided the ordaining prelate has used the essential 'matter and form'. The matter refers to the action, and the form to the words. St Thomas had understood the matter of Orders to be the handing over of the instruments of office. Thus the matter of priesthood would be the handing over of chalice and paten; and the matter of diaconate the handing over of the book of the Gospels. There were many other theories as to what was the true matter. Cardinal Van Rossum contended that the only part of the rite that had always been present, in all parts of the Church, was the rite of laying-on of hands, and that this, and this alone, must be the true matter of Orders.

The Van Rossum theory rapidly made headway among Catholic theologians in the first half of this century. In the year 1947, Pius XII declared that, at least from that time onwards, whatever the Church might have ordered at any previous time, the 'matter' of Orders for the diaconate, priesthood and episcopate would be the laying-on of hands alone (Cons. Apost. Sacramentum Ordinis, 30 November 1947, Denzinger, Enchiridion Symbolorum, 2301). Since this document makes no mention of the subdiaconate or the minor orders, it is thought to be a strong authoritative argument that the diaconate, and the diaconate alone of Orders below the priesthood, is truly a part of the sacrament of Orders, and at least virtually instituted by Christ, in so far as He instituted the sacrament of Orders, and gave the Church discretion whether to confer it wholly or partially.

All this controversy about the diaconate remained a speculative matter until this century, when a movement arose, and has been yearly increasing in strength in favour of a restoration of the permanent diaconate to the Western Church, such as existed in the early centuries in all parts of the Church. The first suggestions of importance on the subject were put forward between the two great wars in the pages of the German review, *Caritas*. A further step was taken during the war, above all in the concentration camp of Dachau. Here two priests, the Jesuit Father, Otto Pies, and a curate, Father Wilhelm Schamoni, began to have serious discussions together on the nature and advisability of restoring this permanent diaconate. It was brought home to them that here was an order, having its own sacramental grace, which could be highly beneficial to the Church in our modern world. Aware that such a diaconate had existed in the early Church, and that for long it had ceased to exist in the West, they realized that its existence or non-existence was purely a matter of discipline. In other words, there could not possibly be any dogmatic objection to its immediate introduction, if the Church leaders so desired. What had been in use once could be in use again. On the other hand, they likewise recognized that, since it had so long fallen into disuse, its use could not be essential to the Church. As we would say today, it could not be necessary for the *esse* of the Church, though it might well be necessary now for its *bene esse*.

These two priests had in mind a married diaconate, and many of the advantages they hoped would accrue to the Church from it were bound up with the married state. Thus they expressed the hope that the homes of these deacons would form patterns of family life in the parish, and that priestly vocations would naturally be cherished in them. They thought here of the value of the good example and stimulus to vocations that come from many families of Protestant clergymen. Likewise they hoped that the sermons of a married diaconate might make a useful contribution to the value of the Church's preaching, because of their greater nearness to the ordinary life of the laity. Further, they expressed the view that such deacons would perhaps more often than priests spring from working people, and so would help to form a bond between the priest and the bulk of his people. All this, they said, would soften the Church's feudal aspect. Holy Mother Church would become in a new way the people's Church. The functions they envisaged for these deacons were catechetical and liturgical. They would lead public prayer, preach and distribute Holy Communion, and would be in charge of parish catechism.

After the war, articles began to appear more frequently in the German and Swiss Catholic press. Finally, in 1950, Hannes Kramer declared that he had a vocation to this permanent diaconate, and he applied to the Freiburg Caritas Association. Gradually other young men attached themselves to him. A group of seven youths became known as the *Diakonatskreis*. Among those whose writings were translated into English were Dr Josef Hornef and the above-mentioned Wilhelm Schamoni. The latter preferred part-time to professional deacons. He hoped that a part-time diaconate would discourage the spread of clericalism.

The question came up for discussion at the International Pastoral and Liturgical Congress in Assisi, September 1956. On this occasion an Indonesian Bishop spoke in favour of this restored diaconate. Later, at the International Congress for Mission and Liturgy in Nijmegen, September 1959, an Indian bishop added his recommendation. Since then Latin America and Africa have entered the lists. Contributions from the former continent naturally looked upon the permanent diaconate as a new hope for solving the problem of vocation-shortage in South America. Opinion in Africa has been divided. Many were strongly in favour. On the other hand, a group of Banundi priests came out strongly against such a restoration. They expressed a fear that many of the deacons would be ill-instructed. They thought that there was a danger of scandal in a diaconate chosen less carefully than were present-day priests. They feared moreover that it might lead to a drop in vocations to the priesthood.

The final stage in this debate came during the Second Session of Vatican Council II. The promoters of this change had succeeded in getting the matter discussed during the debate on the Church. Two questions tended to get confused during the conciliar debate. One was the principle of a restored diaconate. It was simply proposed that this might be sanctioned for those parts of the Catholic world where there seemed to be a need for it. The other was the subsidiary question of relaxation from the law of celibacy. There was probably more discussion on this latter question than on the main one. The idea of a married diaconate came to be viewed with more universal favour, however, when it was made clear that what was really needed was that married men, in countries where there was a shortage of priests, could be allowed to exercise at least diaconal functions. They could look after a parish, preach, lead prayers, distribute communion, baptize, and preside at marriages. This would take a big load off the shoulders of overworked clergy, and would also ensure the pastoral care of a parish in the absence of a priest. Many bishops from South America, Africa, and the Far East spoke passionately in favour of the restored diaconate, and were supported by Cardinals Doepfner and Suenens in Europe. The bishops of Latin Europe were very anxious that the ideal of celibacy should not be damaged or destroyed in the Church.

Eventually the principle was accepted; and a compromise solution was reached with regard to the question of celibacy.

However the final draft of the Constitution did not confine itself to the two questions of permanence and celibacy. An entirely new statement was made on the functions of deacons, whether permanent or not. It will be seen to widen considerably the scope of the diaconate in the Church's daily life. It declares: 'On a lower level of the hierarchy are situated the deacons: hands are laid on them "not for the priesthood, but for the ministry".' With the strength of sacramental grace they serve the People of God, in fellowship with the bishop and his body of priests, in the service of the liturgy, the word, and charity. The function of the deacon is proportionate to the assignment granted him by the competent authority. It consists in the solemn administration of baptism, the reservation and distribution of the Eucharist, being in attendance in the Church's name and giving the blessing of matrimony, taking viaticum to the dying, reading the sacred Scripture to the faithful, giving the people instruction and exhortation, presiding over the faithful's worship and prayer, the administration of sacramentals, taking charge of funeral and burial rites (*Const. de Eccl.*, 29, C.T.S. translation).

What is here said refers to the diaconate everywhere, whether or not in any part of the Church it is made again a permanent order. In other words, the Council has considerably widened the field of diaconate service beyond the practice of the West up till 1964. Presiding at matrimony, taking viaticum to the dying, presiding over worship and prayer, administering blessings, and taking charge of funerals and burial rites are all new. Moreover, these appear to be assigned to the deacon without any restriction of cases of necessity or absence of priest or the like.

In addition to such liturgical functions, the Constitution adds duties of charity and administration. (*Const. de Eccl.*, loc. cit.)

Finally, on the specific question of a restoration of a permanent diaconate, the Constitution says: 'These functions are supremely necessary to the life of the Church, but, in the discipline of the Latin Church now in force, it is difficult for them to be fulfilled in many districts. For this reason, it is to be possible, for the future, for the diaconate to be restored to a proper and permanent grade of the hierarchy. It is for the competent regional conferences of bishops, which vary in kind, to decide, with the personal approval of the Supreme Pontiff, whether it is opportune to have deacons of this kind appointed for the care of souls and exactly where. With the Roman Pontiff's consent it will be possible for this diaconate to be conferred on older men, even if they are living in matrimony, and on younger men of the right sort, too, but in their case the law of celibacy must remain in force' (*Const. de Eccl.*, loc cit., C.T.S. translation).

The final solution accepts more or less the custom of the Eastern Church for the married diaconate, i.e. they must be married before receiving the order. It differs from the East by confining this privilege to 'older' men. But no definition is offered as to the exact significance of 'older'. For younger men, the present legislation of the West remains in force.

It remains for future history of the Church to record the countries that will make use of this permission, the manner in which they will apply it, and the extent to which it will bring blessings to the Church. To anyone following the recent debates during the Council, it seems certain that it will not only be in mission countries that the permanent diaconate will be restored. However, there will be many practical difficulties to be overcome before it becomes a workable proposition. To say nothing of any others, there will be the problem of training these deacons. Whatever the problems are, it is eventually only time, apart from the grace of God and the goodwill of those who are called and those who will train them, that is needed. It is the conviction of many of those who have fought for the principle at the Council that it will answer a great need in our day, and bring many blessings to the Church.

BIBLIOGRAPHY

Karl Rahner and Herbert Vorgrimmler, *Diaconia in Christo. Ueber die Erneuerung des Diakonates* (Freiburg, 1962). This book gives the result of a series of studies undertaken in recent years on a restored permanent diaconate.

A Functional Diaconate. Such is the title of a document sent to the bishops of Vatican Council II, signed by many theologians of central Europe. Published in English in *Worship*, U.S.A., vol. 37, No. 8, Aug.-Sept. 1963.

Wilhelm Schamoni, *Married Men as Ordained Deacons* (London, 1955) (tr. from German).

Josef Hornef, *The New Vocation* (Cork, 1962) (tr. from German).

Johann Nepomuk Seidl, *Das Diakonat in der katholischen Kirche* (Regensburg, 1884). A monograph on the whole question of the diaconate in the Catholic Church.

H. Kramer, *Das Diakonat der Liebe* (Lucerne, 1953), vol. 8/9, p. 289.

For the history of the question:

A. Gréa, *De l'Eglise et de sa divine Constitution* (Paris, 1885).

Zt. *Caritas*, Switzerland, Juli & Aug. Heft, 1934, article on Das Caritasdiakonat und seine Erneuerung.

Zt. *Caritas*, Aug. 1936. Hanns Schütz, 'Diakonie der Liebe'.

H. H. Gehle, 'Das Diakonat, das Laienamt der Kirche', Beitrag der *Deutsche Volkschaft*, May 1949.

Damasus Zahringer, 'Ein Berufsdiakonat der Kirche' in *Benediktinische Monatschrift* (1952), vol. 11/12, p. 489.

Josef Hornef, 'Der Priester und sein Diakon, Tübingen' in *Theol. Quartalschrift*, 1953, vol. 4, p. 437.

Otto Pies, 'Block 26, Erfahrungen aus dem Priesterleben in Dachau' in *Stimmen der Zeit*, Oct. 1947, vol. 1, pp. 27ff.

M.-D. Epagneul, F.M.C., 'Du rôle des diacres dans l'Eglise d'aujourd'hui', *Nouvelle Revue Théologique*, 79, Feb. 1957, p. 153.

P. Winninger, 'Vers un renouveau du diaconat' in series *Présence Chrétienne* (Paris, 1958).

François H. Lepargneur, O.P. 'Laicat adulte: Premier problème de l'Eglise en Amérique latine', *Nouvelle Rev. Théol.*, 83, Dec. 1961, p. 1051.

Cardinal Van Rossum, *De Essentia Sacramenti Ordinis* (Rome, 1931).

Diakonia in the Reformed Churches Today

J. L. M. HAIRE

I. RECENT DISCUSSION

There has been a considerable amount of discussion in the Reformed or Presbyterian churches in the recent past on *diakonia* in general and on the office of the deacon. Three factors have led many of these churches to ask themselves whether their provision for diaconal action—for service—fully accords with the will of God for them.

1. *Ecumenical Encounter*

When they have begun to consider schemes of union with other churches they have found that these churches, too, wish to find a place in a united church specifically for the office of deacon. They have generally found also that these other churches have had a very small place for such a specific office. Discussion has been especially keen when Presbyterian churches have been in conversation with either Anglican or Congregationalist churches. The conversations with Anglicans have made much clearer to the Presbyterians that there are historically two quite distinct interpretations of what the office of deacon is. While they themselves have long taken for granted that it is primarily an office of service to the poor and the sick or, even more frequently, a service of administration, concerned with the temporal possessions of the congregation, they have discovered that in the Anglican tradition it is principally an office akin to and subordinate to that of the presbyter. When, on the other hand, they have had conversations with Congregationalists, they have learnt that here those who take the principal part in the government and life of the Church along with the ministers are called deacons and perform a function very much akin to that of Presbyterian elders. The experience of the Church of South India has also suggested to Presbyterian churches engaged in conversations about union that it is important to try to define more clearly the office of deacon before union. In South India it had been hoped that the exact nature of the deaconate would find clearer expression within a united Church, as churches with different traditions of the deaconate came together, but in fact this has not happened. The Church of South India has now asked the World Council of Churches to give guidance on what this office should become.

2. Biblical Theology

Recent New Testament Scholarship undertaken by men of many traditions has shown Reformed Churchmen what a variety of expression there is within the New Testament about the nature of service (*diakonia*). Neither the Western tradition which made the diaconate a stage towards the priesthood, nor the Reformation identification of the deacon with the seven in Acts 6 correspond very closely to the total New Testament picture. In the few passages where there is specific reference to the office of deacon, as in 1 Timothy 3^{1-13}, the exact nature of the office and its differentia from that of bishop is not wholly clear. There is a great variety of the kinds of service which the people of God are called to render to one another and to mankind, and there are people with specific gifts for performing many of these acts of service, but it is far from clear that all acts of service, other than those performed by a bishop or a presbyter, should be performed by a deacon. There are, however, many diaconal services which must be performed if the Church is to be the Servant Church of her Servant Lord.

3. Confrontation with the World

Presbyterian churches along with others have found themselves forced to rethink the forms of service they should be rendering to the community in face of great changes in the structure of society.

The State in its capacity as the provider of welfare for the community has taken over many duties traditionally performed by the churches, in education and in the care of the sick and the poor. The churches, therefore, have had to ask themselves how far they should accept this, or how far they should attempt to continue to perform these offices also themselves. If they accept the welfare state as an expression of the divine care for men, they then have to ask themselves whether it is not their duty to provide from their membership men and women with special gifts to serve God and man through the State service. They have also considered whether there still remain services which the State is not rendering, and which the Church must render until the State is moved to take these also as its responsibility or, in some cases, always claim the right to render. There appear to be a good many waifs and strays who, perhaps by the very nature of their weaknesses, do not qualify for State aid, but for which the Church is bound to have a concern. In all these services good personal relations, real personal concern, is obviously a matter of great importance. Men and women who are convinced of God's concern for them in Christ, despite their unworthiness, ought to be the very people, given these gifts, both to serve the State in its welfare services and to care for those who are not provided for by any government department.

II. RECENT EXPERIMENT

Before there was any State aid for the poor or the sick, the Church did make constant provision for these people, and there were generally men in the congregations responsible for funds for the sick or the poor, though often in English-speaking Presbyterian churches this was a function carried out by the Session. In the more recent past, especially in North America, the deacon has been chiefly concerned with the financial welfare of the Church. While in many Presbyterian churches the administration of the congregation has been carried out, not by deacons, but by a committee or a board of trustees. In some churches provision has been made for the appointment and the ordination of deacons for these purposes, but even there this provision has itself often not been used.

A completely different development has taken place in parts of the continent of Europe, especially in Germany in the nineteenth century. Both men and women were selected and appointed to care for the new poor in the great industrial cities, and for those who were now out of Church connexion, or to render some real Christian service to prisoners and those discharged from prison. Deaconesses also were appointed, especially to care for the sick, and Reformed churches contributed both people to, and financial support for, such movements.

In the recent past several new forms of service have become prominent in the Presbyterian churches. The dissociation of large numbers of people from the Church and the apparent irrelevance of religion for these people led to movements aimed at showing how closely related religion is to everyday life, how it is in one's daily work that one can serve God best as a Christian, and bear witness to the Grace and Truth of God, as one does in one's ordinary work. In Scotland the Iona community sought to render service to the Church and the world in this way. In Germany the Evangelische Akademies brought together men in various professions and skilled occupations to consider the relation of their work to the Christian faith. In Holland the Kerk en Wereld has equally sought to relate the Christian service to everyday work, and a similar movement has been established in the United States, where the Faculty Christian Fellowships have tried to relate academic life and Christian faith.

Very recently in the United Presbyterian Church of the U.S.A. there has been a proposal to create along with ministers and theological professors a third order, of deacons. These deacons would be responsible for the educational and social service of the Church, they would be ordained to this office, they would be distinct from pastors and theological teachers, but possess very much the same status. This proposal has met with a good deal of criticism from those who would prefer that the service of the Church should be the concern of the whole congregation rather than of special officers appointed for it. The very proposal, however, makes clear how concerned the Church is with the service which the Church should be rendering. Many fear, however, the danger, which did appear to arise in nineteenth-century Germany, that congregations as a whole left this work to the hands of the full-time workers and showed much less concern for it than Christians should.

The conception of Christian stewardship, the devotion by many members of congregations to the work of the Church both by larger financial contributions and the giving of their own time, is still another form which the desire for service has taken, especially in North America. Yet it would be hard to say that the churches as a whole have been greatly roused towards that call to service which the New Testament sets before Christians as a central mark of their calling. But certain men within the churches are conscious of the danger that devotion to administration alone makes the Church far too concerned only with itself, or involves it in some vast organization, some promotion of projects, which gives it no real time to be of service.

III. THE DIAKONIA OF THE WHOLE PEOPLE OF GOD

Recently it has been common in the theological thinking of the Reformed churches to think of our Lord Himself as *the* servant or minister and of all ministries within the Church as derived from Him. So the whole people of God are called to be servants, and within the people certain men and women with special gifts to perform special acts of service. The Church, set almost everywhere now in a missionary situation, is being called to a deeper awareness of her witness to Christ as a witness of service. Just as our Lord Himself revealed the power of God both in word and in healing, so the Christian is called to bear witness both by his word and by those acts of service through which God reaches out to heal and to help men. There has been a tendency to identify Christianity with intellectual assent, with doctrine, moral advice or sentimental feeling. The Church is being constantly reminded through Scripture that the Word of God is with power, and this divine power is mediated through the service of His people, and this service is rendered in two ways:

(*a*) Every man in his daily vocation is being called to be a witness. Not only is he to bear witness in what he says and in the honest and considerate performance of his work, he is called to bear witness by his concern in the place of his work for the total welfare of the undertaking. He is to render service as employer or employee by concern for all those involved. He is called to be active in an employers' federation or a trade union, as a Christian showing there God's concern for justice and mercy. The enthusiasm of the Marxist to bring political and social life under Communist control is, in the providence of God, a challenge to Christians—not to adopt the Marxist methods, which at many points are inhuman—but to be no less concerned that the Will of God is manifested in the carrying out of everyday work.

It has been claimed that in the nineteenth century the centre of Christian life was the congregation; here one met for worship and for social life. In the twentieth century, it is said, it will have to be for many people the place where they work. In fact, the Christian has to render service in both places. There is service to be rendered within the congregation by giving one's time, by sharing one's friendship and by offering any help one can to other members of the same people of God. There is, however, a very special service to be rendered in the places where men work. In the great industrial societies of the West it is only too clear that boys and girls often break their Church connexion as soon as they enter industry. The atmosphere is so different from the school, and religion seems so much out of touch with both the practices and conversation of the factory, that young people feel uneasy when they return to the Christian community. This may well reflect the unreality of much Christian social life as well as a sub-Christian level of much life within industry, but Christian men and women, meeting to study and pray and think together in their places of work and to guide those who come in as boys and girls, have clearly a very great service to render in the second half of the twentieth century. If, in the nineteenth century, it was chiefly in church that men had their domestic virtues clarified, the church should continue to be a place where this is done for their whole way of life, but witness to and application of it may have to be done even more obviously and courageously on the factory floor.

Especially in the rich Western part of the world, there is a community service of a very costly kind, of which men are very aware at the moment. An affluent society is very much beset by the idolatry of money and the status which it gives. There is a real call to a sharing of wealth. A community like the Iona community has set out a certain discipline in the use of wealth for its membership. We have, as Dr Ralph Morton says (*The Household of Faith*, p. 105), 'to make our social interdependence and our public responsibility the deliberate expression of our faith'.

(*b*) While the whole community is clearly being called to service—and of this men in the churches are aware—at the same time it is clear that there are specific jobs, both within the Christian community and in the world outside, for which special training and full-time freedom are required. Thus, as we have seen, Reformed churches are beginning to face the question whether they should now think of setting aside certain people to be deacons or deaconesses in these two spheres. If they do so, however, the churches are being constantly reminded that the appointing of these people must not be the way by which a Christian community through monetary subscription buys off its own responsibility, as we are all tempted to do. The great advantage of the service which the whole community is called to render is that this is often something humble and something done secretly. Many of the acts of service rendered in the Church by the preacher or theologian or pastor can so easily become places where man is magnified as great orator or thinker or soul-doctor. Service to one's fellows possesses a certain element of humility about it which enables us to follow more closely the Lord of the Church.

IV. STATE SERVICE AND CHURCH SERVICE

As we have already noted, modern welfare states have taken over many of those services to the community formerly rendered exclusively by the Church. This is especially so in the case of education. In the centuries following the Reformation the minister in each parish, where Reformed churches were the principal churches in the country, was the chief person responsible for local education, and had the principal part in appointing the schoolmaster, who with him was responsible for the moral and spiritual as well as general education of the community. But the Presbyterian tradition has not generally been inclined to maintain special Church schools and in the recent past in western Europe the Presbyterian churches have been more ready, wisely or not, to transfer their schools to the State, believing that the State now has this duty to perform, and has resources both in buildings and in training such as the Church cannot have. Yet Reformed churches are aware today of the depth of man's need and the reality of that restoration of human nature in its totality which is only possible through Christ. In many places, as the pioneers in education, they have retained rights in the appointment of teachers and in directing religious education in day schools. As the relation between the State provided education and the religious education within the schools varies very much throughout the world, the Reformed churches, like other churches, are aware of the varied problems of how the Christian understanding of the world may be rightly related to general education. Many teachers are active members of Christian congregations. There is a service which they can render by their Christian understanding. There are many helps that the Church should provide for teachers, both in religious education within the schools and in the relation between the Christian faith and the many subjects which they teach. In Britain, for example, quite a number of men trained for the Presbyterian ministries are teaching as specialists in religious education in grammar schools. This is a sphere of Christian service to which the Church should give a great deal of thought.

The majority of those who are sick, and in many cases those who are old, are being looked after by the provisions of the State. It is difficult, however, to exclude from welfare services a certain impersonal attitude, in which people are treated as cases rather than persons. It is here that a special Christian service can obviously be rendered, not only by the pastoral care of the minister of a congregation, but by that of elders and of deaconesses. In large urban areas other members of congregations, too, have been organized as regular visitors to the sick and the old, and Presbyterian churches, like those of other denominations, have established homes for the old. This is a constant form of service to which the Church is called, and one to which it is called in a more extended way today.

V. THE CHURCH AS CRITIC OF THE SOCIAL STRUCTURE

There has been a strong anti-Erastian element in the Presbyterian tradition which statesmen have, from time to time, accused of itself being a desire for theocracy. However such criticism of the State and of society may have been misused, it represents a service which the Church must render. Need in a society may be due, not to lack of social services, but to something fundamentally wrong with the society itself. The social or political structure may need radical reformation which the community is incapable itself of carrying out. The Christians and the Christian Church in such a society may believe themselves called, unpopular though it is, openly to criticize the whole political or social structure. In doing so the Christian community has constantly to ask itself how far it is to blame by its past silences for the social and political ills of its day. Equally it must undergo certain self-criticism of the failure of its members to take part in politics or in trade unions. It is clear to us now how closely nineteenth-century Protestantism was aligned to a capitalized society. One of the services which the Church may have to render is to urge radical changes in a community structure. It is not unnatural that pastors, elders, deaconesses, and other church workers should be aware of certain ills and injustices and possess information about them such as no other people have (see Karl Barth, *Church Dogmatics*, English translation, vol. IV, 3, part 2, p. 892).

VI. THE WORK OF THE DEACON

There is considerable variety of opinion as to whether the deacon should be a full-time officer of the Church or should be a member of the congregation chosen for this task as a voluntary part-time job, but probably on the whole the latter opinion is the most common in Presbyterian churches. As in the case of the eldership, there would be no general hesitancy to ordain a man to such an office. It would also be fairly commonly agreed that there may well be certain special times and places where there should be full-time deacons. Some of the services which a deacon should render clearly require special training, and for this special training some central training centre may well be necessary. While the work which deacons perform within the Church will, in many cases, be primarily centred in the congregation, it is no less clear today that not only a congregation but a presbytery will require certain services to be rendered for the whole area. A special work for sections of the community not provided for by the State or the co-operation of the Church with the State in the care of those in special need will almost certainly require men trained to work over a considerable area.

The Church in this age is giving more thought to the special place and function which *women* may perform within the service of the Church. It is interesting that it was to diaconal service that the Church first opened its doors to women. A special place found for widows in the primitive Church points to a type of service that almost certainly can be rendered today. There are many acts of kindness and of service which women perform in an outstanding way, both in the care of the sick and of children. By and large Reformed churches have, in theory, seen very few barriers to the functions that women also may perform within the Church, but in practice, they have been given, since the Reformation, a very small part to play. Some Reformed churches admit women to the eldership, others do not. In many Presbyterian churches deaconesses or church sisters do a great deal of missionary and of social work. Their position in the polity of the Church, however, has often been not worked out at all. If Reformed churches, with others, find a greater place for the diaconate in the life of the Church, there is no doubt that women's place within this office will have to be thought out much more clearly.

VII. SERVICE AND WORSHIP

In contact with Anglican churches the Reformed churches have been made aware of the fact that traditionally the deacon has played a part both in the service of worship of the Church and in the care of those in need. In certain schemes of union it has been assumed that the two different conceptions of diaconate can fairly easily be united. The experience of South India, already referred to, casts some doubt on this. It is argued that those who serve the Christian community or the world at large throughout the week can best make clear the nature of their service by also taking part in the public worship on Sunday. There is danger here of mere ecclesiastical joinery, or the attempt to give ecclesiastical status to those who are deacons. But it is none the less important to make clear that worship and service are two sides of one reality. It has been suggested that it is the deacons in a congregation who should present the congregation's offering at the Sunday service. It has also been suggested that those whose task is to care for the sick or the needy should have some part in leading the intercessions of the congregation. It is they above all who will know what the real needs are. While Presbyterian churches have given a very special place to those who proclaim the Word and administer the Sacraments, they have also been insistent that these are not a caste apart. Presbyterian churches have constantly hesitated to draw a distinction between clergy and laity. They rather see the ministry as a body of men within the people of God who, possessed of special gifts, are called to exercise them within the Church. If gifts necessary for the diaconate also include certain functions which they best can perform within the public worship of the Church, then certainly they should have a place in such public worship. Traditionally, in many Presbyterian churches, it has been the elders who have assisted the minister at the Holy Communion, though some Presbyterian scholars hold that any member of a congregation has an equal right to be invited to do this. It is clear that deacons also might well be considered as those worthy to perform such a function. The Presbyterian churches would be hesitant to introduce deacons into the conduct of public worship purely as a means of uniting churches which have deacons performing functions in public worship, but Presbyterian churches clearly have no right to refuse to consider such a possibility, if the service which deacons perform points to their rightly taking this place, as appears to have been the case in the early Church.

Diakonia in the Methodist Church Today

GORDON S. WAKEFIELD

The name 'deacon' is absent from Methodist nomenclature and polity. 'Its omission may be accounted for on the ground of Mr Wesley's unwillingness to adopt Church terms to distinguish his office-bearers, while the Methodist Societies, according to his apprehension at first, constituted a kind of order in the Church of England, a society which had ordained deacons of its own.'[1]

When Wesley abridged the *Book of Common Prayer* to provide a service book for America, he changed the titles of bishops and priests in the ordinal to superintendents and elders, but retained deacons. This threefold ministry was continued in the British edition of 1786, and subsequently until the middle of the nineteenth century, but since there were no Wesleyan ordinations from Wesley's death in 1791 until 1836, it is clear that failure to revise was due to disuse. Alteration to the present form of 'Ordination of Candidates for the Ministry' was made in 1848, but there has never been other than a single order of ministry in the Methodist Church. 'Ministers on trial' or 'probationers', though they often exercise full pastoral functions with dispensation to administer Holy Communion, are not ordained.

The debate on the proposals for union with the Church of England has produced from an eminent layman the suggestion that the *Service of Reconciliation* could be made more palatable if Methodists would recognize that they were a 'one-ordination church' being invited to enter the further stages which the Anglican doctrine of the ministry deems essential.[2] This ingenious idea is not likely to find much favour. It cannot be rid of the implication that the present Methodist ministry is a perpetual diaconate, i.e. a lower order, which displeases most those most anxious to insist that the minister has no priesthood differing in kind from that of the layman.

Methodist theologians of the nineteenth century strongly maintained that though the name deacon might be lacking from the Methodist title-deeds, the concept of *diakonia* was of the *esse* of the Church of Christ. What puzzled them

---

[1] Alfred Barrett, *The Ministry and Polity of the Christian Church: Viewed in their Scriptural and Theological Aspects: And in Relation to Principles Professed by the Wesleyan Methodists* (London, 1854), p. 208.
[2] David Foot Nash, *Their Finest Hour* (London, 1964).

was the question 'Where in Methodism is the diaconate?' Granted that it is not an order of the ministry, is it exercised by the local preachers or the various stewards of the societies and circuits?

In *A Comparative View of Church Organisations Primitive and Protestant* (1891), J. H. Rigg refers to the office of lay or local preacher 'which some have regarded as a branch of the diaconal service, and others as a modern equivalent to the office of prophet in the early Churches'.[1] Alfred Barrett had held the former view in his *Essay on the Pastoral Office as a Divine Institution in the Church of Christ* (1839).[2] It is arguable that this is due to a vestigial Anglicanism—a local preacher corresponds to a deacon because he shares part of the ministry of the man in full connexion. But no one seems to have believed that the whole of *diakonia* could be fulfilled by those whose task was almost exclusively preaching. Barrett included class leaders in the diaconal body as well as local preachers.

By 1854, however, he had changed his mind. 'Further reflection has convinced me that this arrangement is incorrect, inasmuch as the *original* ordination of deacons was not to the care of souls but to the serving of tables'.[3] Barrett maintains that pastors are directly ministers of *Christ*; deacons are directly *ministers* of the Church, though, of course, all are ultimately responsible to the Church's Lord. He would, I think, have agreed with the question and answer of Benjamin Gregory:

Who in the present day hold the corresponding office to that of a New Testament deacon?

The officers of finance, who, in some churches, still bear the same name, but in other churches are called stewards.[4]

Barrett claimed that the duties of the diaconate were discharged in the Wesleyan system 'upon a scale larger than is known in any communion of Christendom', and chiefly by society stewards ('they arose before any other subordinate functionaries'), circuit stewards, and stewards of the poor.

These offices still exist in the Methodist Church, and they all include important financial responsibilities. The society stewards

shall be the Treasurers of the Society Fund, which is the local Church Fund for the maintenance of the Ministry in the Circuit. They shall receive from the Leaders all contributions made in the Society Classes or otherwise by the members, and also such of the Sunday collections, or sums allocated from the collections by the Local Finance Committee . . . excepting always such collections or allocations as may have been made for Trust or Connexional Funds or for other specified objects. They shall meet all financial obligations on behalf of the Society, and present a statement of the account quarterly to the Leaders Meeting. On behalf of the Leaders Meeting they shall, quarter by quarter, pay to the Circuit Stewards the sum allocated to the Society by the assessment of the Circuit Quarterly Meeting.[5]

[1] op. cit., p. 222.   [2] op. cit., p. 128 n.   [3] *Ministry and Polity*, p. 211.
[4] Benjamin Gregory, *A Handbook of Scriptural Church Principles and of Wesleyan Methodist Polity and History* (London, 1888), p. 10.
[5] *The Constitutional Practice and Discipline of the Methodist Church, 1963*, p. 157.

The society stewards are also responsible for seeing that all services, meetings and other engagements appointed on the circuit plan are duly held, and 'for welcoming and being in attendance upon the Preacher before and after the Service'. A very interesting standing order instructs them to make all necessary arrangements for the administration of the sacrament of baptism. The circuit system means that these lay officials have a far closer concern with the preparation of the externals of worship than is customary where there is invariably a resident minister.

This is seen even more clearly in the case of poor stewards. They prepare the table for the Lord's Supper, as well as ensuring that a collection for the poor fund is taken at the sacrament. This means that there is no offertory in the technical sense in the usual Methodist communion service. In this, perhaps, it corresponds to Cranmer's intention in 1552, which was obscured by the Caroline reinterpretation of his rite. More important for our purpose, however, is the consequence that by virtue of the office of poor steward the laity are closely involved in the Lord's Supper. The service is not the peculiar preserve of the clergy, as is the Anglican tendency, at least according to the experiences of John Robinson in the parishes of rural Somerset some years ago.[1]

Circuit stewards, these days, are regarded as the 'leading laymen' of the group of societies known as a circuit. They are financial officers, though they are also very closely concerned with the invitation and appointment of ministers.

Alfred Barrett was inclined to lament the fact that these officials were called stewards and not deacons; also the absence of 'those solemnities connected with the appointment, such as prayer and the imposition of hands, which were observed in apostolical and ancient days'. But he recognizes that any form of ordination would be unseemly when an office is held only by annual election and for a limited number of years. He half craves for a separated order and for a greater dignity to surround these offices, but he concludes that 'the lowering of individual importance is the price men must pay for an honest democracy'.[2]

Earlier, Barrett had shown himself aware that *diakonia* in Methodism is not really limited to those who hold office. He was doubtless thinking of the vast philanthropy and mutual aid for which Methodism has been renowned all over the world. In many a depressed village or hideous slum, Methodists have shown to one another, and to all in need, without discrimination, the 'little, nameless, unremembered acts of kindness and of love'. There have been and still are Methodist magnates and tycoons, but much of their charity has been given in secret, with no trumpetings, much less the spirit of patronage, the rich condescending to the poor.

But Methodism has organized its philanthropy. Every contribution to a local society is taxed for the benefit of the underprivileged, whether to subsidize the building of church premises or the provision of ministerial help for those who could not raise sufficient money on their own, or to aid missionary work overseas,

[1] cf. *Layman's Church* (London, 1963), pp. 13f.
[2] *Ministry and Polity*, pp. 209f.

which means schools and hospitals as much as direct evangelism. The Christian Citizenship Department has a Methodist Relief Fund, which exists to meet International emergencies such as earthquakes and hurricanes, to transmit monies to the Freedom from Hunger Campaign and Christian Aid, and even, in some instances, to relieve personal distress beyond the capacities of the local poor fund.

Undoubtedly the most signal instance of Methodist *diakonia* is the National Children's Home. Wesley himself founded an Orphan House in Newcastle upon Tyne, but it was more than a century later that Dr T. B. Stephenson began the work which now spans Britain. It is interesting to read in the report to the Methodist Conference of 1964 that a substantial proportion of the income is derived from non-Methodist sources, and 'shows the result of an appeal which is becoming increasingly national rather than denominational'.

But it is the evolution of Dr Stephenson's women workers into the Wesley Deaconess Order which is most relevant to our theme. There is a distinction between the home sisters, who are trained and commissioned, and the deaconesses, who receive a theological education in their institute at Ilkley, and, after a probationary period, are ordained, by the laying-on of hands, and with these words:

Take thou authority to fulfil the office of a Deaconess in the Church of God now committed unto thee, in the Name of the Father and of the Son and of the Holy Ghost. Amen.

Before the imposition of hands a badge is presented to each candidate and afterwards a Bible, as with ministerial ordinands. The Gospel at the service is the story of the pedilavium in John 13, and the President of Conference reminds the sisters of 'the various and exacting services' which their calling requires:

It may fall to you to preach the Gospel, to lead the worship of a congregation, to teach both young and old; you may be required to feed the flock of Christ, to nurse the sick, to care for the poor, to rescue the fallen, to succour the hopeless, to offer friendship, even at cost, to many, who but for you may never know a Christian friend. But in all this you must be true evangelists of Our Lord Jesus Christ, translating your Gospel into the language of personal service. . . .

In 1874 a deaconess movement began in the small German Methodist Church. Of this, the writer in *A New History of Methodism* (1909) remarked—'Only those who have been with them month after month in the sick room can know and appreciate the gentle, calm mysticism, yet true devotion of the "Sisters of Bethany", and of the "Martha and Mary" association.'[1] This German movement had important repercussions in the Methodist Episcopal Church of America.

This short account of *diakonia* in Methodism raises several matters which demand theological evaluation, and to this we must now turn. Since the

[1] op. cit., vol. II, p. 49.

nineteenth-century writers referred to, there has been little Methodist thought on the subject, and, therefore, we shall doubtless find ourselves making some tentative, pioneer, and probably unacceptable and misguided suggestions as to future developments.

It is becoming a cliché to speak of Methodist pragmatism, but our study has provided a good example of it. For Wesley and the early Methodists the diaconate was the lowest rank of the ministry in the Church to which they half belonged. But *diakonia* in the New Testament senses arose spontaneously as the Methodist societies sought to promote Scriptural Christianity. It sprang from the closeness of *koinonia*, and the awareness of human need and Christian responsibility which the Spirit gives. This has much to commend it. 'By their fruits ye shall know them.'

Alfred Barrett says that the diaconate is a plastic office, which may be moulded by circumstances and necessities. It deals with temporalities and may be varied as they are. In this, it is unlike the pastorate, which must remain fixed.[1] On the latter point we shall have more to say below, but while *solvitur ambulando* is often a good rule for Christian organization, *diakonia* is too Scriptural an office, too closely related to the very heart of Christianity to be left entirely to chance, even to 'providence'. The very elect, with Christ's true love in their hearts, may sometimes be deficient in imagination, or simply ignorant of the real needs of men. It has been suggested that it may be quite as important for the British churches to take into their systems 'a diaconate primarily concerned with ministering to Christ in the persons of the needy' as to adopt episcopacy or eldership.[2]

Perhaps the nineteenth-century view that in Methodism a deacon is primarily a financial officer needs some revision. Does the function of steward precisely correspond? May we not need to think of stewards as a further order in the Church of God concerned chiefly with financial administration, while the deacons are much more propagandists, organizers and participants in the work of personal service?

The poor steward may appear to be the true Methodist equivalent of a deacon, because he combines treasurership of the fund devoted entirely to the relief of distress, the nucleus of which is the monetary offering at Holy Communion, with the service of *the* table. He is involved in the liturgy. But is his position used as fully and consciously by the Church as it ought to be?

In him, the ordinary, inarticulate worshipper is brought very close to the sacred mysteries. He is sometimes chosen for sheer humble worthiness. In some societies he is expected to graduate to the Society stewardship, but in others he —or she—may be someone without notable presence or gifts, or one of the younger members. He is less clericalized than many local preachers, and without the sacristy-mindedness which is reputed to be the occupational disease of Anglican servers.

Yet there is a price to be paid for these manifest advantages. The only place

[1] *Ministry and Polity*, p. 207.
[2] C. E. B. Cranfield, *The Service of God* (London, 1965), p. 32.

for the poor stewards in the actual service is to take the collection and motion the communicants to the table. The presiding minister does not normally look to them for help in the distribution when there are no other ordained ministers present. They are charged with the disposal of any of the elements that remain, which means that the wine is usually poured back into the bottle, and the bread thrown to the birds. One must admit that if poor stewards preserve Methodism from fastidiousness, undue scrupulosity, and excessive clericalization of the sacrament, as they operate at present, they help to deprive Methodist celebrations of a *mystique* for which many worshippers crave, and which could restore a whole new dimension to Methodist spirituality.

If there were, in Methodism, a diaconate 'primarily concerned with ministering to Christ in the persons of the needy', would it not be appropriate to involve its members in the liturgy as assistants to the presiding minister, particularly, perhaps, as distributors of the cup? They would need to offer themselves, be chosen, undergo a short and simple course of training, and be solemnly commissioned for an indefinite period. Democracy (*pace* Barrett) would no more be assailed than by the order of local preachers, though it might be advisable to legislate for an elected and changing representation of the diaconate in the Church courts. This could be a means of revival for the worshipping life of many Methodist societies.

Any discussion of *diakonia* in the Methodist Church today is bound to raise the problems of women and the ministry. From early days Methodism has been extremely cautious here, though the smaller denominations in their revivalist period were less inhibited in the use of women as preachers than was the Wesleyan body. Today women are accepted for every office save that of the full-time, itinerant ministry. The Methodist Conference in 1948 debarred them from this, and attempts to raise the matter since have been frustrated by the desire not to embarrass the unity discussions with the Church of England. It is perhaps valid to argue that a departure from Catholic tradition should be decided by a united Church, especially when large administrative changes are involved.

It is impossible to avoid the suspicion, however, that the traditional Methodist mentality regards woman's place as the diaconate not the full ministry. Few today would write or speak in the patronizing tones of Dr Waddy Moss in *A New History of Methodism*—'though a woman does not seem to everybody to be in her best place when she is in the pulpit, there are confessedly some ministries for which she is better fitted than men, and others which should even be committed to her exclusively. . . . For work amongst the sick poor, amongst women in trouble and girls in peril, these sisters of the people are an indispensable part of the equipment of a fully organized church; and their devotion and modesty, the warmth of their sympathy, and the quietness of their ways, are telling directly to the glory of Christ in the relief of human distress.'[1] But the majority of Methodists have felt like that (the women themselves not least), and postponement will not make the decision easier, particularly if the feminist cause becomes

---

[1] op. cit., vol. I, p. 455.

identified with anti-Anglicanism, which, mercifully, does not seem probable.

Meanwhile, there is a dearth of candidates for the Wesley Deaconess Order, and the considerations which are influencing men to fulfil their Christian vocations in secular pursuits as teachers, psychiatrists, social workers and the rest, weigh even more strongly with women. There is also the fact that the era of the dedicated spinster is coming to an end. The modern woman wants marriage *and* a career, and neither society nor the churches have adjusted themselves to the realization of this, though it seems likely that Wesley deaconesses will no longer be required to resign from the order when they marry.

At the same time, we must not ignore the revival of the 'religious' life in our time, and in all denominations, those 'living springs' of which Dr Olive Wyon has written, the women's communities of Grandchamps, Darmstadt, and Farncombe, the last of which numbers a Methodist retired deaconess among its members. There are particular gifts which women can bring to the service of Christ. Dr Waddy Moss's list is not wholly the redundant catalogue of a patronizing male, nor must we forget the mysticism which the description of the German deaconesses mentioned.

These qualities are not, however, exclusively feminine, and the decisive scriptural word would seem to be 'In Christ there is neither male nor female'. Almost certainly we shall move towards a Church in which, while there are still diversities of gifts and, differences of order, sex will no longer be so influential as formerly in deciding who possesses or has a right to exercise them.

No discussion of *diakonia* can properly conclude without some specific attempt to consider its implications for our understanding of the ministry as a whole. The Wesleyan Methodists at any rate had a high doctrine of the ministry. Alfred Barrett regarded it as fixed and unchangeable. This was partly due to his distinction between spiritual and temporal, those offices which are concerned with the content of the Gospel, and the everlasting salvation of souls, and those which are organizational and help to provide the setting and circumstances for the offer of Christ. Today such a distinction, which admittedly can be derived from Acts 6^2, is unfashionable. Indeed, the whole account of the ordination of the seven reads uncomfortably beside the reiterated words and actions of Christ 'I am among you as he that serveth'.

One of the great rediscoveries of our time is that the whole Church must take the form of a servant, and those appointed to its chief tasks must be the servants of all. John 13 ought not simply to be read at the ordination of deacons or deaconesses. A recent editor of Charles Wesley has headed the following lines 'For a Candidate for the Ministry':

> Meanest of all who Thee confess,
> The least of all Thy witnesses,
> Oh that I may be counted meet
> To wash Thy dear disciples' feet.[1]

---

[1] J. Alan Kay, *Wesley's Prayers and Praises* (London, 1958), p. 139.

It is a problem in the Church to reconcile orders with humility and rule with service. Bonhoeffer's suggestion, so eagerly taken up by our new radical theorists, that 'the clergy should live solely on the free-will offerings of their congregations, or possibly engage in some secular calling',[1] could point to a solution, though lack of financial independence could inhibit courage, while it would seem misguided to suggest that the pastorate and the leading of worship are not tasks which demand the whole of a man's time and thought and energy. Some, surely, must continue to be set apart and to 'direct all their cares and studies this way'.

Ultimately, no human contrivance can protect the Church or its individual officers from pride or self-assertiveness. But an open and free colleagueship may help. And if the one ministry is seen to be Christ's, delegated to the members of His Church, and divided among them severally as He calls, then one might hope for a new and wide collegiality of bishops, presbyters, deacons, and stewards, men and women, some part-time, some full-time, but each finding his chief joy as the servants of the servants of God.

This looks beyond the present structure of Methodism, and it might seem to omit the local preacher completely. His position today is somewhat ambiguous. Is he a member of an order, so that he could be, as by Barrett in 1839, mistaken for a deacon? After all, he now must undergo examinations and be recognized at a special service. Or is he, in fact, outside the ordered ministry, the prophet from among the people, who emanates from revivalist movements rather than from the Catholic Church? If, today, the former is his true role, then we had better rank him among the part-time presbyterate, and ordain him, and give him the ministry of the sacraments as well as the word. But no living Church can be so well ordered as to exclude liberty of prophesying, the right of the ordinary, unordained member to give utterance to the faith that is in him, sometimes from the church pulpit, but more often in less conventional ways and in unconsecrated places. Sometimes his task may be to rebuke the Church: more often these days it will be to convict or convince the world. But this takes us beyond *diakonia*. It has been necessary to mention it because in Methodism *diakonia*, like *episcope*, has not been so much defined as shared in a variety of forms. It has been vastly effective. But 'the coming great Church' and the needs of the world alike will demand reappraisal, experiment, and adaptation.

[1] *Letters and Papers from Prison* (1953 ed.), p. 180.

Some Reflections on Secular Diakonia

D. M. MACKINNON

This paper is concerned with some aspects of the contemporary significance of the concept of *diakonia*. I say some aspects, for I must be necessarily selective; but I am concerned to inquire whether the concept effectively illuminates the present-day scene. Do we, by asking questions concerning its applicability, learn something not only about modern society, but also about the content of the concept itself? Or does the application emerge as something forced and consequently distorting?

Here, however, it is worth recalling that theologically all *diakoniai*, whether personal or institutional, are parables of the archetypal, fundamental *diakonia*, the mission of Christ, who came οὐ διακονηθῆαι, ἀλλὰ διακονῆδαι. That once for all *diakonia* was the fundamental service men demanded. In John the pediluvium was performed to express its inwardness, an action at once menial and suggestive. But in itself Christ's mission promises the norm of *diakonia*, and if it illuminates its depths by parabolic samples of *diakonia* in human affairs, they are themselves illuminated, and, still more important, succoured by it. Indeed, their ultimate health is in it.

If we turn to the world we live in, we find parables of the ultimate *diakonia* in all sorts of unexpected places. If I begin by selecting examples from work that is fundamentally theoretical, I do so because in such work the assumptions are inevitably articulate, and the paradox consequently more sharply revealed. Take, for instance, the work of Baroness Wootton, on such subjects as the social foundation of wages policy, and more particularly the function of penal institutions. There is no doubt that men and women of traditional mind are often on edge in the presence of projects of penal reform, especially those which consciously aim at subordinating altogether the concept of retribution to that of reformation. We find various reasons given for this hesitation, some of them more intellectually respectable than others. But it would be wrong to ignore altogether the extent to which inadequate *Versöhnungslehre* has given certain evangelical Christians a kind of vested interest in the retributive conception of punishment. We have all of us met self-styled evangelicals for whom the *Anknüpfungspunkt* between men and God is found in the institution of retributive punishment, following guilt incurred. They write and speak as if sovereignty were predicable of a set of abstract ideas, and not of the Father who sent His Son to be the saviour of the world. But an honest, theological critical spirit will find *diakonia* most certainly present in those who, like Lady Wootton, search out the inconsistency, the unacknowledged cruelties, the informing prejudices (e.g. in the different esteeming of even trivial offences against property, on the one side, and motoring offences, which could easily end in the maiming or death of the innocent, on the other) of our judicial procedure and the penal administration. Her standpoint is utilitarian; she finds the values she would promote more or less adequately contained in a relatively unsophisticated concept of human happiness, and she refuses to concede any independent sanctity or venerable dignity to institutions, tradition and procedure which impede a measurable advance towards the increase of that happiness. At first she seems a long way removed from the Good Samaritan of the parable—likely indeed to be embarrassed by the comparison! But in the world we inhabit we must seek the 'Good Samaritans' (parables themselves of the ultimate Samaritan) in those who by their works, their energy, their disciplined effort, prove themselves neighbours to those who fall among thieves. Take another example from prewar history; I refer to the late Lord Keynes on unemployment. The memory of the fall of the Labour Government of 1931 is one that is still vividly alive. The policies of its so-called 'National' success or—and I refer especially to the continuing acceptance of unemployment, with the unemployed men's benefit slashed in the name of economy, as a built-in feature of our society—have left scars that remain to this day, Keynes is remembered as the man who challenged those assumptions as an economist, and argued powerfully for another way. He did not achieve a final wisdom, a panacea for all times and all places; but in the Britain of Ramsay MacDonald, Stanley Baldwin, and Neville Chamberlain, he was neighbour to those who had fallen, if not among thieves, at least into places where there was none effectively to help them. Those of my age smile as they recall their guilt-ridden amateurish efforts at first-aid in unemployment centres and the like in those days; but we do not smile when we recall the extent to which we owed, for instance, our final educational opportunities particularly, to policies which, if they squeezed the wage-earners and left the unemployed to rot, were calculated to give wider opportunity to those whose resources were differently derived. Here was surely an experience of what Marx called 'alienation'—estrangement from one's fellows—that we learn unconsciously to accept as part of the inherited scheme of things. It is not the least of Keynes's services that he sought, by intense intellectual effort, to find the means of eliminating a destructive source of guilt.

It should be noted that his intensely interesting paper 'My Early Beliefs', read privately in 1938, and published posthumously in 1948, reveals that Keynes accepted to the full the late Professor G. E. Moore's drastic criticism of hedonistic utilitarianism, and he himself in later life learnt something of the inadequacy of the highly sophisticated doctrine which Moore and Lowes Dickinson sought to substitute for Benthamism, which they rejected. Yet he remained one of the greatest humanists of his generation, marked, one can hardly deny indelibly, by the lessons concerning the nature of values he had learnt from Moore.

We find comparable *diakonia* today in the work, for instance, of Professor Richard Titmuss, who has made a most careful study of the workings of the welfare state, and seeks, as a social scientist, to grapple with the obvious crisis of the National Health Service. But we find analogous and related manifestations of what we must surely regard as *diakonia* in the laboratories of research workers. For instance, I think of those who are investigating conditions of the ageing of bodily tissue, hoping thereby to lay the foundation of a more adequate geriatric medicine. Their service is of a different order from that of those who face daily the utterly depressing duties of nursing in the geriatric wards of our hospitals; but we cannot deny the title 'service' to what the research worker has undertaken, with the peculiarly exacting disciplines that it imposes.

Such a man may be, by profession, a humanist, or his concentration may exclude him from the consideration of general ideas, with resultant refusal to label himself at all in such terms. But as much in his way as Baroness Wootton, the late Lord Keynes, and Professor Titmuss, we must regard him as truly of the Samaritans' school.

So far I have concerned myself with men and women whose contribution has been, at least in part, on the plane of theory. But *diakonia* is to be found at the level of practice, likewise in quite unsuspected places. If I may take an immediately contemporary example, to which I shall return later, we must surely find *diakonia* in the work of those who would, by their effort, make the United Kingdom economically healthy again, able in the many critical areas of international tension, for instance in central Europe and in the Far East, to make its voice heard in a way hardly possible at a time of an ever-present threat to sterling. In a time of economic weakness any nation is inevitably restrained in the counsels she offers to those economically stronger than herself, by knowledge of her possible dependence on them for support, even survival. These are hard facts of life which moral idealists, deeply aware of the follies and worse to which their position and responsibility may tempt the strong, must recognize.

Again, to turn for a moment to wider issues, we must surely find *diakonia* among those who concern themselves theoretically and practically with the issue of the ever-increasing menace of the 'population explosion'. It is very easy for the simple-minded to see *diakonia* in the fund-raising activity of those who raise large sums of money, for instance for Oxfam; it is harder to see it in the devoted labour of biological and social scientists who are seeking, day and night, the means of tackling a supreme emergency, of whose imminence a large majority are still blithely unaware. But most certainly it should be seen there as well. At first sight, it may seem a paradox to describe as *diakonia* the effective dissemination of proper contraceptive skills; but in the situation with which the whole world is faced in respect of ever-increasing numbers it would be hard to disqualify the work from its claim to that title. There is certainly a tragic element in the fact that increasing mastery of various killing diseases has given rise, in its turn, to the tormenting issue of overpopulation. As we shall see later in this essay, the tragic elements in human life are elements with which the most sketchy treatment of *diakonia* in the world today must concern itself; but recognition of the tragic must not be allowed to inhibit action, even if it must deepen perception and, in consequence, purify the motives and intentions from which men act.

Already this brief study has made us aware of the extent to which a treatment of *diakonia* in the world today involves us in questions of politics and of economics, in the fundamental sense of the conditions of the creation of wealth. No one who recalls the details of the Suez adventure in 1956 will wish to claim too much for British wisdom and moderation in international affairs. But equally there are conflicts, destructive in themselves and infinitely menacing to the peace of the world, in which Britain could intervene on the side of moderation, were she not hobbled by an unfavourable situation. Although its correction calls for political decision in control of the economy, allocation of priorities, etc., the actual work of the creation of wealth is something still in our society, to a considerable extent, left in the hands of individuals, even though highly organized in productive units. As soon as one recognizes the dependence of political attitude on wealth, one is plunged into a world of frightening ambiguity. Few works make the depth of this plainer than Joseph Conrad's great political novel, *Nostromo*, not only one of the greatest novels in the English language, but a major contribution to the fundamental anatomy of politics. But even if we leave on one side detailed attention to the conditions under which wealth is created, and attend only to the business of government, involved today in every allocation of priorities and consequently a necessary condition of every effective initiative in the field of welfare, the matter is complicated enough. Suppose we say that we must discern a great act of *diakonia* in the work which the late Mr Aneurin Bevan did in establishing the National Health Service. In the months in 1948 that followed the establishment of the service permanent officials of the Ministry of Health regularly received most touching letters of thanks from old people, now, for the first time, equipped with spectacles, and able to relieve the boredom of their days by the delights of reading. It could be argued that it was Bevan's battle with the B.M.A. that helped make this relief of distress possible. No doubt the seeds were also sown of present discontents with the National Health Service structure; but something was accomplished, and it was on the plane of government and administration that it was done. It is a commonplace to point out that problems of politics are problems of power; but it is perhaps less often recognized by the devout that for effective action today political power is an essential lever, whether directly exercised or influenced by overwhelming extraordinary pressures in one direction rather than another. If we are to face the actuality of *diakonia* in the world today, we cannot take refuge in a fantasy world wherein the motives and methods of those who do good, or seek to do good, are alike pure. In fact, we know that in private life the motives of 'do-gooders' are muddied in their depths; but they can be more effectively disguised, alike from agent and observer, than is possible on the plane of politics, let alone the related plane of economics. Again we touch the frontiers of the tragic, the conditions of existence, with which men must live, avoiding alike the escape routes of Utopianism and despair.

It may be thought that the approach followed in this essay has given to the concept of *diakonia* restricted application; we now come to the vastly different questions of its relevance to the situation in which the individual man or woman seeks to exert his influence to make his protest, to insert his insight into the decision-making processes of our society; we come, in fact, to an aspect of the plight of democracy, and I propose to illustrate it by turning from the relatively restricted plane of national affairs (to which I have largely but not entirely confined myself), to the tormenting field of international relations, where at first sight it must seem that the significance of the individual is nil, but where, in fact, the overwhelming gravity of the issues, the apparent smugness of those who hold the future of the human race within their power, and a kind of neo-metaphysical concern, have combined to make intrusive protest a feature of our age.

Diakonia means service, and so far this essay has been largely occupied with examples of service in the work of men and women who, by their commanding intelligence, have shown themselves properly equipped to serve their fellows. It has been concerned to rescue the concept from definition in terms of an uninformed goodwill, which may too easily conceal the personal self-indulgence of the *poseur*. In conclusion of this section, there has inevitably been reference to the role of the State in co-ordinating the activities of properly informed agencies of welfare, in establishing priorities between them, in initiating their enterprises, and in providing the resources without which even the best-informed intentions are doomed to sterility. It is clear that reference to the function of the State is necessarily reference to the actualities of power, both in the sense of the resources available to men, in their environment, and of the methods whereby those resources shall be disposed and organized.

And here we meet an element of paradox, familiar in part to those who know something of the history of ethical and political thought, but still in the manner in which we have to deal with it, novel and startling. It is not for nothing that the examples of *diakonia* mentioned so far have been quite concrete; it is not for nothing that their practice has been made possible by a humanism, sometimes vaguely agnostic in temper, at other times almost overtly atheistic. One is tempted to say that an aloofness from metaphysical questioning is part of the equipment of the contemporary *diakonoi*, yet when one recognizes the involvement and role of the State in *diakonia*, one is immediately reminded that it is at the level of the State's organization of the power resources of our society that questions begin to assume a metaphysical, as distinct from a practical, form. To some extent, as well as, and in so far as democracy, understood as a set of methods for holding power, accountable to those in whose name it is allegedly exercised, is effective, metaphysical perplexity is kept at bay. Although it is Utopian fantasy to speak of the individual citizen as exercising any appreciable effect on the decision-making processes of modern government, where internal affairs are concerned, we can still in the ballot-box say some sort of Yes or No to aspects of public policy. But when we pass from the field of internal politics to that of international relations, to speak of any sort of effective participation by the individual becomes a mere *flatus vocis*. There he finds himself confronted with a power system that seems very nearly immune from effective human direction. Inevitably the sheer immensity of the dangers confronting mankind, coupled with the individual's sense of his impotence, and the irrelevance of his personal scruples, begets a sort of deep spiritual malaise in any who may have become imaginatively aware of them, the imminence of these dangers encourages a kind of scepticism concerning the worth of the familiar. This scepticism may, of course, be no more than an adolescent self-indulgence, but it is one which can also be a point of departure for a new formulation of the radical question how a man must live his days.

There is a certain continuity here with the mood in which, in the second book of Plato's *Republic*, the issue of the ontological significance of moral excellence is posed by the two young men Glauco and Adeimantus. There is something of the same awareness of the sheer irrelevance to what happens in the world, to the effective spring of human action and choice, of the aspirations and self-discipline of the saint. In the world of the young men of Plato's dialogue, it is energy, not scruple, that reveals itself as decisive; in the international society in which we find ourselves today, the achievements of our urgent technological genius stand over against us as a monstrous process built into the very structure of our world.

In the thirties Maritain wrote that 'The very crises of the economic order compelled us to study metaphysics'. Today we say that it is the sheer enormity of the possibility of thermonuclear warfare which gives its impetus to a mood of existential revolt. To men and women in such a mood the present organization of international relations, the extent to which they rest on continual unstable 'balance of terror', seems to embody a kind of ultimate 'alienation', wherein the human family is in trembling bondage to its achievement. Against such an alienation they protest, seeking to ground their *non possumus* in some general vision of the human scene. Yet, as one looks back, one sees how little such a study as the one Maritain advised contributed to the resolution of those crises of which he spoke. It could be regarded as a way of escape, both by those who went to Spain to fight in the International Brigade and by those who followed Keynes's example. There is a kind of metaphysical preoccupation which is less *diakonia* than personal self-indulgence. It is not only the positivist who insists on the sterility of metaphysics; anyone who is serious about the problem or set of problems facing humanity must have his suspicions about it. After all, Aristotle himself recognized the practical futility, even destructiveness, of Plato's profound engagement with the metaphysical problem of the foundations of morality, to which we have referred, and which issued in Plato's central doctrine of the 'Idea of God'.

So we do well to suspect what withdraws us off the paths of practical *diakonia* into vague, general perplexity concerning human origins and destiny, and presents the withdrawal as a kind of substitute for resolute action. Such an attitude is a besetting sin of the intellectual, and in our day and age it may take the shape less of overt metaphysical preoccupation than of a generalized attitude of revolt, an attitude that is very nearly completely vacuous. Once we recognize how nearly completely vacuous the attitude is, we may quickly return to a ready acceptance of the concrete realities of the human scene; we may say that we have learnt humility in the school that circumstances have provided for us. The powers that be are 'ordained of God'.

Ideas are here, as always, what we make of them. Acceptance may inspire resignation and political quietism; or from it may spring a truly reverent empiricism. Yet always it seems to be at war with the temper of revolt. And this emerges most clearly at moments of crisis. One must allow that a healthy political and social order will seek to minimize the frequency of such moments, and that it is a vast mistake to extrapolate as principles of a general political theory anxieties relevant to a period of appalling extremes. Thus one cannot, it is argued, extract from consideration of the sorts of decision facing men and women in countries occupied by Nazi Germany between 1939 and 1945 significant illustrations of the principles of political obligation. Here is indeed the stuff of tragedy, rather than the matter of political theory. Yet one must ask whether it is quite as easy as that. We certainly live, however quiet the temper of our individual lives, in an age of extremes; and an age of extremes is one in which tragic drama can sometimes provide more powerful sources of insight than the measured argument of the political theorist. We live in an age in which men and women may suddenly find themselves exposed to themselves by public circumstance, as well as by the more familiar and often more searching ways of private failure, grief, or ordeal. While it is always true that it is in the privacy of his home that a man is most shown for what he is, in such an age as ours the public sometimes so presses on the private that the test, when it comes, is felt at both levels. Thus, a young man in France in 1943 had not infrequently to risk the welfare of his family, if he was to serve the cause of resistance. The demand came from public circumstance; but its searching depth was experienced at the more intimate level of personal choice. So, in a measure, it is true today of all of us at some time or other. We must be concerned about the war in Vietnam; but we do well to suspect that concern, lest it be an attempt at escape, even at the level of imagination and feeling, from the pressure of personal failure.

In both the circumstances mentioned literature often helps men and women in the way of self-knowledge, and therefore in that of responsible decision, more than the political theorist, or even the spiritual writer. Thus Shakespeare's *Julius Caesar* remains (as Mr R. H. S. Crossman has pointed out) the one work in English that really engages with the predicament of the heroes of the July 1944 plot against Hitler. Again, Conrad's exploration of the mind of the *miles gloriosus* in *Lord Jim* (which I agree with Mr Tony Tanner in regarding as one of the greatest studies of conduct in the English language)[1] throws, or may throw, a flood of light on the mind, conscious, subconscious and unconscious, of the nuclear disarmer. For such a protester may (I do not say necessarily does) see himself as a man matched with a supreme hour, and rising to it; but this vision of himself may be a perilous fantasy, or worse. A man's protest may be a deliberate aversion from the costly business of coming to terms with himself. Yet, if he does come to terms with himself, he will not do so as long as he fears that anxiety is offered him only as a mechanism for obliterating his vision, or silencing his voice. There is, very often, in such a protest a tragic quality or, in its more youthful manifestation, a pathetic. Yet what is tragic is found only in that which has a measure of validity. In a continuing age of extremes such as ours undoubtedly is there is a place for the temper of protest. There is a crying need, therefore, for what I can only call a spirituality of protest, a new sort of essay in self-knowledge, rooted and grounded in the sort of perceptions in which great literature abounds, but which also belongs to the Christian tradition. After all, it was Freud himself who said that the poets knew it all already. And what is true of the poets is also true, where the subject-matter of this essay is concerned, of works of fiction, such as *Lord Jim*.

At an early stage in this essay it was suggested that theological examples of *diakonia* which were taken were parables of the ultimate *diakonia*. May not something of the same parabolic quality be found *mutatis omnibus mutandis* in the kind of malaise of which I have more recently written? Its sterility, even its destructiveness, may have a kind of tragic quality that we need to perceive; but when we have once perceived it we may also be made vaguely aware of the extent to which such experience complements the more spiritually protected, because more austerely concentrated, awareness of the practical servant of his fellows. Such judgement may seem harsh and unfair, when one recalls, for instance, the deep awareness of such a man as Abraham Lincoln of the tragic quality of the burden of political power. Yet in the present we have to reckon with the extent to which a prevalent utilitarianism, with all its strengths and weaknesses, may blunt the sharpness of human perception, may atrophy the consciousness and may diminish or altogether destroy our sense of the profoundly parabolic character of human existence. To write in these terms is not to suggest that the tragic is a sort of *Anknüpfungspunkt* between creature and creator; rather it is to remind ourselves that it is at the level of personal self-interrogation, to which tragic perception belongs, and not at that of abstract speculation that metaphysics often finds its home. We need to revise our concept of the metaphysical, to do justice to its situation in the stream of human life; inevitably such a revision will enable us to take stock of its human role, and therefore of its tragic quality. If in faith we see men and women as encountered by God in their manhood and womanhood, we cannot allow that these aspects of what they personally are shall fall outside the scope of that encounter, of that interrogation of all interrogations, of that servicing of all our services.

[1] See his valuable monograph on *Lord Jim* (Edward Arnold, 1963).

It is indeed in the context of the ultimate *diakonia* that we are alone enabled to take hold of our service one to another, to apply the category of *diakonia* to experiences as varied as those I have contrasted in this essay, and therefore to interpret them anew. The schisms in our culture are varied; yet if anything significant has emerged from this essay, it is the recognition that one of the most crucial of them concerns the contradictions between our attitudes to the power element in human life—contradictions which issue in virtually irreconcilable definition of what power is and which also, indeed, show themselves in the ways in which each one of us copes with the world in which we live. To set these contradictions in the context of the ultimate *diakonia* is to see them anew, to see them as *diakoniai*, no more, no less.

The Church's Diakonia in the Modern World

ALAN A. BRASH

The service which Christians, individually or corporately, offer to their neighbours springs from their relationship and obedience to Jesus Christ as Lord. But its form at any particular time and place depends on the nature of the neighbourhood. Whenever organized service fails to take seriously and adjust freely to its environment it becomes barren and irrelevant.

Throughout the churches of the world today there is an increasing awareness that many of the methods by which Christians serve are no longer appropriate to our modern circumstances. These methods, many of them expressed through inflexible institutions, may have been the most relevant possible when they were first adopted. But people both within and without the churches are raising fundamental questions today, and implying that perhaps the enterprises of Christian service should be radically reshaped in response to the characteristics of human life in our time. The debate continues. There will be no easy or rapidly accepted answers. But the churches everywhere have much to learn from the thinking and acting of Christians in Asia, where the tensions have been acute, and the leaders are being forced, often against their wills, to the adoption of new kinds of policy and programme.

The forms of Christian service inherited from the nineteenth century are more or less the same throughout Asia. As missionaries arrived in most areas they found vast numbers of people, not only without any knowledge of God as their Father through Jesus Christ, but also without the means of education or of the healing of their many diseases. Along with the preaching of the Gospel, therefore, and intimately related to it, came all the forms of compassion for the sick and ignorant. At first there were simple schools and clinics. But in the face of the need the work inevitably expanded until there were great colleges and hospitals, operated by qualified and specialist staff.

Various questions about such services have always been discussed. What is their relation to the 'central missionary task' of 'converting' people? Are they just the means to an evangelistic end? Or is service only 'pure' when it is rendered 'for its own sake'? From the point of view of any adequate understanding of the Gospel, of course, these questions are somewhat academic. There can be no real bringing of salvation to any man unless it is concerned with his whole life. There can be no expression of genuine compassion that is not interested in more than a man's bodily state. Be that as it may, the real issue is deeper. Are the methods by which we show Christian caring the ones most relevant to man's need in Asia today? Are there other forms which would be more relevant to that need, and therefore a more adequate expression of the Gospel?

The only characteristic true of almost every part and aspect of Asian life today is change—irresistible, revolutionary change. Newly independent nations enthusiastically adopt the objectives of the welfare state, and their peoples experience the dignity as well as some of the frustrations of freedom and a growing selfhood. Governments increasingly want to undertake the overall task of providing medical and educational services for all their citizens and inevitably want to use the resources of skill, experience, and equipment which previously they had subsidized, although it remained under the exclusive control of the Christian minority. In some cases the Christians are permitted to continue their institutions if they want to, and if they can find the resources—but in competition with the State services. In other cases they are given no such opportunity.

However disastrous such changes appear to those most intimately involved, there is an increasing number of Church leaders who see them as the pressure of God, compelling them to rethink and perhaps reshape their service in terms of the present circumstances. One of the very first results of such rethinking is the recognition of the holiness of the 'secular world' and the responsibility of Christians to serve far beyond the bounds of Church-controlled institutions. As D. T. Niles declares: 'To be possessed by Christ is to find oneself delivered from religious preoccupations and involved in secular life, because that is the life in which He, the risen Lord Himself, is involved' (*Upon the Earth*, p. 52). Or Masao Takenaka: 'Thus we are coming more and more to take worldly affairs seriously, not because of our sociological interest, nor because we have a ready-made blueprint for the ideal world, but precisely because we believe the redemptive power of God is at work in the concrete social reality of our changing world for the restoration of true humanity in Jesus Christ' (*John R. Mott Lectures*, Series II, p. 12). Or from India: 'Where Christians keep apart from movements and adherents inspired by secularism or non-Christian faiths, they keep apart from Christ Himself' (*Christian Participation in Nationbuilding*, p. 266).

One discovers the fruit of this kind of understanding in many places. For example, in the devising of rehabilitation programmes for refugees in Calcutta the two points of view were clearly expressed. Most of the expatriate staff in this operation had a clear preference for providing employment for the refugees by establishing small industries of some kind, under the control of Bengal Refugee Service. Such industries were then part of its 'programme' which could easily be identified, and for which, incidentally, it was easy to raise funds overseas. But other members of the group, including the local Christian businessmen serving on the committee, strongly preferred to study the economic needs of the Calcutta area, and then train refugees in skills that were in short supply, so that they could be fully integrated and permanently rehabilitated. They had no desire to keep the 'Christian' enterprise separate from the purely secular one.

A group of Korean Christians who work in a Seoul factory spend their discussion periods trying to answer the question 'How can we make this factory a more "Christian" place?' From listening to these discussions one quickly becomes aware that their concern is not to make the factory a 'religious' place, but to find practical ways to make it part of the world as it is meant to be, overcoming the tempting corruptions of a money economy and of ruthless competition.

It is obvious that such thinking will bring great changes in the forms of service, for example in terms of hospitals. It is easy to distinguish a Church-controlled from a Government-controlled hospital. But this is by no means to be identified with the distinction between a Christian and a non-Christian hospital. A hospital can be said to be Christian when it fulfils effectively the true purposes of a hospital. It may well be contended that some at least of these ends will not be served unless there is a leaven of Christian participants in the institution; but even so it can clearly be a Christian hospital without any form of Church control. Here is one of the strongest arguments for spreading Christian doctors and nurses throughout the nation's hospital service instead of concentrating them in Church-dominated institutions, for such a diffusion may leaven the whole service, redeem it, and enable it to be Christian in the sense of being its true self.

Sometimes the thinking comes *after* the change is imposed upon the churches by Government action. When the twelve hundred previously subsidized schools were taken out of Church control by the Government of Ceylon it seemed the most devastating blow they had ever suffered. Much, in fact, was lost. But increasingly today one hears statements which indicate that the scattering of the Christian teachers throughout the whole nation and its entire educational system can also be a tremendous gain in Christian leavening power. Similarly with the loss of Judson College in Burma; unburdened by the tasks of administering a great university, Church leaders have begun more fruitful work in providing hostel accommodation and pastoral services to the students. If there is loss, there is also gain. And there are some who claim that the gain is greater than the loss. On the other hand, in Chandigarh, India, where a new and planned city is springing up almost overnight, the churches are planning *in advance* to provide hostels for women students, rather than build a separate university college—thus integrating their service into the total community programme, at the point of one of its greatest needs.

One of the great difficulties in clarifying the strategy of service in Asian countries is the fact that the whole service life of the churches is so substantially paid for by people in other countries. On the one hand, those who provide these large resources are rarely aware of the degree to which the situation in Asia has changed. Their understanding of the methods of service is stereotyped, and is largely determined by a propaganda created by those whose task it is to raise the money, rather than by those who fully participate in the local situation. On the other hand the Asian churches receive 'designated gifts', tied by specific wording, or by traditional agreement, to certain kinds of operation. They hesitate, even if they are theoretically free, to respond in a revolutionary way to a new set of opportunities. More often than not, the very people who are the recipients of such resources are the ones with the greatest vested interest in not disturbing the existing pattern. In such circumstances the Asian churches long for a situation in which those who support them with help from outside will regard them as, and enable them to be, the *subject* of Christian service, not its *object*. They want to break free from the comfortable position where they are pampered recipients of special aid, to become the co-operators in a Christian service to the neighbourhood as a whole.

Two other characteristics of the Asian setting must be noted. First, the problem of the gulf between the affluent and non-affluent peoples of the world—a gulf which affects the interrelations of both nations and churches. One of the great problems of our time is to find some means of handling the inevitable giving and receiving that such a gulf demands in ways that will not be corroding to the selfhood of all involved. This remains a problem for the Asian churches in the context of their service; but they are already striving toward the mutuality of giving and receiving that is one of the keys to a wholesome solution. This is evident in their appointment of over two hundred Asian missionaries, in their response with gifts to disaster situations in East and West, and in their allocation of contributions from the Fellowship of the Least Coin to projects in Europe and the United States, as well as in Africa and Asia.

A second characteristic is the hard fact of population expansion. This challenges the Asian churches directly to a new and unexpected form of service—as evidenced by the Consultation on Responsible Parenthood and the Population Explosion, held in Bangkok in February 1964, and by the proposal of the East Asia Christian Conference to establish mobile teams of experts to aid the churches in making their contribution at this point. Ever since the Middle Ages Christians have been moved to make some provision for 'unwanted' or deserted children. The provision of orphanages has been typical of Church programmes everywhere, not least in Asia. But in many places today—including India, Malaysia, Thailand, Formosa, and Japan—Christians are active also in support of Government and community movements to teach methods of family planning and birth control. But the indirect consequence is in some ways even more important, for it faces the Christians with a task of evangelism and service that for sheer size is far in excess of that faced by any other Christians in all history. How can the churches avoid the conviction that their Lord is compelling them not only to understand the task together, but to think and pray together about their overall strategy of service, to select priority tasks and to work daily together? Such mutual love and respect will make them not only the reconciling servant people within the nations, but also the reconciled people of Jesus Christ.

Asian Churches Confer

It is the judgement of Abrecht (*The Churches in Rapid Social Change*, p. 47) that 'It is doubtful if Christian concern for political and social affairs has been anywhere expressed more boldly and vividly than in the series of study conferences held by the Asian churches 1949–1959 (Bangkok 1949; Lucknow 1953; Siantar 1957; Manila 1958; Kuala Lumpur 1959). At Kuala Lumpur they affirmed their "common conviction that the church should be a full participant in the new life of Asia".'

Between the Kuala Lumpur Assembly of the East Asia Christian Conference in 1959 and the following Assembly at Bangkok 1964, two committees held a series of consultations on the theme 'New Forms of Christian Service'. It is significant that the committees concerned were, on the one hand, 'Church and Society', and on the other, 'Inter-Church Aid for Mission and Service'. The intention was to bring together in each consultation two types of people— Christian experts on various aspects of the economic, social or political life of the nation, and those actively involved in works of specifically Christian service. The discussions were held in Nasrapur, India (including representatives from Burma, Pakistan, and Ceylon), the Philippines, Indonesia, Korea, and Japan. Another similar consultation was held separately in Uduvil, Ceylon. The thinking and forms of Christian service reflected in these consultations indicates radically new and excitingly relevant ways in which Asian Christians are beginning to serve their neighbours in the circumstances of the time. There is a determined attempt to read the 'signs of the time' in such a way as to distinguish between the efforts and achievements of men which fit into God's purposes, and those which are denials of all that He has revealed to us.

Service by Participation

General Simatupang, former army leader in Indonesia and the convener of the consultation in that country, expressed in a useful analogy the essence of the new emphasis, in an address to the W.C.C. Committee on Specialized Assistance to Social Projects (Bangkok, March 1964). He described 'the long march of the nation' on its way to the fulfilment of its revolution and the achievement of social justice. What is the function of the Christians in that march? They have always ministered to the casualties of one kind or another who fall by the wayside, and they must continue to do so. But they must also share as Christians in the ideological exchanges leading to the defining of national objectives, and in the long struggle of the whole community to achieve them. They must no longer stand on the perimeter, but must be the permeating leaven, the first fruits of the Kingdom, in the very heart of the national struggle. In the past, Christians have been far too concerned that their particular service should be distinctive, identifiable, and of a character not seen elsewhere. They have wanted to be separate and, preferably, to receive the adulation accorded to pioneers.

Obviously this is partly a matter of whether the Church will run its own separate institutions, and inevitably draw qualified Christians into them, or whether such trained Christians can do a better service to their neighbours and make a better witness to the Gospel by being in the more difficult posts under community direction. Whereas in many places Church institutions were at one time the very best available, it is obviously impossible for a religious minority to compete against a Government whose conscience is aroused to the needs, and whose resources are very much greater than those of the minority. The result, in not a few places, is a desperate and hopeless struggle by the Church and a steady loss of prestige.

But the loss to the community is also very great. It is to be regretted that in Korea, for example, so many 'Christian' universities have been established, mostly by endowments from overseas. These draw Christians to themselves, with the result that the great community universities, though of the highest standards and strategic importance, are almost completely bereft of Christian staff.

A good illustration of what is involved for the individual Christian is given by one of the participants of the Madras Consultation of the Department on the Co-operation of Men and Women in Church, Home and Society (W.C.C. Report, p. 26): 'Individual witnessing should be done dangerously rather than comfortably. It is easy to be a Christian and to witness inside a church or church related institution. It is more difficult in a non-christian world. Forgive my using a personal illustration. Some fifteen years ago I had to choose between a government job with a large salary, and a teaching job in a church-related institution with a small salary. This kind of decision had already come up in our family. Two of my sisters had taken government work. I took the humble one and felt rather self-righteous that I had undertaken sacrificial living. Today I reverse my position, for I have learnt that it is far easier to be a Christian on a christian campus, than it is in a government job under constant non-christian pressure.' And of course it is quite clear that it is not only more difficult in the community at large, it is often a more effective sphere of service, a greater and more fruitful act of obedience.

But it is not only or primarily a matter of institutions. The relevance of the Church maintaining its own institutions will vary from country to country. In some circumstances, for example, the Church can make a real contribution to education by having a limited number of independent schools, provided this is not the sole Christian contribution to education. In other circumstances the Church will require to keep its own medical institutions primarily as a training-ground for personnel being sent out into service in the wider community. In Hong Kong many Christian leaders claim that the Church institutions remain as one of the primary centres of evangelism—a claim that cannot be supported in most parts of Asia.

There is more at issue than the finding of new answers to the practical and difficult question of institutions. What is happening is a rediscovery of the meaning of faith in an *incarnate* Lord. There is a new trust in the ultimate consummation of His redemptive purpose for the world, and the relevance of our working with Him as He suffers to redeem it—because He is, in fact, Lord over it. It is the beginning of an outpouring of service and caring *into the world* of sin and pain, in endless patience and trust, because it is His world. It is the falling of the seed into the ground, even though the ground is dark and full of death, in the confident knowledge of the resurrection into new life at His good time.

The shattering changes that are taking place round about the Asian churches are forcing them to think again of the fact that the Gospel is for the world, and for its redemption, and to see their service as no longer a sideline ambulance operation but a deep involvement—a means of God's redeeming activity in the whole body. When plans were made for the Indonesian consultation on New Forms of Service, the theme chosen by the local leaders was 'The Gospel and the Revolution'.

The real crisis in the life of the Church today is surely our discovery, under the guidance of the Word of God, and under the disciplines of worldly movements around us, that God is not calling us to be 'more religious' but to a persistent caring for His world and His children. We need to discover and confess that we had ceased to care about the life of the world. In the words of the Japan consultation, 'The church must not only share the burden of man's sufferings but must determine what God wills His people to do at this very moment. It must also rear the kind of men who will stand up and fight to improve the structure of our society.'

It is obvious that if we are to regard Christian service in this light, if we are to bring the dynamic faith right into the life of our congregations, it will bring about a radical alteration to the familiar structures of our congregational life, and a new mutual dependence between the minister and his people. The minister will truly become the servant of his people for Christ's sake (and not their master as chief organizer or agent in all the work of the Church). The calling of the layman will not be conceived as his 'spare-time' devotion to the needs of the Church, but as his full-time life in the world. And the worship life of the congregation will become the inspiration and power house of its whole life, for the relevance of the Gospel that is powerful, because of the fellowship of His people in worship, will become clear to them.

What is implied is a revolutionary change of direction, of understanding the structures of Christian service, one of the main characteristics of which will be that every Christian will be aware that he stands as a minister of Christ's redemption in the life of a world which, whatever its appearance and present reality, is being redeemed.

'What can we, who belong to Christ and bear His name, expect? We must expect to be taken by Him and mixed by Him in that aspect of the world's life in which he wants us to be the leaven. Once the leaven is mixed with the dough it has no other function except to lose its identity. . . . We must expect also to be taken by our Lord and set upon lampstands from which we can radiate the most light. When men light lamps they do not hide them. God does not do otherwise. He too will set the lamps He lights where they can be set to most advantage. But these places of advantage are also the places where the winds blow. A sudden gust of wind and the lamp may go out. But that is part of the lamp's adventure.

Always facing death in order that it may communicate life—that is the Church's unavoidable role' (*Upon the Earth*, p. 103).

The New Cities

A clear example of the application of this new emphasis is the thinking of the churches about the challenge of the cities that are springing up all over Asia. As long ago as 1951 well over 100,000,000 people lived in Asian cities of over 100,000. The move to the cities continues at incredible and irresistible speed. Apart from refugee movements and overall increase of population, the most widespread factor in all this has been the adoption of industrialization as a necessary and desirable method of increasing the wealth of the nations and raising the living standards of the people.

But the provision of physical amenities has not kept pace with the need. In India in 1953/4 a survey revealed that 25 per cent of city dwellings were made of mud, 44 per cent had only one room, and 46 per cent had less than 100 square feet per person. Conditions of extreme overcrowding are widespread. It has been quite impossible for the civic authorities to provide the basic necessities for health, let alone adequate facilities for a wholesome existence.

Inevitably there has been a degeneration in human life under such circumstances. The loss of stable conditions, of moral values, and of accepted community authorities and disciplines, has led to the breakdown of family life and of individual character. Family obligations are neglected. Children whose parents are both obliged to work grow up in uncontrolled conditions. The drudgery and loneliness of the overcrowded industrial city breed gambling, alcoholism, and prostitution. Indiscipline grows, particularly among students and industrial workers. Human values disappear.

And yet, at the same time, the city is the pride and glory of the Asian nations as it has been in other parts of the world. It is felt to be the mighty symbol of the new era, the coming-of-age of the nations, and the achievement and skill of the new leaders. Its industrial potential is the primary hope for material welfare in the future. Not all the streets are ugly, nor are all the suburbs scenes of overcrowding and degeneration. Even the visitor to Tokyo, Djakarta, Rangoon or Calcutta is conscious not only of the horror and gloom of human existence for many citizens, but also of the pride and achievement and beauty of the works of man's hand and the planning of his mind. Above all, he is conscious, if he looks at all beneath the surface, that it is utterly futile to bemoan the modern city. It has come into existence as a result of compulsions that cannot be stayed. The process cannot be reversed, but it can be modified and guided if men have the character and will and competence to control it. Men do not have a choice as to whether or not ours will be an urban civilization. But they do have, in the long run at least, the choice between degradation and glory, both of which are visible in the cities of today.

The churches have not really grappled seriously with the problems of the city. They have poured out their resources in sideline acts of organized mercy which, however commendable, have not touched the heart of the matter. Such charitable service has made little or no impact on the shape of the city itself, nor on its hectic rush to shame or glory. The dimensions of the problem have frozen the Church into inaction.

If, as Christians, we are sent into the city to dominate its development in the strength of our own resources and in terms of our religious ideals, we are indeed irrelevant—and would be wise to recognize it. If, on the other hand, we are called to be firstfruits of a process of redemption which is in the hand of the Lord of all the earth, we can indeed go forth with joy into the problems and wounds of the city itself, confident that He can solve and heal them. There was an agreement on one essential point in all the Asian consultations—that the task of Christians is to understand and share in the total struggle of the emerging city.

Thus in the consultations there was a real effort to define how the Church as a community, and Christians individually, can contribute to the provision of adequate living conditions, for example in using Church lands, providing hostels, and giving better conditions to their own employees. There was far more emphasis on 'social justice' than on 'social work'. It was agreed that pastoral help, as well as service to the community, should be aimed at helping city dwellers to understand the nature of work, to overcome the dehumanization implicit in mass society, to establish trade unions, to preserve the family unit, and to contribute through individuals of integrity to the economy and government of the city. Not all these things are foreign to the service of Christians in the past. But some of them are, and in most the understanding and the objective is new.

The fruit of this new understanding is by its nature not always visible. The primary result is the change in the approach of Christians to their whole environment of work and city life. It is the growing awareness of such Christians that, specifically as Christians, they carry a responsibility for the conditions of city life, and that there are some things that they can do about it.

But there are, nevertheless, identifiable changes in Church activities also. In almost every Asian country there are the beginnings of programmes to help lay Christians define their daily-life responsibilities. Everywhere there is talk about the need for lay-training centres. There is a particular emphasis on work among industrial workers. The Church of the Holy Carpenter, with its image of Christ the labourer, and the carpenter's tools surrounding it, standing as it does in dockland Hong Kong, embodies this witness. The house-churches in Kyoto, Japan, welcoming people who would be uncomfortable in conventional congregations; the non-church-centred seminars sponsored by Japanese Christians, in which workers can discuss their work and its conditions; the sending of theological students in Korea, Japan, and Hong Kong into terms of industrial labour; the special approaches made to industrial workers and trade unionists, particularly in Bangalore and Durgapur in India, and in the Philippines—these are just some of the outward evidences that the new understanding is, in fact, bearing fruit in the cities that dominate Asian life in our era.

The Christian and the State

The Asian churches—like all churches—have to negotiate with the State so that they can have room to live and witness. But they are also asking new questions. The statement of the W.C.C. Assembly at Delhi on the Christian as citizen does not really touch these new questions. The statement reaffirms the Christian view of the State—that it is ordained by God for the creation and maintenance of just order—and the belief that the Christian is 'called to be a citizen and in his membership of the State to obey God and love his fellow men'. Yet 'Christians can never give the State their ultimate loyalty. The Church must see both nation and State under the judgment as well as the mercy of God as known in Christ. Churches must be prepared for conflicts with the State in any nation and under any political system. . . . The existence of a Church may have great indirect effects on the nation's political life, for the Church is the clearest case of an association within a nation which has its own foundation independent of the State.' Even if it admits that 'as the Church struggles to preserve and widen its own freedom to witness, it may open the door for the freedom of men as men', the latter remains a possible by-product of the main objective—the freedom of the Church to do its 'spiritual work'.

There is a serious lack here from the point of view of churches in Asia. They, too, are concerned for their own survival and for the protection of their rights to worship and witness. But they are in a much more precarious position than the report envisages. They live in the midst of young states struggling desperately to survive as human communities, to give to their people the bare means of existence and the beginnings of welfare and decency and dignity. These are the ends for which the State is struggling—by whatever path—in Asia. Is the Christian's chief concern here to protect his communal rights to witness? Is the Church as a whole, and the Christian individually, not called of God to serve the ends of the State itself, being its servant in the name of the Lord, protecting it from the demonic forces within and without, and seeking its redemption? The traditional position of the relationship, as stated by the Delhi report, is a tremendous security for us in the times ahead—times that will demand of us clear thinking as well as courageous action. But it is not enough; not nearly enough. For example, Delhi rightly warns us against the corruption that threatens the heart of every authoritarian régime; it rightly points out the superiority of less dictatorial forms of government; yet its only comment on such governments is that 'there is no greater desecration of the human in men than to intimidate and torture them in order to force them to obey the political authorities against their consciences'.

This is apparent. But there is an equal desecration—the adoption of political institutions that may guarantee all the appropriate freedoms to the religious institutions and communities, but whose ineptness at government in other respects results in the continuing existence in the degradation, illiteracy, and early death, of a multitude of citizens. It is the task of the Church to bring these citizens into faith, but it is the task of the State to give them the *possibility* of a human life within a redeemed society.

There is the choice between forms of government. There is the issue over freedom of religion. What responsibility does the Christian have for the ends of the State? What is the value to God of the secular ends of human life? Is it not a betrayal when the Church can ignore these ends unless they happen to be served incidentally in the Church's struggle for her own rights?

At the Bangalore meeting of the E.A.C.C. in 1961 a great deal of attention was given to the State, not in terms of its dealing with the Church, but in terms of its own calling. Many at that meeting endorsed the view Mr M. M. Thomas had expressed two years previously: nationalism and nation-building are a divine preparation for the Gospel. They are creating a situation in which Christian social thought and action and the preaching of the Gospel are integral to each other in raising the question and giving the answer. The Church, therefore, in its participation in the tasks of repatterning society and in nation-building, is really pushing the ultimate questions regarding the nature and destiny of man to a decisive answer. 'Nationalism is therefore an essential preparation of Asia for the gospel. We cannot have a new vision of the christian mission in Asia without a christian interpretation of Asian nationalism' (*Kuala Lumpur Report*, p. 51).

When the consultation on New Forms of Service was arranged in Korea by the E.A.C.C. it was 'the first time throughout seventy-five years of history of the Korean churches, that theologians, social scientists and practitioners who are working in various fields got together in response to the need to look together as Christians at the rapidly changing social scene in our country' (*Consultation Report*, p. 1).

The consultation began with a realistic examination of the actual state of both the churches and the political life of the country. The churches had been extremely pietistic and other-worldly, with a strongly moralistic attitude to the world. There was need for repentance—but a new kind of repentance. There had been repentance meetings held through long nights, consisting of the confession of the sins of bowing before Shinto shrines in the Japanese era. But 'the repentance required of the Korean churches today is for their failure to respond to God's call to serve in the midst of the revolutionary changes in the light of God's purpose' (p. 9). 'As Christians we cannot leave aside politics because this is one agency which plays an increasingly large role in influencing the lives of the people in our society' (p. 15).

A very good example comes from Korea itself. Every year there is a rice shortage in the south, and, according to Government statistics, nearly half a million bags of rice are needed annually to assist the destitute farmers in the area. In 1961 the Korean churches decided to take action. They organized a massive relief appeal among their own members. The response was generous, and in some cases sacrificial. Here was a compassionate programme, aimed at feeding the hungry.

But its inadequacy as a method is apparent. Not nearly enough help was available to meet the need. Even if there had been enough for that year it would have left the basic position unchanged. Famine for the farmers would come again the following year. The Rev. Dr Won Yong Kang of Korea made the comment—'A more helpful approach would be for the churches to stand for the enactment of legislation which could deal with the problem itself, and not just its surface expressions. But this was received coolly by the churches, when proposed, because this involved political action and required a degree of imagination and self-forgetfulness which we did not have. In our world today sentimentalism cannot be considered a responsible approach to social reality, and Christian love must seek to manifest itself through social structures towards greater justice for all' (*Church and Society*, March 1962, p. 60).

Such insights do not readily produce clearly defined programmes of service. This is not so much because the approach is as yet relatively new; it is not so much that the Asian churches are all very small relative to the states within which they live; it is rather that by the nature of the case the essential acts of service that a Christian does are to be found in the very tissue of his daily work and involvement in politics. They are invisible from outside the actual situation. They are concerned with the way he does his technical job, with his competence, with his objective, with his activity in a political meeting or State agency, with his attitude of constructive hopefulness and realistic caution in face of cynicism or over-optimism. In other words, the real concern about such service is with what a Christian *is*. It has to do with his whole being as a servant of his Lord, and of his neighbours. It implies a whole-hearted rejection of the pietistic conviction that a Christian must keep himself separate from the community's normal life, and particularly from its politics.

There is an interesting illustration in Indonesia. In that country the Christians have established two 'Christian' political parties—one Protestant and the other Roman Catholic. Many would question such a policy. But it is important that the Protestant churches as such do not officially support any particular party, and, in fact, Christians serve in many parties. They appear in extremely high positions in the State. It is quite clear that the small Christian minority must protect its religious rights in such a Muslim community—but it is also widely understood that as *Christians* they must participate in, and accept responsibility for, the overall life of the nation. None would doubt the temptations and tensions that result from such an involvement. But who can estimate the significance of the hidden leavening that cannot be achieved in any other way?

The churches can render a Christian service to their communities by their understanding of the ambiguity of human nature—its potentiality and its corruption. One of the most corroding factors in any democratic state is the frustration and hopelessness that is created in the common mind by the fact that ambitious or optimistic programmes are never realized in any completeness. As was said at the Japan Consultation (p. 27), 'The Church knows that a completely reformed society stands better in righteousness, but also that it is still a temporary set-up in the non-redeemed history.'

The series of consultations did, however, attempt to set out some specific tasks for the churches, against this background. Those particularly mentioned included the following:

> To emphasize the Biblical and theological basis on which all Christians can understand the meaning of their calling to involvement in the political life of the State.
> To give clear support to forms of government which permit a democratic participation by citizens in the decisions of the State—and at the same time to devote special efforts to educating both Christians and others in the meaning of the issues in the decisions in which they are involved.
> To produce study books, articles, and pamphlets on political issues.
> To support Church members already active in Government services.
> To encourage Christians of ability to enter both public service and the political parties.
> To clarify the major issues at stake in political elections.
> To form specialist advisory groups to watch the legislation being introduced into Parliament.
> To exercise a prophetic and critical function over against the actions of the Government.
> To facilitate the establishment of groups of politically minded Christians.

Each of these proposals needs careful analysis, but together they indicate clearly a change of policy and direction as Asian Christians face the states in which they live, and are called to serve.

Conclusion

All that has been said of Asian thinking about the forms of Christian service in the cities and within the states is illustrative only. The consultations indicated an increasing grappling with all the tasks implied by the new interpretation of Christian involvement—the tasks in community development, in strengthening the new concept of the family, in the search for cultural foundations, and in the objectives of economic development. The change is an adaptation to the circumstances of the time. But it is more than that. It is a renewal of the theological insight that 'the leading force of history is God, and that all social changes should be directed according to our understanding of God's purposes' (*Korean Consultation Report*, p. 50).

We stand today at the beginning of a revolution of Church life in Asia—a changed understanding of service is only one of its fruits. If that revolution should wither, the churches would become increasingly introspective; all would wither, and many would die. If under the leading of the Spirit it goes on to obedient fulfilment, none can say what will happen to the structures and programmes of the churches as we know them. But by faith we can say that the people of Jesus Christ will truly be the living witnesses to His Gospel and the firstfruits of His Kingdom.

Ecumenical Diakonia
(Inter-Church Aid, Caritas, and so forth)

JOHN COVENTRY SMITH

Diakonia is at least as old as the Christian Church. What is new in our time is an *ecumenical diakonia*, and it is quite possible that it represents the most meaningful and significant aspect of the ecumenical movement. It would be a mistake to say that Protestant denominations pooled their resources to be used in postwar reconstruction, Inter-Church Aid, and work for refugees just for the sake of greater effectiveness and economy of funds and personnel. There is something much deeper and more significant than these, important as they are. At New Delhi in 1961 the World Council of Churches said, 'It is the conviction of the World Council of Churches that unity grows as the churches learn to fulfil their mission together . . . The World Council of Churches seeks to promote this co-operation of mutual service, not merely for the sake of organizational effectiveness, but also for the sake of the deeper unity for which they prepare the churches.'[1] Inter-Church Aid grew out of an awareness of the Biblical concept of the one-ness of Christians in the body of Christ, expressed in their desire to be mutually helpful in time of need.

Diakonia in the early Church was on a small and very limited scale, but an effective one; today it is a complex and immense undertaking, both in depth and extent of operation.

A writer in the field of world history recently established the thesis that the history of mankind has been moving toward an *oikumene*, and that by virtue of this movement people all over the world have come to the realization that they are part of a world-wide community of peoples. During the past one hundred years, and more especially in recent decades, this historical process has accelerated until today there is a growing consciousness of the existence of a world community.

Christians believe that God has been speaking through this movement in human history, not only to establish in the minds of Christian people the oneness of the human family, but also to bring home to them the fact that they belong to a world Christian community. Moreover, within this world Christian community there has emerged a new sense of responsibility for one another, and a realization that their plans must grow out of this feeling of responsibility, which is inherent in the concept of unity in the body of Christ.

[1] *New Delhi Report*, p. 346.

One of the exciting features of this realization since World War II has been the emergence amongst almost all of the Christian groups of a new sense of 'ecumenical *diakonia*'. This is roughly defined as the necessity of every Christian's feeling the responsibility for being of service to the world Christian community of which he is a part. Wherever anyone is in need, all of his Christian brothers should come to his assistance. This service is not limited to those who are members of the Christian Church; but where a Christian Church is faced with the emergency of service to its own community it can expect that it will be assisted by the whole of the World Christian Community.

Origin and Development of Inter-Church Aid

The idea of churches rendering service to other churches and Church people who are in need, goes back to the period immediately following World War I. In 1921 the Federal Council of Churches financed a meeting which was held in Denmark on 22 August, under the joint sponsorship of the Swiss Church Federation and the Church of Denmark. In seventeen European countries reports revealed the serious plight of many Protestant churches. Not only was there a need to rebuild or to repair churches which had been damaged during the war, but pastors and their families, professors and students in theological seminaries, were in dire circumstances, while Church life itself, disrupted and curtailed, had to be rehabilitated.

The Conference in Denmark established a 'Central Office for the Relief of the Evangelical Churches of Europe', with an International Executive Committee meeting in Switzerland. The name of the organization was changed some time later to 'European Central Office for Inter-Church Aid', and as such it served as a co-ordinating agency in a programme of reconstruction and rehabilitation among the churches, both Protestant and Orthodox. In 1937 the International Executive Committee stated that 'the time of Protestant individualism is over, and ecumenical thinking has started'.

When the World Council of Churches in Process of Formation was formed in 1938, Dr Adolf Keller, the Director of the International Executive Committee urged the World Council to undertake a programme of inter-church aid. For the next six years the two organizations worked closely together, and in 1944 the Department of Reconstruction and Inter-Church Aid was established by the World Council of Churches, still in the process of formation.

During the mid-1930s the refugee situation in Europe became desperate, due to Hitler's systematic campaign against non-Aryans. An International Committee for Christian Refugees was formed in Britain under the chairmanship of the Bishop of Chichester of the Church of England, with the purpose of drawing the attention of Christians to the plight of the refugees and also to seek social aid for them. The urgency of the refugee problem was placed before the Provisional Committee of the World Council of Churches, and Dr Freudenberg was asked to co-ordinate the activities of various refugee committees and to appeal to the churches for assistance. At the outbreak of World War II, Dr

Freudenberg's office was transferred to Geneva, where the World Council of Churches established an Ecumenical Commission for Refugees. A few years later massive deportations of people from Holland, Belgium, and France greatly increased the number of refugees, and in 1945 the Department for Refugees became a part of the Department of Reconstruction and Inter-Church Aid.

Thus even before the first Assembly of the World Council of Churches in 1948, at Amsterdam, and before the World Council of Churches itself had been formally established, its potential Division of Inter-Church Aid was organized and active, with experience enough to indicate the direction of the future.

Of course, this coming together of the churches in order to be of assistance in relief and reconstruction in Europe was not the first instance in which churches had been challenged together to be of assistance in times of emergency. In the United States any reference to such activity recalls the emergence of various relief committees for China, in the early 1900s. The formation in 1911 of a new Central China Famine Relief Committee indicates the direction in which churches in both Great Britain and the United States moved in a time of crisis.

The same procedure was followed again in relation to Near East Relief at the time of and following World War II. However, it is clear that the development of this conception of ecumenical *diakonia* and its procedures has never been so clearly defined and so widely implemented by churches across the world as within the World Council of Churches itself.

Relief and rehabilitation in Europe after World War II was a major project for many of the churches in North America and a surprising number in Great Britain. The tragic aftermath of war left many communities desolate. In their midst Christian congregations still existed and were at work. Christian brethren from across the world now came to their aid. Some of this was done within the narrower limits of denominational fellowship: Presbyterian for Presbyterian, Lutheran for Lutheran, Methodist for Methodist, and so forth. But the major characteristic which soon came to dominate the scene was the emergence of a common concern among Christian churches for Christians no matter what their denominational allegiance might be. Christian congregations were aided, churches were rebuilt, and refugees were served regardless of creed. The extent of this service will never be accurately known, but it included aid to thousands of congregations and to millions of people. The characteristic of this service is perhaps best exemplified in the service to refugees. In our time '. . . the refugee problem of the world is a human tragedy unparalleled in modern history'.[1] 'Though 7,000,000 persons had been re-established in their former homelands by the end of 1946, it was seen that there would be a special group of refugees who would need some form of international assistance toward finding new jobs and homes again.'[2]

By 1948, at the time of the First Assembly, it had become evident 'that the day

[1] *Europe's Hopeless* (1951), W.C.C. Report.
[2] ibid.

had passed, or was passing, for the short-term repair work and that the day for long-term planning had arrived'.[1]

'The change in the Department's function was signalized at the Central Committee meeting in Chichester in 1949 by a change in the name of the Department. The old title had been "The Department of Reconstruction and Inter-Church Aid"; the new title was "The Department of Inter-Church Aid and Service to Refugees".'[2] Thus the various streams of relief, rehabilitation and service to refugees which had started separately had become a permanent obligation of the World Council related to the spiritual task of the Church.

The Central Committee decided to remind the member churches that Inter-Church Aid is a permanent obligation of a World Council of Churches which seeks to be true to its name; that many of the churches in Europe are in dire need of assistance as they take their part in the great spiritual struggle of our day; that the millions of refugees in Europe have an urgent and incontrovertible claim upon the help of the churches; and therefore that a fresh approach must be made, by the churches which are in a position to help, to their members for renewed and generous giving on behalf of their fellow Christians in Europe.

The newly named Department continued to serve effectively the needs of churches and of refugees in Europe through the support of churches in other parts of the world. But the work of the Department was still limited to the continent of Europe. However, as the service of the World Council became more and more adequate, and as relief and rehabilitation were far enough along, so that committees could begin to look into the future, the anomaly of having a Department of Inter-Church Aid of Service to Refugees of the *World Council of Churches*, which limited its activity to one continent while Christian communities and their fellow citizens on other continents were in need, became more and more evident. Christians in churches in Asia, Africa, and Latin America began to say, 'We also are members of the World Council of Churches. Europe's needs immediately after the war were critical, but long-term needs in our part of the world are at least as urgent. Why cannot the World Council acting through its Department of Inter-Church Aid and Service to Refugees be a channel of assistance to us?'

This matter came to a head at a meeting of the Joint Committee held in London in the beginning of July 1952 and was further developed during the course of the meeting of the International Missionary Council in Willingen, Germany, later that month. The result was that at the beginning of 1953 the Central Committee, meeting at Lucknow, adopted a report which reads as follows:

The Reference Sub-committee has studied the proposed plan for co-operation between the International Missionary Council and the World Council of Churches for emergency inter-church aid and relief in countries outside Europe.

[1] *The First Six Years 1948-1954*—Report of the Central Committee W.C.C.
[2] ibid.

It welcomes the suggestion that the Department of Inter-Church Aid and Service to Refugees should be entrusted with this responsibility. . . .[1]

This statement highlighted the necessity of co-operation between the two ecumenical organizations. It also explained, in part, why the World Council of Churches had not extended service operations beyond Europe. The International Missionary Council, having been organized in 1920, was the older ecumenical body. It was composed of Foreign Mission Councils in Europe and North America, and of National Christian Councils on the continents of Asia, Africa, and Latin America. The International Missionary Council, though organizationally separate, was in co-operation with the World Council of Churches. The 'sending' churches of the West exercised their Christian accountability for physical and spiritual needs through the International Missionary Council in Asia, Africa, and Latin America. Though the magnitude of human need on these continents exceeded the resources of the mission societies, the World Council had been hesitant to expand its services to these three continents. The Lucknow Report was adopted with the understanding of the International Missionary Council and with the expectation of its co-operation.

Moreover, during the formative years of the World Council of Churches the realization that churches outside of Europe, the Middle East, and North America had equal stature with the long-established churches was only growing. They were 'mission churches'. The stature of 'younger churches' had not yet been achieved. Several years of living together were required before these terms were recognized as derogatory. The Lucknow decision to include them as part of the church family had meanings beyond the extension of relief.

The decision was confirmed by the Second Assembly of the World Council of Churches at Evanston (U.S.A.) in 1954. Subsequently, at joint meetings of representatives of the World Council of Churches and the International Missionary Council, the categories of requests from needy churches were studied. The differentiation between 'mission' and 'emergency inter-church aid and relief' was necessary to avoid an overlapping of responsibilities between the two ecumenical bodies.

The emergence of a 'total strategy' on behalf of the needs of humanity necessitated a distinction of categories. Meetings for this purpose were held at La Rosse and St Albans in 1955, and at Herrenalb in 1956, resulting in the 'Herrenalb Categories' which extended the responsibilities of the Division of Inter-Church Aid. The seven areas in Asia, Africa, and Latin America, the Division was authorized to explore and meet were:

(*a*) Needs arising from situations which are strictly of an emergency character creature by natural disasters, economic crises, political and social upheavals, etc.
(*b*) The needs of refugees and homeless people.
(*c*) The needs of churches not in regular relations with any missionary society and therefore not normally receiving help from this source.

[1] *The First Six Years 1948–1954*—Report of the Central Committee W.C.C.

(d) Urgent inter-church and ecumenical projects, whether designed for the strengthening of the churches' witness or the service of the community, in so far as these cannot be supported adequately either from local sources or through mission board action.

(e) Church work originally aided by a missionary society which can no longer continue its help although the need for assistance is still recognized.

(f) New projects in the fields of social service or relief clearly demanded by the local situation, but beyond the resources of the churches or the missionary societies co-operating with them.

(g) Experiments aimed at ensuring the self-support of the Church or Christian community, where these have been adequately examined and duly commended.[1]

With the categories approved, the Department prepared a 'Project List' of requests from National Christian Councils, which churches and Christian service organizations were encouraged to underwrite.

The 'service' or 'inter-church aid' listing by the World Council of Churches and the churches of Europe was similar to most of the projects carried by North American Churches through their Boards of Foreign Missions. The artificiality of the line between has become increasingly evident. By 1966, upon the recommendation of the Division of World Mission and Evangelism, and the Division of Inter-Church Aid, the Central Committee abolished the 'Herrenalb Categories'. The project list now includes needs of the churches both in 'service' and 'mission'. Bona fide 'mission projects' are certified by the Division of World Mission and Evangelism in expectation of support from both missionary and service agencies. Thus *diakonia* or service, which mission agencies from both Europe and North America had initiated in various parts of the world and which had been carried out through the generous giving of the churches, now came within the scope of consideration along with the service projects which were sponsored by the newer ecumenical organization of the World Council.

The New Delhi Assembly also reformulated the responsibilities of the World Council of Churches as it established this Division of World Mission and Evangelism. This change was spelled out in an amendment to the constitution concerning the new Division of World Mission and Evangelism, as follows:

The programme of the new Division . . . will provide . . . a new dimension to the World Council. We have made a general outline of its task. We cannot now define all its deeper meanings nor the extent of its activities. Only the experience of living and working together can teach us these. Our temptation will be to think of the Division simply as the continuation of the interests of the International Missionary Council with emphasis on Asia, Africa, and South America. We must resist this temptation. This is the Division of World Mission and Evangelism of the World Council of Churches. We are concerned not with three continents, but with six. In co-operation with every department of the World Council and with the full resources of the Christian community in every land we

---

[1] Minutes of Joint Committee of World Council of Churches and International Missionary Council, St Albans, October 1955.

would help the churches to confront men and women with the claims of Jesus Christ wherever they live.[1]

This 'six-continent policy' has opened new avenues of communication to, and sparked new activities, by the Division of Inter-Church Aid, Refugee and World Service. Thus the project list in 1965 included requests for assistance in Mississippi, Chicago, and Detroit. The Mississippi Delta Project received spontaneous and enthusiastic support from churches in Europe and Asia. The distinction between 'sending churches' and 'receiving churches' no longer is tenable.

At the Third Assembly of the World Council of Churches, in New Delhi in 1961, the Division of Inter-Church Aid and Service to Refugees (DICASR) became the Division of Inter-Church Aid, Refugee and World Service (DICARWS). This last additional term 'world service' recognized that 'inter-church aid' includes more than the assistance extended by one Christian Church to another. The designation 'inter-church aid' also refers to projects in areas where there is no Christian Church, or where a given church is too weak to administer a programme even with help from abroad. The corporate World Council of Churches community conducts aid programmes on behalf of suffering humanity. Inter-church aid now can be defined as 'churches helping one another at their total task in the world', thus including both world service and inter-church aid.

Financial resources for such activities have gradually increased. Cash contributions in 1964, from more than thirty different countries, totalled $7,708,843. Contributed goods totalled in excess of $46,000,000 for projects in fifty-five countries and on every continent.

Support for this programme, which had come primarily from North America, comes now from many countries. European churches that formerly received aid now underwrite new projects. The East Asia Christian Conference has channelled assistance to and from churches in Asia during crises.

Autonomous and semi-autonomous developments in North America as well as in Europe have strengthened the World Council of Churches' programme. China Famine Relief, U.S.A., Inc., organized in 1920, was but the first of a number of ecumenically oriented relief bodies established to deal with particular needs. Several organizational streams converged on 1 May 1946 to produce Church World Service Inc. This body was merged with the Division of Foreign Missions in 1965, as the Division of Overseas Ministries of the National Council of Churches of Christ in the U.S.A.

Certain Church families also have developed their own programmes of relief and inter-church aid. For instance, the Department of World Service of the Lutheran World Federation channels annual contributions approximating $2,500,000 and materials valued at several times this amount, from a dozen Lutheran Church bodies of North America, Europe, and Australia to areas where there are strong Lutheran constituencies. Two major areas where the Lutheran

[1] *Minutes of New Delhi*, 1961.

World Federation operates are Hong Kong and the Jordan. Since its world service operation was initiated in 1947, the Lutheran World Federation together with its related agencies has distributed approximately one-quarter billion dollars in cash or value. The responsible departments of the Lutheran World Federation and the World Council of Churches share information to evaluate priorities and avoid duplication. Member churches of the Lutheran World Federation also contribute substantial amounts each year to the cost of administration and to the relief and inter-church projects of the World Council of Churches.

Space does not permit even a sampling of the activities that run parallel within the World Council and the Roman Catholic Church. Actual data concerning this development in the Roman Catholic Church is not as easily available. Protestants have been surprised to discover that there has probably been less co-ordination of service programme in Roman Catholic circles than in the World Council. There are at least as many centres of initiative and the emergence of CARITAS INTERNATIONALIS has not yet resulted in adequate co-ordination. The purpose of this Roman Catholic international body is 'to animate the charitable action of all its members and to assure its efficacious presence in front of the world's misery'. This desired efficiency is still being sought. The report of a Roman Catholic conference states:

On the Catholic level the total distribution made on an international level is gigantic. But certain areas are fed at the same time by five or six organizations which ignore each other. Whilst next-door abject poverty is disregarded by all. The establishment of a central and confidential file for distributions would enable the partial limitation of useless repetition. This file would be more efficacious if it also contained a reference to the distributions of the Propagation of Faith.[1]

SECTION II

Theological reflection has followed upon the World Council's participation in what has become known as 'ecumenical *diakonia*'. What was begun as a response to human need was now interpreted in theological terms, some of them fresh and stimulating. This is not surprising. One can enlarge upon the times in the history of the Christian Church when new theological stimulus came not from those whose professional business was theology, but those who were engaged at the level of mission and service on the frontier. God often speaks through what He is doing in the world as well as through the heritage of our Christian faith.

The first theological reflection began with the scriptural basis for Inter-Church Aid. The earliest known account of Inter-Church Aid, dating almost to the very beginning of Christianity, is found in the Acts of the Apostles (Acts 11: 27–30).[2] The basic principles for present-day Inter-Church Aid were drawn from this Scriptural experience.

Theological development followed rapidly. There were articles written and

[1] 'Advantages of a Central File for Distribution.'
[2] 'Fellowship and Christian Sharing'—Geneva, 1954.

even books published on 'ecumenical *diakonia*'. I remember as an American trying to understand this development when I attended the First Assembly of the E.A.C.C. in Kuala Lumpur, in 1958. I asked Dr Visser 't Hooft, the General Secretary of the World Council, and he referred me to Professor Freytag, who was present. Dr Freytag laughed when I asked him my question and said, 'This will take six hours'. We began at Kuala Lumpur, we continued the next summer at La Brevière in France, but I had only completed the first half of my education in ecumenical *diakonia* when I said farewell to him, never to see him again.

I quote now from a memo which I wrote in the summer of 1959 concerning some statements,

'Diakonia' is, of course, first defined as aid to needy people: the widows in Jerusalem, the cup of cold water, the visit to those in prison. This is described as having no relationship to Mission. This is done out of love and not as an evangelistic witness. Those who have must help those who have not, the strong must help the weak. This, of course, is Christian and compelling.

But this is now extended to include aid to churches, the strong to help the weak. And it is defined as having no necessary relationship to Mission. It is like the offering Paul collected for the churches in Jerusalem. We are now one fellowship of churches in the W.C.C. and should help one another in all things, including financial aid to Church programmes. This has had a response in some European countries which were helped after World War II and are now financially able to give assistance. They give it through Inter-Church Aid rather than through traditional missionary societies. . . .

'Mission' is described as that which definitely crosses into the non-Christian world, in pioneer areas, and with non-Christian religions. And mission agencies are said to be 'bogged down' with doing 'inter-church aid' in institutional programmes rather than being free for their original task of direct evangelism.

The above is an oversimplification of the case. It is nowhere quite so clearly defined.

Perhaps six years later I would add the following: 'The work of Inter-Church Aid rests upon a growing ecumenical awareness of the Biblical concept of the Body of Christ, in which all members of the Body suffer when one of its members suffers' (see 1 Corinthians 12^{26}).[1]

My education in ecumenical *diakonia* has been continued by reading a number of statements, one of them by Dr Freytag, made in 1955 at the St Albans Consultation. He remarks that Inter-Church Aid began 'at the smallest possible scale as an agency for co-ordination' and is now described 'on the largest possible scale as a new step into a very comprehensive service of the Ecumenical movement'. He then prepared to define what he means by the relationship of 'mission' to church. He describes the impossibility of detaching mission in the Biblical sense from church. 'Biblically speaking, there is no Church which is not part of this action of God, no Church which does not have her particular position

---

[1] *Inter-Church Aid Report*, 1951.

in His design towards the end, no Church in the service of which men do not become new men and through baptism become included both in the eschatological and temporal fellowship of those who belong to Christ.' And then he says, 'Neither is it possible to detach from this background what the Scriptures say about the life of a Christian and, thereby, about love.' And he concludes by saying: 'A separation of the tasks of Inter-Church Aid and the International Missionary Council, is on principle, not feasible.' . . . 'We can speak of a separation of functions within the common mandate'.

It is not surprising in the light of this statement to reflect that in 1961, when the International Missionary Council became a part of the new Division of World Mission and Evangelism of the World Council of Churches and a serious attempt was made to describe the functions of the Division of Inter-Church Aid and the Division of World Mission and Evangelism, it was found that they could be described only by making their overall definition the same and by then saying that within one Division the *focus* was upon crossing the barrier between belief and unbelief and in the other Division the *focus* was upon service to needy mankind.

We cannot but agree with Professor Freytag's summary, 'All attempts to make "ecumenical *diakonia*" something entirely separate from "apostolate" are doomed to failure.' The history of the Church, beginning with the days of the disciples, is the history of the fact that God approaches man with integrity which involves concern with his 'wholeness' in both a physical and spiritual sense. Jesus never made these distinctions. Sometimes through His action the healing of the body and the healing of the soul occurred in the same person at the same time.

Perhaps in summary it would be fitting to quote from a theologian of the Orthodox Church. In recent centuries the Orthodox Church has not been involved in missionary activity and was not a participant in the International Missionary Council. It welcomed the Division of Inter-Church Aid and participated enthusiastically. Dr N. A. Nissiotis comments:

When we speak of *diakonia* we usually mean the action of the churches in the service of the world as one of the most important factors in their missionary activities. The churches are sent to the world not only to preach and to save men but also to establish communities through which they serve the world in its material and spiritual needs. In this sense, the act of *diakonia* is equivalent to the fulfilment of the duty of the churches to offer help to the suffering people outside their membership or to provide answers to the problems of man in economic, political, personal or family life. Through this kind of *diakonia* the churches enter into the world and render their witness to their Lord evident, vivid and realistically present in practice. Without this action a church would seem to be deprived of the fundamental expression of her inner life.[1]

The growth of this activity, which is so inadequately described in this brief compass, has arisen in my estimation because of three things:

[1] *The Ecumenical Review*, vol. XIII, No. 2, Jan. 1961.

First of all, the realization in our civilization, where need for help can be communicated across the world, that one-half of the world's people are hungry, one-half have never had medical attention, and two-thirds are illiterate. No Christian who knows his New Testament and seeks to follow Christ can be insensitive to this fact, especially if he lives in an affluent country. The news that he reads and the television programmes that he sees describe to him the sharp contrast of his own situation and that of many other parts of the world. The less-fortunate peoples, who are hungry, have a right to say to affluent Christians, 'When I needed a neighbour, were you there?'

The second reason for the expansion of the Division is its real crystallization of the necessity of expressing the unity of the world Christian community. Assemblies and committee meetings are symbols of this, but participation is only by a few. In the Division of Inter-Church Aid this instinct for expression finds an outlet. Human need is met, not nearly adequately enough, but still met in substantial proportion and as an expression of Christian love and concern. The amazing response of the churches to the challenge is strong indication that this division has been established and continues to operate in its central thrust under the guidance of the Spirit of God.

But a third reason for the growth of the Division of Inter-Church Aid is a negative one. To put it bluntly, the churches have found an ecumenical expression of their concern for all of humanity through a Division that emphasizes 'service' because at that moment in history missionary societies failed to fill the vacuum. For a hundred and fifty years they had operated as separate agencies, often with a denominational and national emphasis. The work they had done was tremendous. Without it there would have been no World Council of Churches and no Division of Inter-Church Aid. Beginning in Edinburgh in 1910, it was the thrust of those concerned with the mission of the Church who were preparing for the organization of the World Council. We all owe a debt we can never repay to that movement of the Spirit which led people in these last two centuries to leave their homes and venture across the world in order that God's love and forgiveness may be made known to all people in Jesus Christ.

But the missionary societies had hesitated too long in making a decision to become a part of the newly emerging ecumenical organization of the World Council of Churches. They were in co-operation with but still separate from the World Council. This provided the opportunity for churches, especially in Europe, who sought to express their concern for humanity to find an opening for this expression through the Division of Inter-Church Aid. The World Council could not long continue without an avenue for this expression. It was finding a channel and enlarging it rapidly when in 1958, belatedly, the International Missionary Council made its decision and in 1961 became the missionary arm of the World Council in its new Division of World Mission and Evangelism.

It still remains a question as to whether a missionary movement with a hundred and fifty years of history and with a commitment to past programmes, can make the changes that are necessary in this new kind of world that will enable it to participate alongside the Division of Inter-Church Aid, under the common mandate that the churches serve the physical and spiritual needs of all of mankind.

Actually, Inter-Church Aid is a descriptive term, but not accurately descriptive in any definitive way for a particular Division of the World Council. The words 'inter-church aid' do not describe *what* is done, they do describe *how* it is done. That this is true is evident by the refusal of the East Asia Christian conference to make any distinction between their requests for 'mission' and 'service'. Their Working Committee when it was established in Kuala Lumpur was challenged with the responsibility for 'inter-church aid for mission and service'.

Here the historical difference between the growth of the missionary movement in Europe and its growth in the United States have contributed to the confusion. In the United States for the most part missionary agencies are official boards of the Churches. They do not have a separate existence from the Church and, therefore, more readily are drawn into participation in the World Council as their own Churches become participants.

Moreover, in the United States, perhaps for the reason mentioned above, there has been a much greater tendency to unite in one agency responsibility for both mission and service. This is common enough so that the new organization in the National Council of Churches is the old Division of Foreign Missions and the old Department of Church World Service united into one Division, the Division of Overseas Ministries.

Any administrative solution will not impose one of these patterns upon all, but it should provide that no matter what names we give to our task and no matter what our own denominational and national structure may be, we may still be able to do together the things that God requires of His people in our time. Thus that which was begun out of the needs of World War II, and which has come to fruition so effectively in a few short years, will continue to be the stimulus for an even greater effectiveness as the churches seek to represent the eternal dimension in God's concern for every individual in all the wholeness of his physical and spiritual existence.

Dr W. A. Visser 't Hooft has said, 'The calling of the churches to serve has now a new global dimension. We must increasingly create a type of *diakonia* which is world-wide in its outreach, its strategy, its spirit. This common service may become an increasingly powerful factor in the growth of Christian unity. This will not happen automatically. It will happen only if the service is undertaken as a welcome opportunity to show that the Lord who became Servant intends us to serve together.'[1]

[1] *Ecumenical Foundations*, p. 61.

www.ingramcontent.com/pod-product-compliance
Lightning Source LLC
Chambersburg PA
CBHW070251230426
43664CB00014B/2492